# BUDGET TRAVEL

Dear Reader,

I'm so thrilled you have acquired *The Everything® Family Guide to Budget Travel*. This topic is so broad it's difficult to cover "everything." In this book I've tried to encapsulate the best places for affordable family travel that I've come across in eleven years of writing about the world.

Even when your family travels to places you've been time and again, you'll continue to learn new things—about the destination, about traveling, and about each other. I encourage you to chronicle your travels with your family. Take thousands of silly pictures. Write everything down in a travel journal. Go places where the whole family can learn about other cultures, interesting foods, and cool customs.

This book is full of travel secrets and trip suggestions. But love is in the details, so do your homework! Thoroughly review websites before booking tickets. Things like last-minute travel deals and hot-button specials can change in the blink of an eye, so check often. Never be afraid to ask tough questions—after all, it's your money!

And remember, family doesn't have to be limited to mom or dad or the kids . . . family can also include friends, coworkers, and even your pet. Travel with people you care about and want to spend time with. That's what makes great family travel, and that's what makes traveling fun!

Kelly Merritt

# WELCOME TO THE

# EVERYTHING®

## FAMILY GUIDES

*Everything*® Family Guides are designed to be the perfect traveling companions. Whether you're traveling within a tight family budget or feeling the urge to splurge, you will find all you need to create a memorable family vacation. Review this book to give you great ideas before you travel, and stick it in your backpack or diaper bag to use as a quick reference guide for activities, attractions, and excursions. You'll discover that vacationing with the whole family can be filled with fun and exciting adventures.

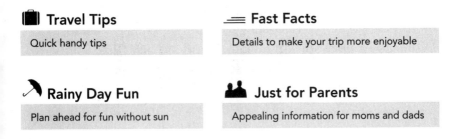

### 🧳 Travel Tips
Quick handy tips

### ═ Fast Facts
Details to make your trip more enjoyable

### ⚓ Rainy Day Fun
Plan ahead for fun without sun

### 👥 Just for Parents
Appealing information for moms and dads

When you're done reading, you can finally say you know **EVERYTHING**®!

**PUBLISHER** Karen Cooper

**DIRECTOR OF ACQUISITIONS AND INNOVATION** Paula Munier

**MANAGING EDITOR, EVERYTHING® SERIES** Lisa Laing

**COPY CHIEF** Casey Ebert

**ASSISTANT PRODUCTION EDITOR** Jacob Erickson

**ACQUISITIONS EDITOR** Lisa Laing

**SENIOR DEVELOPMENT EDITOR** Brett Palana-Shanahan

**EDITORIAL ASSISTANT** Ross Weisman

**EVERYTHING® SERIES COVER DESIGNER** Erin Alexander

**LAYOUT DESIGNERS** Colleen Cunningham, Elisabeth Lariviere, Ashley Vierra, Denise Wallace

Visit the entire Everything® series at *www.everything.com*

# THE EVERYTHING®

## FAMILY GUIDE TO

# BUDGET TRAVEL

Hundreds of fun
family vacations to fit any budget!

Kelly Merritt

Avon, Massachusetts

*This book is dedicated to my precious nieces, for*
*whom I would travel the world, Savannah and*
*Sierra Johnson. I love you dearly and thank you for*
*introducing me to the world through your eyes.*

An Everything® Series Book.
Everything® and everything.com® are registered trademarks of F+W Media, Inc.

Published by Adams Media, a division of F+W Media, Inc.
57 Littlefield Street, Avon, MA 02322 U.S.A.
*www.adamsmedia.com*

ISBN 10: 1-60550-120-4
ISBN 13: 978-1-60550-120-8
eISBN 10: 1-60550-669-9
eISBN 13: 978-1-60550-669-2

Printed in the United States of America.

10 9 8 7 6 5 4 3 2 1

**Library of Congress Cataloging-in-Publication Data**
is available from the publisher.

This publication is designed to provide accurate and authoritative information
with regard to the subject matter covered. It is sold with the understanding that
the publisher is not engaged in rendering legal, accounting, or other professional
advice. If legal advice or other expert assistance is required, the services of a
competent professional person should be sought.
—From a *Declaration of Principles* jointly adopted by a Committee of the
American Bar Association and a Committee of Publishers and Associations

Many of the designations used by manufacturers and sellers to distinguish their
products are claimed as trademarks. Where those designations appear in this
book and Adams Media was aware of a trademark claim, the designations have
been printed with initial capital letters.

*This book is available at quantity discounts for bulk purchases.*
*For information, please call 1-800-289-0963.*

# Acknowledgments

I would like to thank the following people for their unwavering support as I completed this book. First and foremost, I thank my editor, Lisa Laing, at Adams Media for being so patient with me as I survived two life-threatening illnesses within six months of each other while writing this book. Her patience and direction were invaluable, along with my development editor at Adams Media, Brett Palana-Shanahan. My thanks especially go to my agent, Bob Diforio; Barbara Lawing; Joanna Nix; Mike Prasse; and my camping resource, Travis Johnson. Most special appreciation goes to Catharine Hamm, my travel editor at the *Los Angeles Times*, one of the most knowledgeable experts in the travel industry, and one of the kindest. In further gratitude I acknowledge the brilliant writers of the International Thriller Writers Association, Johnny Jet of JohnnyJet.com for a world of travel wisdom, Roberta Braun, Catherine Lee, Keri Morris, Tammy Schuft, LeeAnn Rawson, Cassie Brinkley, and talented actress of stage and screen Mary McNeil for her inside scoop on Hawaii. I owe Julie Ellis Levine for gifting me with the travel bug in the first place through our beloved Paris, and my grandmother Melba Wilson, who shared generations of knowledge with me as we sat side by side for many months as I wrote this book. I thank Pat and Brad Johnson, Peggy and Buzzy Merritt, my beautiful stepdaughter Madeline Merritt, author William Graham Carrington, and Pamela and Tom Newton. Most of all I acknowledge my husband, Kevin Merritt, for putting up with eons of family budget travel talk, never once complaining and always providing support.

# Contents

## Appendix B

## Appendix C

## Appendix D

# Top Ten Tips for Successful Family Budget Travel

1. Remember that spending quality time together is the most important part of family travel.

2. Be realistic: Only take trips you know you can comfortably afford.

3. Avoid destinations that don't appear legitimate. If it seems too good to be true, it probably is.

4. Work with an outfitter whenever possible, especially when traveling to remote destinations.

5. Save, save, save. Expand your destination options by saving for your trip in advance.

6. All-inclusive vacations are tempting because they can limit the number of times you have to reach for your wallet. But be sure to check for "hidden" expenses before booking travel.

7. Consider taking an educational vacation—it's a great opportunity for your family to learn something together.

8. Long-term travel planning can help you save, but some of the best deals are for last-minute weekend getaways.

9. Combine business or trips to see extended family with your vacation for extra savings.

10. Can't decide where to go on a day trip? Put ten doable destinations in a hat and let each family member draw one each month until you've been to each.

# Introduction

Traveling as a family is a great way to spend quality time together. From day trips to long-term travel, adventure, ecotourism, and educational travel are increasingly popular family activities. As a result, destinations are responding to demand with great deals and more flexibility to accommodate families on a budget.

There are many ways to save on travel and still have a wonderful vacation. Bringing food from home for staple meals, dining out only to enjoy special regional cuisine, and taking day trips until enough money is saved for a long-term trip, are just a couple of ways to save money. Packing equipment like mountain bikes and Frisbees saves on activities at a destination. Combining a business trip with vacation can cut trip expenses in half. There are so many ways to get out of town without it costing a fortune.

Long-term planning is all about patience. With patience and a little fiscal discipline, you can go just about anywhere. Some families plan months, even years in advance for major destinations. They save diligently and only take their vacation when they have the funds. Patience puts travel within reach that's otherwise unaffordable if you're willing to wait until you save enough to make it happen.

For families who love last-minute travel, travel bargains abound. But these hot deals can change in seconds, so diligence is a must.

Signing up for every travel newsletter and watching for specials every day are the keys to getting the best deals.

Until you can set aside enough funds to take an adventure of a lifetime, travel close to home. Family budget travel is all about being able to have a nice vacation with those you love, without spending so much money that it stresses family finances. Travel only when it will alleviate stress, not cause it. There are enough weekend getaways and day trips that won't break the bank to satiate the wanderlust of even the most travel-loving families.

This book will help you find ways to travel to the places you love and discover new destinations your family can experience together within your budget. How to understand the economy of travel and what you need to do to prepare for your trip are also important things to know if you're going to travel within budget. This is a broad topic, but many of the tips in this book will apply to any destination you choose. Use this book as your guide to make the right choices and select destinations that will have everyone smiling on your next vacation.

Happy travels!

# CHAPTER 1

# A Vacation Doesn't Have to Break the Bank

It's a common tale. You and your family need to get away to spend some quality time together. But between homework, careers, soccer practice, and getting dinner on the table, time is limited. Most families are on a tight budget. Travel options are numerous, so it's easy to get confused. With so many vacations to choose from, travel options can seem like salt in the ocean. Relax! Travel planning can be fun.

## The World Is Your Playground

So many places to go. How to choose, when the world can be your playground? Today, families are positively besieged with promotional messages about resorts, hotels, destinations, and travel package deals. The number of advertisements is overwhelming, but the good news is that this competition between resorts and destinations for your business puts you and your family in the driver's seat. You can go anywhere if you plan and budget in advance.

"Kids eat and stay for free," "two-for-one," and "get a free night" deals abound online, so why not start there? In this book you'll find hundreds of tips and resources for the best travel destinations and places for finding the hottest travel specials that are just right for you.

As you begin your research, keep in the back of your mind that once you confirm a trip you are unlikely to be able to make significant changes to your plan without financial penalties. Most travel companies will allow you to make alterations to your itinerary, but it is usually at an additional cost to you. Request a change and that $235 plane ticket deal could morph into $500 or more, with change fees and fare differences factored in. With marketers dangling enticing deals around every corner, it will be tempting to book travel quickly. Proceed with caution and always read the small print. Travel deals come up every day. To avoid impulse purchases, make a short list of where you want to travel. Then consider your choices and make your reservations. By using the web, your good sense, and keeping your budget in mind, you really can make the world your playground.

## ═══ Fast Fact

Keep in mind, special deals change *hourly*—that's right, hourly. To get the most out of your trip, become adept at using the Internet and tracking frequently updated sites for the latest travel deals.

## Off-Season Travel Deals

Everyone wants to be married in May, cruise Alaska in July, and ski Snowbird in December. But how about the off-season? Family travelers willing to be flexible with their schedules can save up to *half* the cost of a traditional vacation by traveling in the off-season.

Vacation rental houses, apartments, and condos, whether at the beach or in the mountains, are typically more affordable during autumn than during peak months of summer or winter. Property owners are more flexible when it comes to price. The construction boom in recent years has increased the number of vacation properties and made rental property owners more will-ing to negotiate with renters. Do your homework: be sure to ask questions and obtain prices on more than one property.

Places that are very busy during the winter months, like ski resorts, are slow during summer months. Places that enjoy boom-ing business during warm-weather months, like beach resorts, are looking for business during cold-weather months. It's a matter of thinking in opposites. The popular Killington, Vermont, ski resort may appear to be just for skiing, but in the off-season it becomes a mountain biking oasis. The weather is mild and crowds are at a minimum. Families can enjoy hiking, horseback riding, and biking with some of the northeast's most majestic mountains in the back-ground. Nearby family-friendly shopping and the site of unforget-table landscapes complete a Vermont package that can be had for a song compared to the price during ski season.

## Deciding Where, When, and How Long to Go

When deciding where to travel, several factors should be consid-ered. How far do you want to go from home? Will you need pet care? If so, you'll need to budget for that. How much time can the kids be away from their activities or school? Does your family have frequent-flier miles? What are the top ten destinations your family would like to visit? Can you combine your vacation with a visit to your favorite aunt and uncle?

By visiting friends and family you can kill two birds with one stone. You know Aunt Esther would love to meet the kids, but little Stevie loves dolphins and you've promised to take him to an aquarium. Suppose you only have two weeks allotted for vacation—you can't do both. This is where your research can really swoop in and help you save big. There are aquariums all over the country—Florida, Georgia, South Carolina, and Mary-land to name a few locations. See Chapter 18 for a complete list. If Aunt Esther lives in Birmingham, she's a hop, skip, and a jump from Atlanta's world-renowned Atlanta Aquarium. You'll have no trouble thinking up great two-for-one vacations for your family to enjoy.

Who says you can't mix business with pleasure? You can, and taking the family along on a business trip is a great way to stretch your travel dollar. Sure, you'll have work to do while you're away. But nearly every major city is teeming with low-cost or free activities your family can enjoy while you're at that trade show or conference. Bookend a business trip with a few extra days and you'll be joining them in no time. If your business trip is from Monday to Thursday, consider adding a weekend stay-over. Chances are your company is paying for your flight or mileage, so in bringing the family you're saving the cost of one air ticket—yours.

## 🧳 Travel Tip

The easiest way to plan the length of a trip is to tally the number of days you can be gone from work, home, school, and so on, and then subtract two days for travel time. Anything can happen while you're away (car trouble or flight delays, for example) and allowing the two additional days to leave and to return will minimize stress. You'll be glad you planned the buffer to bookend your trip.

You may be working during the day and even some nights, particularly if your job is in sales where entertaining clients is part of the job. But even then, your spouse and the kids can enjoy time together away from the everyday stresses of home. Save the best activities to do as a family until the weekend. When it's time to close the briefcase, you and your family can go have fun. Plus, you'll have extra spending money—thanks to the money you saved on your airline ticket, gas, or mileage.

# "Stay-cations"

At-home vacations, also known as stay-cations, are among the latest trends in budget vacationing. It may surprise you to learn how many great activities are waiting to be discovered right in your backyard.

How many times have you driven by a local museum and scolded yourself for not going? Your local Armory or civic center is hosting another festival—if only you had time to check it out. Your neighbor mentioned a new petting zoo on the outskirts of town, but it's not on your to-do list. Could it be that instead of traveling, you should stay home on your next vacation?

## ≡ Fast Fact

A stay-cation is a great way to discover your community. If you live in a small town, look into activities in neighboring counties and towns as well as your own. Historical home sites, festivals, events, and activities abound in America, and practically every community is full of fun, easy things to do. The effort lies in finding them.

### Planning Your Stay-cation Activities

Nonprofit groups, who don't have enough funds to advertise extensively, organize some of the best events and activities. A notice in the local paper, public service announcement on cable, or some fliers in the church bulletin are all they can usually afford. So how do you find them? Organizations that host events for the public, especially where food and alcohol are served, must have a permit. Your town hall will likely have a list of those upcoming events. Visit their website's calendar of events page. Visit your community library and check out the bulletin board. Your local coffee shop also is a wealth of information on community happenings. Organizations often hold events at local churches, which often list the events taking place on their property on the Internet, even if the organization isn't affiliated with the church.

If you live in an urban or suburban area, check with your local convention and visitor's bureau. They will have the information you need on historical farms where you can enjoy family activities like picking your own pumpkins or strawberries, pawing through back-road antique stores, and much, much more.

## 🧳 Travel Tip

Treat your stay-cation as a real vacation—relax, but get up and out of the house. Experts agree that too much time spent sitting around the house or on the couch actually drains energy.

Local entertainment publications are your best bet for finding out about concerts, events, and the like. Some may contain editorial content that is not family oriented and advertising unsuitable for little eyes. But most also contain community event sections that list everything from concerts to "mommy and me" groups. On a legal pad, make a list of all the events of interest to your family and set it aside.

### Make a Date

Parents know how hard it is to schedule time for each other. Your family's stay-cation is the perfect opportunity to have an old-fashioned date—with each other! Call your babysitter or day care center. Make sure they're available to watch the kids. Here are some tips for a great stay-cation date.

- Recreate your first date or the night you got engaged.
- Have dinner and watch a movie at home. Serve a meal that compliments the film.
- Schedule a couple's massage at a nearby spa.

- Wine and dine each other—order a bottle of your favorite wine with dinner.

On the day of your date, make sure you're rested. Don't be tempted to do chores or work around the house. Focus on the time you're planning to spend with your spouse. Consider picking up his or her favorite chocolate, flowers, or wine. Plan to "meet" for a cocktail in the kitchen before your date—even if it's just seltzer water. Take your time getting ready for your date. At dinner or whatever your date entails, leave work and the kids out of your conversation. Practice being present in the moment and focus completely on each other. Many couples forget as time goes on what makes their partner feel happy, loved, or appreciated. Ask each other those questions. After all, the answers may have changed. Above all, have a fun, relaxing time and enjoy each other's company. The kids will be back before you know it!

## Stay-cation Cuisine

Next step? Where to eat! Trying new restaurants is part of the fun of traveling together. Now is the time to decide where you want to eat while you and your family are enjoying your stay-cation. Think about what's available in your area. Are there restaurants you haven't tried? A type of cuisine you haven't yet experienced? A new restaurant that just opened? Get your legal pad and make a list.

Once you've narrowed your list down to a few restaurants to try while you're on your stay-cation, devote some thought to meals you've always wanted to cook for your family. Spend an hour watching the Food Channel. Pick up a copy of *Cooking Light* magazine from the supermarket. Search the Internet for "special-occasion recipes" or dig out that old cookbook you got for Christmas years ago. Select a few dishes the family can make together. Forget the same old chicken-and-rice concoctions. When deciding on your recipes, go for the gusto—after all, you're on stay-cation!

### Putting It All Together

Once you've made a list of all the events you and your family would like to attend, restaurants to try, and meals to prepare, it's time to sit down together and make some choices. Why not make a fun evening out of it? Make enough copies of the pages from your note pad for every family member. Pick a time when the whole family is together. Provide copies of your list and a magic marker to each family member. Have each family member circle the events or activities they want to do. Everyone should choose two restaurants and two meals. When they're finished, collect the sheets and calculate the results.

# Last-Minute Getaways

To get the best of the last-minute getaways it's essential to register for and read online travel newsletters. They may be made up of words and pictures, but for the family budget traveler they hold the gold. You can register to receive airline travel newsletters for flight deals from just about every major airline. Each travel newsletter is packed with deals for weekend, holiday, and last-minute travel specials. These newsletters are distributed via e-mail at frequent intervals, typically spotlighting travel for the approaching weekend. The caveat is that usually you must be able to leave on the upcoming weekend and stay over that Saturday night. If you're not looking to venture too far from home, a last-minute getaway might be just the ticket.

### Waiting 'til Wednesday Can Help You Save Big on Airfare

As the economy continues to flip-flop, last-minute getaways, which are often cheaper than advance bookings, are becoming increasingly popular. All of the nation's major airlines offer last-minute deals on flights both domestically and internationally. These fares, called everything from e-Savers to NetSAAvers to

One-Passes, are each generally a fraction of the cost of a regular-fare ticket. Most of the time, information on these deals arrives via e-mail or RSS feed on Wednesdays, although some airlines like American and United send their discounted last-minute fare deals every Tuesday. You can visit any major airline website and sign up to receive regular notices about airline discounts. With these last-minute deals, a regular roundtrip flight that usually costs $379 can be decreased to $79 each way on an e-Saver from US Airways, for example. International flights that can cost upward of $1,000 per person can be reduced to $289 roundtrip on a Delta last-minute flight deal, depending on occupancy and other factors. Sounds great, right? These deals provide a great way to save money, but there are drawbacks. Last-minute travel typically requires flexibility in your schedule—you have to be able to leave home on short notice—something that many families can't do, and destinations are limited.

## Easy Ways to Pay for Last-Minute Travel

Let's face it: most families on a budget don't have the disposable income to fly a family of four on a moment's notice. Thankfully, there are so many lodging choices that offer last-minute deals, you don't have to get on a plane to enjoy a last-minute vacation. There are, however, ways to plan for last-minute travel. One way is to start a family fund for last-minute travel. Ask everyone in the family to contribute to it. Older kids can mow lawns or babysit to do their share. Younger kids can do extra chores around the house to earn a dollar for the last-minute travel pot. Before long, you'll have a nice travel nest egg. When that last-minute travel discount to Mexico you've been waiting for pops up in your inbox, you'll be ready to go.

Another way to pay for last-minute travel deals is to accumulate frequent-flier miles. Are your credit cards attached to any rewards programs? They should be. An increasing number of Americans have learned the hard way that paying with credit is a losing game. However, paying with credit attached to a rewards program can also create wealth in the form of travel and discounts. Companies like American Express have aggressive card-holder rewards programs.

## 🧳 Travel Tip

Paying your bills with travel rewards credit cards actually pays you back. Miles you receive are valid on the card's airline affiliate, hotels, and vacation packages.

Often when you purchase airline tickets with an airline credit card, you can increase your miles.

Frequent travelers in the know often pay a large portion of their bills with travel rewards credit cards, and pay off those cards immediately with the cash they would have used to pay the bills in the first place. Sound like a hassle? It's not when you consider the free travel miles you'll accumulate as a result.

### Places You Can Go

Last-minute travel discounts don't apply to every destination. In fact, you can expect to see anywhere from ten to fifty last-minute deals per discount notice, just a fraction of the places that are probably on your list of desired destinations. If you can be flexible, you'll have an easier time being a last-minute traveling family. The key to last-minute travel is preparedness. Keep a running list of places you and your family would like to go. Make a list by season—where would you and your family most like to go to witness the changing of the leaves? Google "fall foliage" and the name of your state to find out which resorts or hoteliers are offering last-minute getaways for fall foliage. Winter blues? Watch online for snow reports and find out which resorts have snow. Snowshoeing is fast becoming one of the most popular winter sports, and it's a fraction of the cost of skiing. Why not take a day trip to a nearby mountain for hot cocoa and snowshoeing together? Summer is perhaps the easiest season to plan a last-minute getaway to a neighboring beach. But during those months often the deals don't seem much like discounts. Consider a lake or river vacation. You can even inquire about lakeside camping, which can be worlds cheaper than renting a hotel room. And don't forget to book last-minute travel in the off-season. In the off-season, last-minute deals gain nuclear strength, as resorts struggle to pay the bills in slower months. For example, ski resorts become hiking and mountain biking paradise in summer months, and the rates can be cut in half.

## Last-Minute Resources

Chances are your state government maintains a tourism division. Visit your state's website and look for links to any hotel, motel, lodging, or hospitality associations. These associations are membership organizations whose member properties often must meet certain criteria to belong—cleanliness, involvement in the community, and participation in state-sponsored tourism campaigns. These properties are likely to be trustworthy when it comes to honoring last-minute deals and discounts.

Contact nearby (within reasonable drive time) hotels or resorts you're interested in visiting. Ask them to add you to their newsletter distribution, or ask the property's reservationist how you can find out about last-minute discounts. For destinations at a greater distance, check destination state and adjacent city websites for tourism information and hospitality associations. There you'll find a wealth of information pertaining to last-minute travel.

There are many last-minute travel websites now online. Choose popular travel websites; obscure sites are obscure for a reason. Either they're too new to have buzz, or they're risky. By the same token, mammoth sites like Travelocity or Expedia are so large it can be irritating to wade through thousands of travel deals when you just want some ideas.

One easy-to-use website is Kayak.com (*www.kayak.com*). This site provides low fares from hundreds of sources. Your luck in landing a great deal is increased by flexible dates. You can find "fire sales" which airlines offer sporadically, but the fares are incredibly low. Airfare Watchdog (*www.airfarewatchdog.com*) includes fares from airlines great and small and often posts airfares faster than other discount airfare sites.

For hotels, often going straight to the source can provide just as much information. Love brand loyalty? Be sure to contact your favorite hotel chain and ask to be placed on their newsletter distribution. Omni Hotels often offer packages in select cities and towns that might not be listed on a travel site. One hotel website called HotelChatter.com (*www.hotelchatter.com*) not only provides information on fares, but also an honest review of the best hotel for the buck, amenities, and cost information.

## Packing for a Last-Minute Trip

Now that you've become an expert on last-minute travel, you'll need a last-minute travel bag, prepacked with a set of your family's toothbrushes, toiletries, and other essentials. It won't matter how good a deal is—you'll miss it if you're not ready to travel. When that two-for-one deal flashes across your computer screen from Ohio's Cedar Point, the roller coaster capital of the world, you'll be ready! The following checklist will help:

- ❏ Medium-sized backpack or roller bag that doubles as a backpack
- ❏ Travel-size toothbrushes, toothpaste, Handi-wipes, baby powder, Neosporin, band-aids, bug spray, and cuticle clippers
- ❏ Over-the-counter medications: Children's Tylenol, Benadryl, and Sudafed
- ❏ Copies of family identification (preferably children's birth certificates and parents' passports)

❑ Printed list of important phone numbers and e-mail addresses
❑ For warm-weather travel, a pair of flip-flops for each family member
❑ Power bars and age-appropriate prewrapped snacks

Some of the items listed may be surprising, but they can make the difference between smiling and screaming children. If too much walking causes a blister on someone's heel—hey, you've got flip-flops. Baby powder prevents chafing. Cuticle clippers are for more than trimming hangnails—they can extract splinters from tiny hands. Your printed list of important contacts will come in handy if you lose your phone and need to call for a replacement. And with some airlines charging $5 per snack box, snacks such as power bars and fruit roll ups brought from home can save a family of four $20 or more.

Traveling with families doesn't have to be stressful. The key is preparation. Be prepared for life's little last-minute emergencies. When they happen, you'll be ready.

# CHAPTER 2

# Planning Your Vacation

Half the fun of going someplace is getting there, and with travel, getting there involves research and planning. It's easier to save money when your trip is well planned and especially when your vacation is combined with a trip to see relatives or for business. Working together, your family can construct a budget and choose activities. You'll enjoy watching your family's anticipation grow with every step in the planning process. Hey, it can even be fun! Vacation planning can bring the whole gang together. Planning, of course, is part of the journey.

## Vacations That Do Double Duty

Combining vacations with trips to visit relatives or for business is a great way to save money. The benefits of merging a vacation with a trip to see Grandma or a work-related event can include less time away from work, fewer miles on the car, and a much cheaper transportation bill overall.

### Family Vacations to Visit Friends and Family

Transportation savings significantly increase when a family doesn't have to fly to a destination, and many parents don't mind a long car ride if it means saving hundreds, even thousands of dollars over flying. And practically any family can find a destination that's within "drive time" of their place of residence. Typical "drive time" (otherwise known as the distance most families are willing to drive to reach a vacation destination) for the American family used to be about five hours. This is the distance many resorts and visitors' bureaus use to measure how far away they will market their destination. Most families have their own set drive time, or the maximum time they'll spend in the car. However, destinations and the people who market them spend the majority of their advertising dollars on reaching families close enough to make a trip to their resort in the typical drive time of about five hours. You may be just outside their reach, but your relatives just a few hours away might see ads for nearby destination specials all the time.

## 💼 Travel Tip

To find out about the best deals from a destination resort or attraction you want to visit, keep an open mind with regard to your drive time. For most families, their set drive time has increased with the downturn of the economy.

Make a list of relatives you would like to visit. Research area attractions near their hometowns. Tell your relatives you're planning a family vacation. Ask them to keep an eye out for specials, and do the same for them. Register for updates and specials on attraction websites. Be ready to travel on a few days notice. Stock up on time off if possible, and start a vacation fund in a cookie jar.

### Shaving Extra Travel Time Off Your Trip

Even on shorter trips where the drive time is just a few hours, smart family travelers know that between packing the car, driving to the destination, unpacking and getting settled, you have to allow for two days of travel time. Let's say you've planned a vacation, and the following month are going to visit your in-laws. Taking these two separate trips means taking four days off from work just to get to and from your destination. Sure it's fun to go away twice, but if you're on a serious budget, it pays to rethink your vacation destination.

Perhaps there are some amazing attractions or things to do near the town where your in-laws live. Add a couple of days onto the trip you're already taking to visit relatives, and you're still saving two days of travel time by rolling both trips into one. Families who combine a vacation with a family visit have to take fewer days off from work, use less gasoline, pay less for food and hotels, and the list goes on and on.

## Mix Business with Pleasure for Big Savings

How does combining business with pleasure save your family money? It would seem the obvious answer is in gasoline, but that's only part of the equation. A family will realize savings when combining business travel with a vacation because the business traveler's lodging, meals, and transportation costs are covered. Combining travel with a visit to relatives can save you money, but mixing business travel with a vacation can really rack up the savings. Are there work-related destinations you need to visit? Perhaps you have been meaning to call on a client several hours from home, but it sure seems like a long way.

The savings continue to pile up if a family joins one of its members traveling on business. Say dad has a convention in Orlando and his company is flying him to the convention. Orlando is a convention capital and home to some of the world's most famous amusement parks. Dad flies for free and the rest of the family joins him on the last day of the convention, meaning the family has saved a roundtrip plane ticket. Or, if dad drives to Orlando, the family can come along and enjoy time together while dad is at work. The whole family can stay a couple of extra days so dad, too, can have time off, and you're still saving two days at a minimum of travel time. Dad will be reimbursed for his mileage or gasoline expense since he was traveling to Orlando anyway. Plus, while they're in Orlando together, the family can have dinner or meet up for lunch.

Perhaps mom has a business meeting in a neighboring state and her hotel is next to one of the country's largest water parks or best museums. Hotels like occupancy, and mom's hotel may offer a discount on additional days if she extends her stay. Mom's company picks up the tab for the duration of her work time, and your family pays a discounted rate for your stay after mom's work is finished. It's a win-win for both parties thanks to the discount for a longer stay.

# Research—Online and Hands-On

As noted earlier in Chapter 1, the Internet has redefined the art of research. The web also makes it more difficult to decipher the factual from the promotional. Nowhere is this more obvious than in the online world of travel. A resort may look like paradise online, but if you don't learn to read between the lines, it could turn into a lemon.

### Decoding Travel Websites

The world wide web is today's wild, wild west. Make no mistake about it: on the Internet, anything goes. Generally speaking, if that all-inclusive family vacation for four to Mexico for $500 sounds too good to be true, most likely it is. When you type "travel deals" into a search engine like Google, hundreds of travel sites will appear. These include mammoth sites like Expedia.com, Travelocity.com, PriceLine.com, Hotwire.com, TravelZoo.com and Orbitz.com, which are considered reputable travel websites. Be sure to scroll down to check out some of the lesser-known sites like Kayak.com and SmarterTravel.com that offer links to additional deals.

Travel portals like JohnnyJet.com and SideStep.com search hundreds of travel websites and list the best discounts from all the major travel sites on one site. Via BookingBuddy.com, visitors to

JohnnyJet.com can simply type their departure and destination cities, dates of travel, and number of travelers, and up comes a list of selected sites. Click on the respective logos to view travel deals. Some travelers prefer searching individual sites, but for those with less time or patience, JohnnyJet.com is a valuable clearinghouse. Note that the site also includes the best travel deals of the day on the home page, so remember to check back often for late-breaking specials.

## Field Trips to the Map or Bookstore

A wonderful resource for your family travel planning is your local book store. If you've already decided where you would like to go, you can also call the tourism division of your destination. They can provide maps and other area information. If you have not selected your destination, physically going to a bookstore, library, or even a local map store, if your city or town has one, to view maps of the world is an educational, fun activity. Other resources include Maps.com and the Rand McNally online map site. Nothing online can hold a candle to the hands-on experience a child can get from running their fingers over the Continental Divide on a map or globe, both of these websites are great tools for you and your family to use together. (*www.randmcnally.com*) (*www.maps.com*)

## Visit the Local Library

Educators agree on the importance of teaching children geography. Children are naturally curious. They want to know where things are. They'll want to know where your family destination is located. Start by showing them where you live, then point out your destination. A child who is curious about geography is a prime candidate for becoming a responsible steward of the planet. Your local library will have at least one atlas. An atlas can serve as a tremendous resource to help everyone arrive at a decision together.

If you so choose, purchase an atlas. A home atlas allows for making notes in the margins and the convenience of having the atlas at your fingertips for the family to enjoy anytime—say, in the evening after dinner when the library is closed. The *National Geographic Atlas of the World* can be purchased on Amazon.com for anywhere from $25 to $185 depending on the edition and whether the atlas is new or used. Used cartography (map) resources can be great fun because they may contain the previous traveler's notations and comments about his journeys.

## ≡ Fast Fact

Each year, vacation resorts and tourism boards spend millions on marketing. You can request their media kit and marketing packages and they may even provide a DVD about the destination.

### Multimedia

As you work together to choose your destination, nothing will serve you better than seeing what a destination actually looks like. Though there are many choices, choose videos such as those produced by National Geographic, Discovery Channel, and Reader's Digest. Interested in seeing America by car? You can get *America's Most Scenic Drives* (Readers Digest) on video from Amazon.com for $14.95. Watching the video together means more family fun. Don't forget the popcorn!

## Cancellations and Contingency Plans

You're excited about your family's vacation. The bags are packed and the dog is already at Grandma's house. You're just about to walk out the door when something happens that requires you to cancel your trip. Cancellations happen—they're just a fact of life. Be prepared with a cancellation action plan.

Before booking travel, be sure to carefully review all relevant cancellation policies. If you're considering a combination travel package that includes air, hotel, and rental car, be sure to review each company's policy to make sure you have all the facts. On pages where you are asked for your credit card information, most websites will ask you to read or if you have read and approved their terms and conditions, which often include their cancellation policies. Make sure you can live with the consequences before entering your credit card information. Still have questions? Call the resort, hotel, or airline to get your answers before booking.

## ■ Travel Tip

Countless vacations are ruined by lousy weather. Before you click "confirm" be sure to check your weather forecast for the dates you are planning to travel. Predicting the weather is not an exact science, but such sites as Weather.com are useful resources for checking immediate weather forecasts around the world.

If you're wise, you will have a contingency plan in place in case you have to cancel your family's vacation. Talk about it as you're planning your vacation. Make a list of activities your family would like to do if vacation plans change. A secondary plan will minimize stress.

## Planning for Long-Term Travel

If your or your spouse's job requires extended travel, you'll need a long-term travel plan. Children can reap tremendous benefits from traveling. If you plan carefully, long-term travel can be one of the best opportunities your family can have for learning together.

### Remote Schooling

Begin by talking with your child's teachers to get assignments due over the course of the time you expect to be away. Find out if you'll be expected to mail completed assignments or deliver all of them upon your return. Fill a three-ring binder with the assignments, and include a three-hole-punched slotted insert after each one. Allow your child to decorate the cover with his favorite decals or drawings. When your child completes an assignment, file it in the slotted insert. If envelopes are needed, addressing them before you leave home is ideal—one for each week you will be away. Then all you have to do is affix the correct postage and drop the envelope in the mail.

## Home Security

If you will be away for extended periods, home security is a special concern. The best way to protect your home is to purchase a home security system. Many security companies offer free systems and installation with a service contract, starting at approximately $20 per month and increasing in cost depending on the type and level of security you desire. Putting one or more interior lights on automatic timers is one of the simplest and least expensive home security measures. They provide the illusion of occupancy. A trusted neighbor is also a valuable crime deterrent. Ask your neighbor to keep an eye on your home, and walk through the house occasionally to be sure nothing is amiss.

## House-Sitters

A house-sitter can be an excellent security measure for your house during an extended absence. Find lists of house sitters and their qualifications at websites like HouseSittersAmerica.com and HouseCarers.com. SabbaticalHomes.com serves as a matchmaker within the academic community, helping to find housing for students and academic professionals on sabbatical or engaged in exchange programs. Have pets? Many house-sitters will also care for pets in your absence for an additional fee.

## Factoring in Extra Time for Travel

When planning your vacation, don't cut yourself short on time. That's a good way to get into trouble. Factor in the possibility of airport delays, car rental problems, misplacing your passport, locking yourself out of your house, and directional challenges (getting lost). A little forethought will ensure that you're ready to handle whatever may occur between your house and your destination.

Always book the earliest flight possible. Not a morning person? Decide you will be this time, because it's a necessity. Getting up at 3 A.M. instead of 6 A.M. seems unpleasant, but it's nothing compared to losing an entire day of your trip because of a missed flight. Multiple legs of the trip—more than one flight—increase the likelihood you will miss a flight. So book direct flights to avoid connections whenever possible. If your first flight is delayed, you will likely miss your connecting flight. The later in the day you choose to fly, the greater the chances of this happening.

The exception to the "don't take later flights" rule is the "red eye." It typically leaves the West coast around midnight and arrives in a later time zone the following morning.

## Odds and Ends of Family Travel

From traveling with your teenage sons and daughters to traveling with an infant, disabled child, or other family member, there are many resources at your disposal. Traveling grandparents and traveling single parents are becoming mainstream. And more families are traveling with other families to shave costs. Travel consultants for virtually every type of travel are available online to provide advice and planning tips. Trade shows are a great place to find deals and referrals for travel that's easy on the budget and family-friendly.

### Traveling with Teens

Traveling with teens doesn't have to be difficult if you make them feel valued! Experts agree that the key to success when traveling with teens is obtaining their input. When making travel plans with your family, be sure to listen to and consider the wishes of your teen. And once on vacation, allow your teen some space to engage in an enjoyable activity. This strategy will go far toward keeping the peace for the duration of your family vacation.

## ≡ Fast Fact

More often grandparents and grandchildren are traveling together without parents present. The folks behind the website GrandTrvl.com organize trips to Washington, D.C., and Williamsburg; London and Paris; Alaska; Italy; and New Zealand.

For an ideal vacation with teens, try a cruise. There is so much to do, and your teen can't wander across a town border or out of your sight for too long. On the other hand, if you have a troubled teen in the house, consider a vacation that's close to home. Another idea is to base a vacation on teens' curiosity about nature. A trek along a trail connects you with nature and expends excess energy, both of which bring out the best in everyone. Check out the location of the nearest national park. See Chapter 18 for a partial listing.

### Single-Parent Travel

The Internet is rich in resources for single parents traveling with their children. One such site, SingleParentTravel.net includes single-parent blogs and connects single parents with one another to plan trips to places as exotic as Costa Rica or as local as New York City. In addition to planned trips and advertised travel deals, SingleParentTravel.net also offers feature stories about how and where to travel. Surprisingly, another resource for you is your local church, synagogue, or community center. Many of them sponsor single-parent support groups and special activities, which may include organized vacations for single parents and their children.

## And Baby Makes Three—Flying with an Infant

Traveling with an infant can be challenging, but a little planning on your part can make things go more smoothly. Something so simple as bringing a firm pillow for baby to sleep on can make a world of difference. Pacifiers can help baby equalize his ears, and timing his feeding during takeoff will minimize stress. Germs abound on a plane, so make sure to bring hand sanitizer (purse size, no more than three and a half ounces) to use on the outside of baby's bottle and everything you touch, before you touch baby.

## Traveling with a Disabled Child or Family Member

Disabled children are special indeed. Depending on the child's disability, parents can employ strategies to minimize complications that might arise when traveling. Keep in mind that traveling in the off-season means fewer crowds. Speak with the manager at your lodging about your child's needs and make sure they are prepared and equipped to help. Resorts like Divi Flamingo in Bonaire have outfitted a large number of rooms specifically for people with disabilities. If your child has needs that will require you to be apart from other guests, ask your hotel to reserve a room without shared walls. Many disabled children prefer familiar scenes and suffer from separation anxiety when their normal everyday routine changes. Items your child enjoys like stuffed animals, toys, or clothing can help ease his anxiety. The American Society of People with Disabilities has produced materials that contain information specifically about air travel for people with disabilities.

### Multifamily Travel

One of the best ways to save money and increase your child's travel experience is to travel with other families. There is safety in numbers, and children have built-in playmates. In addition, traveling with other families makes bringing a sitter a more realistic option, since the cost of the sitter can be split among more than one family.

The cost of food can be cut in half when families share the load, particularly when the group stays in lodgings that include a kitchenette and buys groceries at the onset of the trip. Small children can share meals in restaurants, and snacks—which are outrageously priced at resorts—can be avoided entirely by purchasing snacks to bring along.

### Alternative Family Travel

As the definition of family continues to evolve, families that fall under the category of alternative lifestyle can choose from welcoming resorts all over the world. Grand Lido Resorts & Spas, for example, make a point of stating that none of their resorts discriminate based upon race, nationality, gender, marital status, or sexual orientation.

Southwest Airlines has a dedicated website devoted to gay and lesbian travelers. The website features special offers, gay-friendly destinations, and events. Gay-friendly hotel chains range from intimate bed and breakfasts like the W. J. Marsh House Victorian Bed and Breakfast in Albuquerque, New Mexico, to the second-largest hotel in the world, the Luxor in Las Vegas. GayTravel.com is a credible and thorough resource for alternative lifestyle families who love to travel together.

## Travel Consultants and Trade Shows

Travel planning companies make money by helping you plan your trip. When you're trying to save money, the DIY approach is probably best. But if your family is planning a large scale, long-term vacation, budgeting for a travel planner is a good idea. Using a travel planning company can also benefit group travelers, for example when you and other families plan a trip together. For large families bringing children and their friends, or family members with special needs—a travel planner can help take the stress of extensive planning off your shoulders. Sometimes, money is secondary to convenience and sound planning if it saves you mountains of aggravation.

## 🧳 Travel Tip

There are hundreds of travel companies that specialize in everything from beach vacations to the Amazon rainforests. With so many travel consultants, how do you choose? For starters, choose a travel planner with a proven track record. Spend time on the travel company's website. Check to see if the travel planning company has established partnerships with destinations or holds membership in reputable travel organizations.

### Gap Adventures

"Gap" is an acronym for the Great Adventure People. Gap Adventures offers more than 1,000 expeditions and can count more than 85,000 travelers annually. There are numerous options for active travelers, and travelers interested in culture, wildlife, and eco-travel. Gap Adventures has been so successful, it employs 600 employees and has offices worldwide. Gap's first tours were in Belize, Ecuador, and Peru, but today they handle tours on every continent. The company, like most travel planners these days, is an eco-conscious travel company. Planeterra, Gap's nonprofit organization enables the company to give back to local communities in areas where Gap organizes tours. Visit *www.gapadventures.com* for more information.

**ADDITIONAL FAMILY TRAVEL PLANNING WEBSITES**
- Traveling with Kids (*www.travelingwithkids.com*)
- Go City Kids (*www.gocitykids.com*)
- Trails.com (*www.trails.com*)
- Gordon's Guide (*www.gordonsguide.com*)
- Thrill Planet (*www.thrillplanet.com*)

## Travel Trade Shows—Coming to a City Near You

The next best thing to seeing a resort or destination firsthand is to visit their booth at a travel industry trade show. Ranging from elaborate displays to folding tables and flyers, the Adventures in Travel Expos are travel shows that feature companies in the adventure travel business. Currently four cities—Seattle, Los Angeles, New York City, and Washington, D.C.—host Adventures in Travel Expos.

At these shows, attendees can preview destinations and meet tour operators representing many vacations. From safaris and scuba to archaeology and rainforest tours, there is something for every family to consider at travel shows. Love whitewater rafting? Chances are you'll find numerous booths featuring Class 1 to Class "off-the-charts" whitewater rafting excursions.

The best part of attending these shows is the discounts and specials offered by tour operators. Families can shave hundreds of dollars off of a family trip through travel show connections. See *www.adventureexpo.com*.

## Travel Agent Associations

The American Society of Travel Agents (ASTA) is the largest association of travel professionals in the world. Membership in ASTA includes travel agents, tour operators, cruise lines, lodging companies (hotels and motels), car rental companies, airlines and more. On the ASTA website (*www.asta.org*) you can locate an agent near you.

At Travel.org (*www.travel.org*) you can locate agents by destination and type of travel. And, you can search for providers using an online trip builder portal that will help direct you to the agent best qualified for your vacation destination, number of people traveling, dates, and other preferences.

# CHAPTER 3

# The Well-Managed Budget

B eautiful views. Tantalizing cuisine. Loving couples frolicking on the beach, cocktails in hand. Kids engaged in activities. Those images will get you every time. Marketers know what you want—rest and relaxation and time away with loved ones, far from the office. Every word, every picture is tailored to entice you into throwing caution to the wind. "Come away and forget your troubles," they seem to exclaim. In advertising, vacation spots look wonderful, and the truth is, they probably are. Go on vacation and enjoy yourself, but just remember to ask this question before you leave: after all the frolicking, playing, eating, and drinking, how will you pay for it? Financial worries can turn a relaxing vacation into anything but.

## How to Save Big on Hotels, Transportation, and Attractions

It would seem the answer to this lies in finding the right travel website. Perhaps making advance reservations is the best way to save big on lodging or transportation. Or maybe the shortcut to great deals lies in last-minute booking. All three are correct, but only tell half the story. The best resource for getting the best deal is you. Your choices are what will make the difference between paying full price and getting a discount that will help keep you under budget. Remember that great deals and discounts do exist. Don't allow yourself to be tricked into making an impulse buy before you have all the facts.

## 💼 Travel Tip

> The first step to saving big on vacations is to be wary. Deals that give the illusion that you won't have to spend much money for your family's vacation are false. It costs money to travel, discounts or not. You can aggressively pursue great travel deals, but no one is going to "give" you a free room. Vacation destinations will do what they can to earn a living, just like any other company.

Advertising agencies, media relations professionals, and marketing agencies employ people to do one thing, and that's sell you a product. It could be a trip to Europe or the Caribbean, a quaint bed and breakfast, or a resort package. Their job is to create messaging that entices consumers into making a decision. Look closely at the next vacation ad you see. If it's a good ad, it will have a few key components.

A convincing ad is designed to inform, educate, and persuade consumers to purchase a product or service. There is also something called a "call to action," and that's where you can stop yourself from getting fleeced by the travel industry. A call to action is pressure to "act now" or click to purchase "before time runs out" and other such urgent instructions. Remember, there will always be another deal. The discount that is only valid until a certain date will be replicated soon enough with an even better sounding discount. Don't get sucked into the hype, and you won't get sucked into making a purchase before you've done your homework.

# Budget Travel Detective—Learn to Recognize Travel Scams

Suppose you find an incredible, once-in-a-lifetime deal on your family's dream destination, but it's hard to tell if the offer is real. You don't want to get ripped off, but on the chance the deal really is that great, you're willing to risk it. Read the small print or disclosure statement (if any are listed.) The old adage "if it looks too good to be true, it probably is" is applicable for the most part, but some travel scams are so sophisticated, they can be difficult to recognize. Know that a scam is a scam. That dream trip may indeed exist, but it may wind up costing thousands more than the advertised price.

There are many telltale signs that a travel deal is a scam. Steer clear of deals that advertise all-inclusive rates no matter the season. Your choice of rooms is another lie. An ocean-view room and an oceanfront room will almost always be different rates. When a "travel representative" tells you to go to the website of another company to make hotel or other vacation choices, run the other way. Free upgrades? No way. Unless you have established an escalated status in a travel rewards program, upgrades are typically awarded at check-in or within the hotel package. The promise of an upgrade is a very successful marketing tool, but the destination is not upgrading anything. You will still be charged for your lodging and a destination will recoup the cost somewhere down the line.

This is not to say that hotels or travel companies can't be trusted. Many, most in fact, really do want your business and are willing to go extraordinary efforts to get it. Just remember that slick marketing and advertising can't replace your own good detective work.

## Telltale Signs a Website Can't Be Trusted

Is there a phone number on the contact page of the travel website you're viewing? Call it. Make sure it is legitimate. But even then, be advised. It's not hard to set up a "call center" where scammers practice the traditional bait-and-switch.

Schemes vary. Look for deals that seem impossible to deliver for the asking price. Timing is a key component on website travel marketing scams. Watch out for hazy guarantees or club memberships at extremely low prices. Scam offers can appear to be completely reasonable. Anyone looking for a vacation can be at risk for travel scams if they don't carefully research the details. Does it seem too good to be true? Then it probably is!

# Drafting a Budget

Nearly any vacation is possible if you budget accordingly. The question of whether or not you can take your family to Fiji is one part conscious savings, one part careful planning, and a whole lot of patience. There is nothing wrong with dreaming. Families who really want to take that dream trip to Africa should begin planning. There may be sacrifices along the way, and such a financial undertaking may take a while to manifest. Provided your family has the self-discipline to drop every spare cent into your African safari piggy bank, to Africa you shall go!

## A Family Affair—Getting Everyone Involved

A family vacation is exciting for everyone. Buy a flip chart at your local office supply store and assemble it in the room where your family gathers. Dry-erase boards are not recommended, as you may need to refer to your flip chart repeatedly in the vacation planning process. Gather all your materials and make a date for your family to spend an evening together. Using your flip chart to record the discussion, encourage everyone to make suggestions about activities and discuss the trip. This may take more than one evening. Leave the flip chart out so family members can jot down other suggestions or things they'd like to do on your trip. Eventually, make final decisions. These decisions will be the basis of your travel budget.

## How Much Will You *Really* Need?

The next step is to discover how much money you will need for your vacation. You may be paying for your entire trip with a credit card or money you've already saved, but you still need a budget. Research lodging, transportation, food, and activities based on the decisions you made as a family. Once you've added all of the costs for every family member, tack on the cost for another person— as if you were bringing a guest. This will ensure you have enough money for the trip and a buffer. Make a list of at-home vacation expenses, too, like pet or house sitter expenses, security, and such. Will you need passports? New luggage? Shots? Add these costs to your final dollar amount.

If you want to travel within six months, calculate how much money you'll need to save each week to make that deadline. If you find the amount is unrealistic, move your travel date further out. Do not try to come up with more money faster—this will only place stress on your family and lessen the fun of planning for your trip. If you plan to use a credit card for part of your trip, transportation costs for example, deduct that amount from the funds you need to save. Calculate a plan that includes the dollar amount you need to save each week to meet your goal.

## Sticking to It

The key to arriving at your desired travel budget is sticking to it. It is easier to stick with a plan you have to think about every week. Remain faithful to your plan. If you're saving cash for your trip, place a jar in your family's kitchen for change and dollar bills. As often as your daily budget allows, every time you walk by, drop something into the jar. That money adds up.

## Shortcuts to Paying for the Trip

You've identified the perfect vacation spot. You know how much the trip will cost. The kids are excited and you've put in for vacation time off from work. You and your spouse need new swimsuits, and the kids need passports. If only you could save money faster so your family could go sooner. There are some shortcuts that can help you do just that.

For starters, make sure your credit cards are attached to frequent flyer or other rewards program. In just six months, paying your bills with a rewards card that offers a frequent-flier mile for every dollar spent could result in a free airline ticket.

## 💼 Travel Tip

Use the budget travel snowball. Have you recently paid off a credit card or loan? Instead of spending that money randomly, pretend you are still paying off the balance of the old bill. Take that monthly payment and apply it to your travel fund. Before long, the money will snowball into your vacation.

Many travel rewards programs allow you to use points to pay for travel. Check with your preferred airline and hotel chain to see what programs they offer.

## Be Prepared for Anything

The cost of going to Maine will be entirely different than the cost of going to China, right? Wrong! Maine, beautiful Maine. Home of lobsters. Fine dining. Outdoor activities. Luxurious bed and breakfasts. Skiing. Get the picture? You can spend more on food and wine on vacation than the cost of two airline tickets—and it's likely you will. Lodging can eat more than half of your vacation budget. Headed to one of your neighboring drive states (a drive state is a state that you can drive to in a day or less)? The ad on TV practically yells in your ear: Just a short jaunt from your town! Take the short drive to Bob's Beach Resort! Reasonable rates! Hmm, you might say, we could scoot away for the weekend. That wouldn't be too expensive. It's your money to spend as you wish. But if you're trying to stay in the black, being an informed traveler is your best defense against going over budget.

## Cash, Credit Cards, Debit Cards, and Traveler's Checks

Cash is a necessity for any vacation. As a general rule, however, bring the minimal amount of cash possible on vacation. Theft or something so simple as misplacing your wallet could render you penniless if you don't travel with a credit card or traveler's checks.

Credit cards are the best choice for travel funds, even more so than debit cards. When checking into a hotel, your debit card will be authorized for far more than if you use a credit card. Most car rental establishments will not accept a debit card as a guarantee and will require a credit card to rent a vehicle anyway. Many establishments do not take every credit card, so your best bet is to stick with a Visa or MasterCard, with American Express as backup. Some American Express card plans are designed specifically with travelers in mind, and therefore offer many more perks than Visa or MasterCard credit cards. But it is unwise to limit yourself to just an American Express card, since not every business accepts it.

## The Truth about Credit Card Authorizations

Have you ever gone out to dinner and when paying the check, were told that you're over your credit limit? It's a common tale. And much of the time, people really aren't over their credit limit. Their available credit limit has been reduced because of hotel or other authorizations.

When you guarantee a reservation, reservationists use a tactic that has angered many a traveler over the last few years. The "6 P.M. arrival" guarantee has gone the way of the dodo bird. Now, hoteliers don't care if you arrive by 6 P.M. or before—they'll still require a credit card to "hold" the reservation. Reservationists will tell you when they take your credit card that it will not be charged until you check out, but your card will still be authorized, rendering those funds unavailable for use. It's true that when a company authorizes a card it's not charged, but the hotelier's authorization hold will remain until the card is charged at check out. Even then, depending on your cardholder bank, that authorization could take days to fall off. During this time, those funds on your card will be locked and usually for more than your actual room cost. Your card can be authorized for as much as the full amount of your room in advance of your stay for the total number of days you plan to be at that hotel. Upon check in, your card can also be authorized for additional "incidentals" according to that hotelier's policy. Incidentals can include phone calls, mini-bar purchases, parking, and similar items. This authorization can range from $50 to hundreds of dollars. One way to avoid having your credit card authorized for incidentals is to use your own cell phone when traveling and simply tell the front desk personnel not to enable the phone or pay-per-view in your room. This is called a no-post folio and it alerts room service, valet, and other hotel staff to obtain cash when you request services in excess of your room rate.

The problem with such authorizations is that unless you have a very high credit limit, which is most often not the case with families on a budget, you will not be able to use those authorized funds until they are released by your cardholder bank. People who use debit cards when they check in to a hotel can be subjected to an even higher authorization. Even if you pay cash when you check out, you will still show a hold on the available funds on the credit or debit card you used to check in to the room until they fall off. When you check out of the hotel, you can request that the hotel fax a statement of release to free up the funds they authorized. But this is a pain you don't want to deal with while on vacation. The moral of the story? Make sure you have plenty of available credit on your credit card before you travel.

## Pay-at-the-Pump Gas Authorizations

When traveling, especially to major metropolitan areas, always go inside to pay for gas regardless of whether you're paying with cash or credit even if paying at the pump is an option. Decide how much gas you'll need before you pump rather than fill your tank and wait to see how much the cost will be. Why? A little known fact is that gas stations, particularly in urban and high-crime areas have been known to authorize as much as $200 against your available credit when you pay at the pump. Station owners do this to protect themselves. For years many gas station owners programmed gas pumps to authorize credit card usage for just $1. Criminals realized they could obtain gas at automatic pumps using credit cards with less available credit than the cost of the gas purchase. When actual purchase amounts came through the system, the purchase would be declined leaving merchants paying for the gas. To combat this trend, some gas station owners have upped credit card authorizations at the pump.

This means even if you buy $10 in gas at the pump, your credit card could be authorized for $210 and you'll be the last to know. Even though the authorization will drop off within seven to ten business days, your funds will not be available for use until then.

Not every gas station is adopting this rule. Some still authorize just a dollar when you pay at the pump. But why gamble with your available credit?

## 🧳 Travel Tip

When buying gasoline on vacation, estimate how much gas you'll need, and pay inside in advance of pumping. Otherwise, it's advisable to leave at least $500 in extra available funds on a credit card if you plan to pay at the pump throughout your trip.

### International Currencies

Depending on the country your family will visit, calculating the differences in currency may be an essential part of building an accurate budget. Currencies change in real time, so an up-to-the-minute currency calculator is an indispensable tool. An accurate resource, XE.com is one of many online calculators (*www.xe.com/ucc*). This site has repeatedly been rated as number one by users. To use currency calculators, simply insert the currency you'll be exchanging and the currency of the destination to which you'll be traveling. In most cases, the results of the conversion are immediate.

In a down economy, be aware that the value of the U.S. dollar will fluctuate. For this reason, try to use as little cash as possible when you are out of the country. Get only enough cash to use for gratuities and at places that might not accept credit cards. Unless you have a clear understanding of how the international currency exchange will affect your bottom line on your family vacation, a conversation with your bank representative is highly advisable.

# Budget Travel Dos and Don'ts

The best defense against making budget mistakes is common sense. You should have a handle on your travel budget before you book your trip. Stay with that theme throughout your vacation. Be the guardian of your budget in order to keep your financial sanity. If you feel like faltering, remind yourself that your budget is gospel when it comes to deciding what to buy and what to eat or do.

### Budget Travel Dos

Construct your budget in a software program like Microsoft Excel, which will calculate your budget for you. If you don't have Excel on your computer, check to see if your system has a program called Microsoft Works. They are similar in style and will work accordingly.

Once again, your goal is to come home with something in your pocket—not destitute. Vacationing is a natural aphrodisiac for the wallet. It's easy to overspend.

Bring two printed copies of your budget along on your trip. Keep one in your wallet and one in your room for quick reference. Review your budget before, during, and after your vacation. While away, you'd be surprised how little expenses can add up to big bills. Before you know it, you've spent $100, $200, or even $300 and are over your budget. Keep checking every few days to make sure you're still on track. Stay on track by checking your budget often.

When possible, assign a credit card for each item you plan to purchase. One credit card can be for food. Another for lodging. Another credit card for airline costs. Another for shopping. Reserve the last for emergencies only. Assign cards accordingly and watch how much easier it is to keep track of purchases and stay under budget. Some families prefer to use credit cards to pay for items on vacation to get frequent-flier miles or other rewards, or so they don't have to carry a lot of cash. If you're planning to use credit cards, pay down your balance with your vacation savings before you leave or immediately upon return.

## Budget Travel Don'ts

Relying only on cash when traveling is a mistake of gargantuan proportion. Never bring all your funds in cash. Cash can't be replaced like credit cards or traveler's checks. Having too much cash on hand also leaves too much room for impulse purchases. It's tempting to want to spend your last few dollars on stuffed animals for the kids to take home, or just one more parasailing experience. When you're tempted to do those types of things, picture yourself about to jump from a plane without checking your parachute. Make sure you have the budget to allow for deviations in your budget. Remember, the best vacations are the ones from which you return with something in your pocket.

Families who do opt to bring a laptop may be tempted to use it at coffee shops or in hotel lobbies while on vacation. Don't use your computer to make credit card transactions at public places where the Internet connection is public, that is, a connection where anyone can log on. These open network connections are common at coffee shops. One of the most frequently used tricks by identity thieves are drive-bys in which they drive around neighborhoods with laptops that can "capture" private information like credit card numbers and passwords from your computer.

## Travel Tip

Allow your children to take turns choosing dessert for everyone to share. That way, everyone gets something he wants.

How would like to purchase an additional meal package from your hotel, for the extra low price of $X? You wouldn't, so the best thing to do is say "No, thank you." Kids in general eat far less than adults, and at resorts, the size of portions is often double that of the meals you would prepare at home. Unless your hotel has an exorbitant plate-sharing charge, you and your family should easily be able to get away with ordering a dinner entrée for each adult and one for two kids to split between themselves. You may even have plenty of food left over for the kids from your own dishes. Sure, kids think it's fun to order what they want. But at $18 for a plate full of food your child is unlikely to finish, you'll find that the cost of meals can add up quickly. If your children are inclined to splurge, let them know how much they can spend before you sit down to a meal. The entire family needs to respect the budget so that you can enjoy all the fun activities you have planned together.

# Never Go Over Budget on Vacation

No one is perfect. Even Warren Buffet will admit he's made a few financial blunders from time to time. The problem that leads most families to go over budget is underestimating their financial needs to begin with. In the planning process, don't underestimate the cost of your family's vacation. Always, always overestimate.

The potentially serious consequences of going over budget cannot be overstated. Better to come home with extra funds than to be in a foreign country and unable to pay the departure tax (which can be nearly $100 for a family of four.) This has happened more than you can imagine, resulting in missed flights and other travel hassles.

Finding yourself over budget on vacation is not just inconvenient. It can cost thousands of additional dollars. Sometimes on long vacations room availability may require a stay at more than one hotel. If you have to change hotels, your credit card will be authorized again, with twice the available funds as originally allotted locked up.

A missed flight could cost you hundreds or even more than a thousand dollars in fees and fare differences in order to change all of your family's reservations. Never leave home without enough money to get home.

When planning your trip, if you realize that you'll have just enough saved in your budget to break even, postpone the trip. There's no room for error here. If your trip will wreak havoc on your financial security, *do not go*. Wait, save enough money to enjoy the trip and have a little left over when you get home.

## Budget 911: Emergency Funds

The news is full of stories about people getting hurt or injured on vacation. And although the mainstream media generalizes such stories, becoming ill or injured on vacation is a very real possibility that could occur without warning. Will the hospital take your insurance? Maybe. But do you want to take that chance with your family?

Not every family can afford to set aside funds for emergencies while on vacation, particularly vacationing abroad. Or can they? The fact is that every family who can afford a vacation can afford emergency funds. With enough advance planning and by making small sacrifices for the sake of the trip, a family can set aside enough funds for emergencies.

Before booking your trip, contact your resort or destination's front desk. Ask about available local medical services. Is there a local hospital or at the very least, an urgent care facility? Do not contact reservationists for this information; they are rarely located in the same area as your destination. Get the name and telephone number for the local medical facility. If the front desk can't provide this, ask to speak with the resort manager. Once you have the contact information for the local medical facility, place a call to their billing department. Simply ask about payment policies. Do they accept your insurance and will they file your insurance if you have need of their services while vacationing in the area? Or, will you be required to pay for services and file your own insurance? What forms of payment do they accept? It's worthwhile to make a few phone calls to ensure that you'll be prepared in the event of an emergency away from home.

## Do You Need Travel Insurance?

Insurance is like gambling. You want to have fun, but you don't want to lose your shirt. It's easy to get taken advantage of when it comes to travel insurance, so it's wise to consider your circumstances. The first step is to determine whether or not you need travel insurance. Visiting Aunt Millie in Pasadena for the weekend probably doesn't warrant travel insurance. Taking your family to see the petrified waterfalls in Mexico is an entirely different story.

Speak with your insurance agent. Find out if you and your family are already covered under your existing policy. If not, find out whether your insurance agency offers travel insurance.

## 💼 Travel Tip

Purchasing travel insurance from a company that already insures you is wise—because you're already a customer, you will be seen as less of a risk and could qualify for lower premiums.

American Express cardholders are often already protected with some level of travel insurance, particularly when airline tickets are purchased with your American Express card. Many credit cards also come with travel insurance options. Ask your credit card's customer service department to go over your benefits with you. Ask if travel insurance is available via your credit card and then weigh all your options.

If you discover that you will not be insured for travel by your credit cards or existing insurance agency, ask your insurance agency to recommend a reputable travel insurance partner. When all else fails, go online and compare prices. Companies like Travel Guard (*www.travelguard.com*), InsureMyTrip.com (*www.insuremy trip.com*), Travelex (*www.travelex.com*), and TravelSafe Insurance (*www.travelsafe.com*) all offer search features that let you customize your travel insurance needs.

# CHAPTER 4

# Gas, Food, Lodging

Traveling as a family is fun, and getting to your vacation destination is a big part of that! Traveling together is about those intimate moments you share. On the road, away from work and school, you'll have the opportunity to make those connections. On the other hand, traveling with kids can feel just like work, and for many parents can be more stressful than just spending the weekend at home. Home is all about routine. On the road, families have to be prepared for detours, stops, and emergencies, and parents are responsible for handling anything that comes along. The best way to ensure your family has a safe and enjoyable journey is to be prepared! Know your destination and learn everything you can about how to get there, and all the stops along the way.

## Hit the Open Road—The Basics

Traveling in your own family car has its own unique advantages. You control the pace of the trip. You stop when you want to, and you go when you're good and ready. It can be cost effective in comparison to flying if you're not traveling too far. Traveling by car also provides opportunities for finding new adventures along the way!

Plot your trip. Find a source with a selection of regional and national maps. Printed maps are handy because you can write important details on them for quick reference. Map your journey and notate where you want to stop for meals, sightsee, and so everyone can stretch their legs. Plotting your trip saves money because it can help you calculate an accurate number of meals in restaurants, fuel, and lodging.

## ▮ Travel Tip

Save the maps you use on road trips. They make great additions to scrapbooks and photo albums or even to frame for the family room when you get home.

To make your family's road trip more enjoyable, bring things to keep everyone busy on the longer stretches of road where the view isn't exactly a conversation piece. Include a deck of cards, travel games, and binoculars in your supplies, along with pillows and blankets for napping.

One adventure you don't want to have is motion sickness, or what's often referred to as getting "car sick." Motion sickness is common in toddlers and preschool children traveling long distances by car and often results in nausea. As soon as your child complains of nausea, act quickly to prevent vomiting.

- Open a window immediately to provide the child with fresh air.
- Avoid strong-smelling foods or snacks.
- Stop the car and get out for a few minutes.

Prevent your smaller passengers from getting car sick by having them focus on distant points outside the vehicle, playing car games that encourage them to look outside ("I Spy" is a popular one), providing music or books on tape, and limiting things like reading or video games.

## Vacation Vittles—Dining Out on the Road

Part of the fun of traveling together is eating at great places while on the road. On highways and city streets, in tiny towns and tucked-away neighborhoods, you'll find incredible restaurants that often serve reasonably priced food unique to the region. Most of these places are not franchised and most have a personality all their own.

Casual road food restaurants often feature comfort food: Roast beef po' boys, grilled chicken hoagies, mac 'n' cheese, heavenly cheeseburgers, barbecue, and every variation of the French fry you can imagine. Depending on where you're going, chances are you'll find great food on the road. There is a website devoted to eating on the road that can help you plan where to stop and what to eat. It's called RoadFood.com (*www.roadfood.com*) and on the site you can search for great road food restaurants and dishes by town, ingredient, and forum topic.

If you're paying attention when you're traveling, you'll be able to tell which restaurants are authentic road food gems and which places are designer imposters. Great eateries on the road have character. They stand out. Many authentic roadside restaurants are older and have the signage, lime green booths, or checkered tablecloths to prove it. Diners are hard to miss, and the menu will also tell the story.

## Pack a Lunch, Save a Bundle

Vacation dining sure is fun, but it can get expensive. The key to staying on budget while on vacation is meal planning. When you plot your trip, take a look at your map. Think about places to stop along the way. Research various restaurants located near those stops. Make a rough estimate of meals and budget for the cost of those meals plus 20 percent for gratuity and any extras, like a side dish or special that entices you. Limit dining out to places you can't find at home that serve regional cuisine.

A big part of meal planning on the road includes packing lunches and bringing breakfast. This doesn't mean you have to stay in the car at all times. Get a cooler and stock it full of drinks, snacks, and ingredients you need to make healthful sandwiches. Leave off things like mayo and other wet condiments to keep bread firm and fresh. Grilled veggie sandwiches are a great idea for the road because they can be made in advance and won't go bad as quickly as a meat or cheese sandwich. Store meat, cheese, and condiments in your cooler to retrieve at picnic sites and scenic vistas for family picnics.

## 💼 Travel Tip

Lunch is almost always cheaper than dinner. Ask if a restaurant serves lunch as well as dinner. Flip flop lunch for dinner as the biggest (most expensive) meal of the day. Save sandwiches for dinner and you'll save a bundle on dining out.

Shopping for groceries on the road is another big way to trim travel food costs. Bring your cooler and stop at grocery stores along the way for ice and foodstuffs. When you run out of sandwiches you brought from home or ingredients you used to make them, stop at a local market or grocery store and restock your supply. Be sure to bring extra napkins and plenty of cups—drinks in two-liter containers and a large thermos of water are much cheaper than individual drink servings.

## All Aboard! Traveling by Train

For decades traveling on an Amtrak train was all the rage. And train travel is still a wonderful way to see America! In places like Montana, traveling by train gives passengers a bird's-eye view of some of America's most breathtaking scenery. And using local trains in cities like Manhattan and Chicago is more economical and much faster than other modes of transportation, such as taking a taxi or riding the bus.

Booking train travel online is as easy as booking an airline flight. You just enter dates and departure and arrival points from the station list, and the site (*www.amtrak.com*) will display fares and information. You can purchase your Amtrak tickets as little as three days in advance, making train travel a great weekend or last-minute transportation option.

Overnight train trips, however, can be uncomfortable if you don't reserve a sleeper cabin for your family. Be sure to ask about this option, and visit Amtrak's website to preview what your cabin will look like. Not everyone can sleep sitting up or even reclining in a chair, and just one bad night's sleep can ruin your vacation, especially if it results in tired, cranky children the next day.

# Up, Up, and Away!
## The Basics of Air Travel

Air travel has become more and more common as airfares decrease and airlines struggle to keep customers flying. Traveling by air is in many cases, the fastest way to get to your destination. It is convenient and usually a fun adventure for everyone. In other cases, it can turn into a frustrating experience, especially if you're traveling with small children. Knowledge and preparation will help you make sure your family's flight is safe and harmonious with your fellow passengers.

### Before You Fly

Check with the airline to find their busiest days and times. By avoiding these times you are more likely to be on a flight with an empty seat. Families traveling with kids under age two should ask about an airline's policy regarding empty seats. In some cases airlines will allow you to seat a child who would otherwise be on your lap, in a child restraint in an empty seat at no extra charge.

Ask your travel representative about discounted fares for kids traveling in a child restraint system. The Federal Aviation

Administration recommends children under forty pounds be restrained, however infants age two and under can fly on an adult's lap. Buying discounted or full-fare tickets for your child guarantees his seat will be available to accommodate proper child restraint. Always reserve an adjoining seat for your child next to you, and remember window seats are the best places for children so child restraints won't block escape paths in the unlikely event of an emergency. For families traveling on connecting flights, ask what the airline can do to help you get to your connecting gate to minimize the chance of missing your next flight.

Some children have medical conditions that aren't difficult to manage on the ground, but could pose challenges in the air. Be sure to tell your flight attendant, or counter or gate agents if your child has special needs that would make him more comfortable, and keep him safe.

## 📰 Travel Tip

Young children often can't clear their ears to relieve painful pressure that can build up in flight. Consult your physician before flying with your child. She can prescribe medication to help clear your child's airways to prevent ear pain during flight.

Have a safe (and peaceful) flight by keeping kids under control. As reported by multiple news outlets in recent years, a handful of parents who were unable to control children's behavior to the point that it disrupted fellow travelers and the flight crew were expelled from the flight. Flight staff members are quick to point out that parents are responsible for supervising children in flight and at the airport. Airline galleys are dangerous places for children. A single cup of hot coffee spilled on tender skin in-flight can cause significant scarring.

Don't allow your child to sit in an aisle seat. Kids are explorers by nature! Little outstretched hands can get bumped by passengers, flight crew, and heavy carts that block views of such tiny appendages. To avoid injuries during turbulence, which can happen without any warning, make sure kids are securely belted into their seats. Children should only move about an airplane cabin when the seat belt sign is off, and only when closely supervised by a traveling companion.

## Luggage

Flight delays and lost luggage are an unfortunate reality of traveling. It's understood by most travelers that any and all essential items should be transported in carry-on luggage. Items like medicine; snacks; TSA-approved travel-sized toiletries; and, for families traveling with small children, diapers, teething rings, and anything that can help your child have an easier flight are included in the list of items you shouldn't trust the airlines to deliver. If you're on a specific diet or medication, it's especially important that you keep these things with you on the flight.

Label all of the items in your carry-on bag in large lettering, especially medications, even if your name is on them. For about $39, you can get a compact, portable, handheld labeler that prints custom labels and has a built-in manual cutter. The labeler lets you create labels for just about anything wherever you are, and has a time and date function for medicines, foods, or any dated items you need to keep track of.

## 🧳 Travel Tip

Leave noisy, fragile, or heavy toys at home. Not only are they unsafe in the event of turbulence, they are annoying to other passengers.

To keep luggage check costs at a minimum, pack light and pack smart. Pack dark-colored pants, which don't show dirt or wrinkles as much as their light colored cousins. If the cost of checking your luggage exceeds $100, consider shipping your suitcases home. It's often more convenient because shipping companies will retrieve your packages directly from your hotel. And in many instances, it's cheaper!

## Airlines That Go Out of Their Way to Be Family Friendly

One of the best airlines families can fly is Emirates Airlines because of the amenities they offer children. Statistics show that today's young passengers are far better traveled than their predecessors and many have developed travel preferences. Emirates Airlines is an international airline specializing in long-haul travel, and actively caters to their "jet-set juniors." Their services include kids' birthday celebrations in the air replete with cake that parents can book when they purchase a ticket. Kid-sized headsets connect them to 600-plus channels of entertainment including Disney Classics and other kid-friendly (and parent-approved) programs such as *Tom and Jerry* and *Scooby Doo*, along with music and interactive games. Emirates also features *3,2,1 . . .* and *e-kids*, magazines exclusively for children, and offers the Flying Camera channel on which kids can share the pilot's view of takeoff and landing and scenery for the duration of the flight. They can also follow the plane's altitude and speed on a map through the Airshow channel.

Meals on Emirates Airlines come in briefcase-style boxes and include hot dishes like spaghetti and meatballs, lasagna, chicken burgers, fish fingers, and aircraft-shaped breaded chicken strips plus snacks. Emirates also makes sure flights with young passengers are stocked with stuffed animals and small games to keep little minds busy on long flights. Finally, frequent flyers between ages two and sixteen can register for the Skywards Skysurfers rewards frequent-flier program just like adults can, but with kid-friendly reward opportunities.

Families with fifth graders can look into the Southwest Airlines Adopt-A-Pilot program. The program educates kids in subjects like math, science, geography, language arts and career-planning through pilot mentors who have been "adopted" by a fifth-grade class for about a month. Southwest Airlines pilots volunteer time to visit classes and correspond with students. The classes learn about American cities by tracking their adopted pilot's weekly flight schedule. The "Flight Plan" program was developed with the Smithsonian Institute and education specialists. Southwest also sponsors an online version of the "Adopt-A-Pilot" program, which features a virtual pilot.

## Bon Appétit!

Sampling the culture of an area through its local cuisine is one of the best things about traveling. Tasting regional and local cuisines can be a lesson in culture depending on where you travel. Many areas of the country have flavors unique to their region. And that's how Mother Nature intended it! Soil, water, and plant life all factor into what a region offers, from livestock to produce. Families who learn the cuisine of an area, also learn its culture. What a fun way to teach the kids about a destination. Better yet, families who limit dining out to places that feature regional cuisine can save big on food costs. Some examples of places that feature incredible regional cuisine include Seattle's Pike's Seafood, which features some of the world's best smoked salmon. In Philadelphia, the Philly cheese steak sandwich rules. In the Carolinas and Tennessee, barbecue is a type of food, not just a way of cooking it, and you can choose between pulled pork or beef, and sweet or vinegar-based barbecue sauces. Idaho is home to the almighty potato, which can be stuffed with anything your family's heart desires. Chicago pizza is legendary, and throughout the southwest in places like Arizona, prickly pear cactus fries are a delicious delicacy. When you're traveling to a destination that has great regional cuisine, bring your own snacks and groceries to eat for most meals, and as a special treat, try the regional cuisine at lunch, rather than a more expensive dinner.

## Groceries Versus Restaurants on the Road

Speaking of bringing your own snacks and buying groceries on vacation, this is one way to cut your vacation food bill in half. If your hotel has rooms with kitchens, consider shopping for the bulk of your family's food when your family arrives at your destination. Buying groceries can save hundreds of dollars on vacation. There's no need to leave a gratuity, you can select the items you need, and you can make enough for leftovers the next day, which will save even more money. Families traveling on a budget may spend more on a hotel room with a kitchen, but will recoup that cost and then some by shopping for groceries.

That said, part of the fun of going on vacation is eating out. Choosing the right restaurants will help you enjoy meals that someone else prepares, but not be stuck with an outrageous bill at the end of the night.

## Food Allergies—Eat Smart on Vacation

An estimated 12 million Americans have food allergies, and many of them are children. Allergic reactions can include mild symptoms like rashes or hives to more severe reactions such as breathing difficulties and loss of consciousness. For many children, food allergies can be deadly.

The Food Allergy & Anaphylaxis Network (*www.foodallergy .org*) reports that although labels state ingredients, those ingredients can be found in places you might not expect. On vacation or at home, if allergies are a concern, always read labels on outer and inner wrappers of double-wrapped products (like snack crackers you buy in bulk). Ingredients listed on outer packaging sometimes exclude allergens noted on individual packaging. And some of the same products are made in different plants, which can have varying effects on people with food allergies.

When you're on vacation and away from your regular doctor, it's important that medical providers have all the necessary information they need to make an accurate diagnosis if someone falls ill. Make a list of everything to which your child or adult family member is allergic. Make copies for each parent and laminate allergy ID cards for kids to carry. When eating away from home, it's better to be safe than sorry.

## 💼 Travel Tip

When dining out, refer to your list, and ask your server if the foods on your order contain any of the things on your list. If he can't answer your question, the chef should be able to provide that information.

Food allergies are just one more reason to pack your own groceries for the trip and, if you can, buy groceries when you arrive at your destination. Doing so gives you ultimate control over what your family ingests.

## All about Lodging

Lodging is one of the biggest expenses when you're taking a family vacation. But amazing deals abound, and hoteliers are anxious to fill rooms whatever the cost. Now is the best time to travel. With savings galore, families can stay longer and check in to swankier digs, thanks to the big cuts in room rates hospitality providers are offering in a down economy. And families on vacation have options beyond hotels and resorts.

### Home Exchange Programs

What if you could switch homes with someone who lives in a town where you've always wanted to vacation while that family stays in your house? It's not a movie. Rather, it's a real, viable business for globetrotting families worldwide. Home Exchange is an affordable option for families who otherwise couldn't afford to vacation in Scotland, Hawaii, or even just a few states or towns away. Though Home Exchange programs mean a virtual stranger is staying in your home, you're staying in that same stranger's while they're away. Both parties share the responsibility of keeping their vacation home clean and taking good care of it while the owner is away. Vacation home sharing is a way for families to travel to destinations they could not otherwise afford. Without the expense of a hotel or condo, vacationing families have only transportation and food costs to contend with. For more information visit: *www .homeexchange.com.*

Another benefit to utilizing the Home Exchange program is the chance families have to integrate into the local culture wherever they might be. Homeowners often refer their Home Exchange partners to local restaurants, shows, and activities not found in most guidebooks. In some cases, one partner's travel arrangements allow the two parties to meet.

## ☰ Fast Fact

The blockbuster film *The Holiday* dramatized how two Home Exchange partners portrayed by Cameron Diaz and Kate Winslet became friends and found love through home exchange.

Home Exchange is a membership organization whereby members select the area they want to visit and privately transmit information about themselves, their home, and area to potential Home Exchange parties in that area while at the same time posting their own listing. Membership includes unlimited exchanges and costs just $9.95, billed annually. Most hotel rooms cost far more for one night.

Another home exchange company called HomesAway (*www .homesaway.com*) handles more than one hundred villas in France, Spain, Italy, Croatia, and Scotland. Families can consult with Homes-Away travel advisors to choose their preferred region and villa. The advisors can also help families preplan for their arrival.

Local hosts who are considered regional insiders help guests make the connections they need for things like dinner reservations and local activities and attractions.

## Family-Friendly Hoteliers

Most hoteliers welcome families and offer special discounts just for them. Packages for kids of all ages are a big draw, and hoteliers know it. For today's traveling families, the appreciated but simple "kids eat or stay free" offer isn't enough of an attraction. Hoteliers know they need to provide a lot more than chicken fingers and a cot to win over families who like to travel together.

Convention and visitors bureaus (CVB) in the towns and states where you plan to travel are the best resource for family-friendly lodging. These organizations will have the best list of places to stay based on your family's needs and be able to give you the inside scoop on which hotels offer the best deals and amenities for families.

Starwood Hotels is an umbrella over multiple properties. On their main website, *www.starwoodhotels.com* you'll find a family-friendly feature that makes it easy for families who aren't sure of their destination to decide where to go based on their favorite activities. On the Starwood Hotels family packages web page, helpful links with corresponding icons are divided into categories like museum hotels, zoo/aquarium hotels, beach hotels, amusement park hotels, theatre hotels, ski hotels, and waterpark hotels.

Loews Hotels offers their own "Loews Loves Kids" program as part of a deal the company has with Fisher-Price. All Loews properties stock baby swings and playpens. Children under age ten receive a Fisher-Price welcome gift. The hotelier funds a lending library of children's books as well as numerous other family items. For more information visit: *www.loewshotels.com*.

Perhaps one of the most family-friendly hotel chains in America is the Sky Hotels and Resorts family of hotels. Located in the Orlando, Florida, area, the resorts are made up of condominium lodging that ranges from deluxe studios up to four-bedroom suites. All of the condominium suites come complete with full kitchens, which makes bringing your own groceries and cooking on the road convenient and economical. Within the Sky Hotels and Resorts family of hotels, the Lake Buena Vista Resort and Spa holds a special treat for kids—the pool features a built-to-scale model of a pirate shipwreck with water cannons and a water slide, along with hot tubs and poolside hammocks for mom and dad. See *www.staysky.com* for more information on the family of hotels, or see *www.lbvorlandoresort.com* for information on the Lake Buena Vista Resort and Spa.

## Traveling with Your Pet

Just as Loews shines for providing stellar family-friendly accommodations, they are also a great choice when traveling with your pet. Their Loews Loves Pets program is the cat's meow. If you have more than one cat or dog, that's fine—at Loews they are welcome to accompany you. Loews offers treats and a toy and can facilitate bedding, dog-walking services, and even room-service meals for little Fido or Trixie. Loews stocks pet potty supplies like pooper-scoopers and litter boxes. They also provide a "Puppy Pager" service that allows guests to get regular updates on their pooches via cell phone from Loews staffers when they're out of the room.

Many hoteliers will make room for pets, but traveling with your beloved four-legged family member isn't just about finding a hotel that accepts them. There are many factors to consider before dragging your family dog, cat, bunny rabbit, or guinea pig along for the ride.

The American Veterinary Medical Association website, *www .avma.org*, has tons of tips to help you prepare for a trip with pets. Chief among their suggestions is to plan carefully using the following steps:

- Discuss your plans for pet travel with your veterinarian before you leave home.
- Make sure your pet is comfortable traveling and will be able to handle constantly changing surroundings. Animals who get carsick or have physical impairments can have difficulty withstanding travel.
- Make sure pets are allowed at all of your destination stops or that each place has kennel facilities.
- Hang your "Do Not Disturb" sign on the hotel door anytime you're out of the room.
- Inform hotel staff of your pet's presence.
- Have your pet outfitted with an indentifying microchip before you leave home in case you become separated.
- Make sure your pet's vaccinations are current.

The PetTravel.com website, *www.pettravel.com,* also has great information that if followed will ensure your pet arrives safe and happy to his destination. PetTravel.com also provides links to airline and pet passport forms among other similar resources. On PetTravel.com you can search by destination and region among tens of thousands of pet-friendly hotels and services in more than one hundred countries.

## CHAPTER 5

# Preparing for Your Trip

In the weeks and days before your trip, staying organized is your best defense against poor planning. The second-best thing is to give yourself (and your family) plenty of time to prepare. Don't wait until the last-minute to get everyone involved. If possible, two weeks before you leave, begin making a list of important items you'll need while away from home. It can be costly on vacation to replace important items you left at home. How often have you forgotten your toothbrush? Laptop power cord? Medication? Prevent careless planning by staying organized and allowing enough time to plan for every detail of your vacation.

## Passports

Families traveling abroad must have valid passports. In the past, it was possible to travel to the Caribbean with a driver's license and birth certificate. No more. To travel anywhere outside the United States, a passport is required. First-time passport applicants must appear in person at a passport acceptance facility. There are 9,000 passport facilities in the United States, many of which are located in post offices. The U.S. Department of State website is the best resource to begin the process of obtaining a U.S. passport (*www .travel.state.gov/passport*). You will need to bring two photographs of each person applying for a passport, proof of U.S. citizenship such as a social security card, and a valid driver's license or other form of photo identification.

The passport process, which can be confusing, has given rise to the success of passport expeditors. Rated top visa specialist by TravelTruth.com, A Briggs Passport and Visa Expeditors also was the highest ranked of five independently tested passport service expeditors by *Travel and Leisure* magazine. Working with the U.S. Passport Agency, foreign embassies and consulates, expeditors like A Briggs can expedite travel visas and passports in as quickly as twenty-four hours provided they have all of the correct information from you. There are fees associated with these services that can range from $65 to $245 depending on how quickly you need a passport. Search the Internet for "passport expeditor" with your zip code to locate an expeditor in your area. Expand your search to include county and state if you cannot locate an expeditor in your town.

## Take It or Leave It

Laptop computers are convenient, keep users in touch with the world, and hold important information. Bringing a laptop computer on vacation can be helpful as you travel. Once you arrive at a destination and get the lay of the land, you may need your laptop to search for additional activities or restaurants. However a laptop can be a tempting distraction from relaxation and enjoying time with your family. Teens may be inclined to spend valuable vacation time playing video games, and parents may succumb to the urge to work. Prevent these vacation time stealers by establishing ground rules for everyone to follow, such as limiting the computer for family vacation research purposes only.

Always affix your name, address, e-mail, and phone number to the laptop in the unfortunate event you and your laptop become separated. Many travel insurance policies offer insurance for your laptop. Finally, be sure to back up all your data from your laptop before you leave home. It's wise to back up on an external hard drive and a thumb drive. A thumb drive is a small USB-powered drive that can fit on your key ring—this drive is perfect for backing up your files. An external hard drive with plenty of space should be able to hold all of your data and software. Take your thumb drive with you in case you need to access any files while you're away. Put your external hard drive in a safe place such as in a file cabinet or safe at home.

## 💼 Travel Tip

For about $50 you can purchase a lock for your laptop. To further protect your computer, make sure your laptop is password protected. Affix a label to the top of your laptop that reads something such as "this laptop is password protected."

### Toiletries

Travel toiletries are a conundrum. Ask yourself if your toiletries are absolutely necessary. On one hand, you're probably attached to your soaps, shampoos, and razors. On the other, they're inconvenient. Driving vacations allow for bringing all the beauty goo you can carry. But flying families will be seriously limited to what they can bring in a carry-on. Toiletries can be in containers no larger than three and a half ounces, and must easily fit into a Transportation Security Administration—approved clear plastic zip-top bag. Each person can include toiletries adhering to TSA requirements in a carry-on bag.

There is no limit to the amount of toiletries you can pack into a checked bag, but airlines have been known to misplace and lose luggage. Plus, all toiletries should be enclosed in plastic bags to prevent spillage. Most hotels offer shampoo, lotion, and conditioner, but if you have chosen a budget-conscious destination, you may benefit from bringing your own. Before you leave for the airport, always check your airline website for TSA updates and announcements that may alter your flight plans.

## Leave That Purse at Home

Traveling by car? Purses, knapsacks, and diaper bags welcome. On flights, however, extra bags are a hassle. A purse is a nuisance because it counts as a carry-on, as does a diaper bag. It's best to choose one bag with multiple pockets as your carry-on choice. Select one that can hold the contents of your purse and diaper bag and a change of clothing. Keep identification in a front pocket for quick access at counter and gate check. Pack your purse and diaper bag with your luggage for use when you arrive at your destination. It's unsettling for most women to consider not carrying a purse, but with new airline baggage restrictions and fees, a pocketbook, fashionable or functional, becomes little more than a costly hindrance.

## Toys and Diapers

Toys are a necessity for small children, especially on flights. But most children's toys are bulky and heavy. Bring toys that don't take up a lot of space. Put puzzle pieces in zip-top bags. Buy kid-friendly card games and flash cards. Load your child's favorite cartoons on a small electronic device such as an iPod. Traveling with baby? Get a diaper bag that is travel friendly or let your roller bag double as a diaper bag. Baby or not, the TSA will count your diaper bag as a carry-on. Pack the things you'll need least at the bottom of the bag. Leave things like formula, bottles, and diapers for last to pack at the top of the bag for easy access.

## 🧳 Travel Tip

Formula usually comes in a bulky canister. Measure your baby's formula per bottle. Transfer the right amount into zip-top bags—one for each bottle. Just add liquid and, voilà—instant bottle, less mess.

Diapers are a non-negotiable requirement when traveling with baby. They're lightweight, but bulky. Are you traveling within the United States? Consider shipping your preferred diapers to your destination, or purchase them when you get there. If you're staying at a resort with a concierge, call ahead and see if the hotel would kindly obtain your brand and leave them in your room. An extra fee may be involved, but chances are it will be less than the $25 you'll have to pay for checking an extra bag to accommodate all those diapers.

## Vacation Child Care and Safety

You screen babysitters and day care centers at home. Parents interested in vacation child care must be doubly diligent, particularly if traveling includes time abroad. You will need to provide a caregiver who doesn't normally watch your child with a detailed list of anything that could impact him while in that person's care. Provide your child's caregiver with emergency numbers and information about your child's allergies and food preferences.

### 🧳 Travel Tip

There is no better person to care for your child than you. The next best thing to mom or dad is a child care provider you know and trust and with whom your child is comfortable. The cost of an additional person on a family vacation can be overwhelming. But if spending time with your spouse alone, away from your children, while on vacation is a priority, invest the funds necessary to bring along someone you trust to care for your children.

Be aware of the area where your family is traveling. Your destination may be a beautiful Caribbean island, but does the island have a high crime rate? Are there natural elements that could easily harm your child, such as a high concentration of mosquitoes at certain times of year? Beach-bound families should ask the lodging representative about jellyfish, particularly if you're traveling after a recent storm. Most of the time these factors won't alter your vacation plans, but it's always best to know the facts about your destination before you purchase tickets.

### Plan Ahead and Ask Questions

Don't wait until you arrive on property to ask questions about child care. Research child care facilities before you leave home. Here is a list of questions parents should ask anyone who will be in charge of their child away from home:

- Is the child care provider certified to perform CPR?
- What policies and procedures are in place to ensure the safety of every child in their care?
- Does the facility have a secure web cam that allows parents to view their children in their care?
- What is the provider-to-child ratio?
- What activities are available for children, and what are the child care facility hours of operation?
- What precautions have been taken to childproof the facility?

Ask child care practitioners for references from previous clients. Check your destination or resort website for testimonials about the quality of care the children of other guests received in the care of the facility or person. Also, speak directly with a manager to get a feel for how professional and competent the facility appears to be.

## Giving Each Other (and Yourself) a Break

Even if you've opted not to employ child care, it's important to make a plan for giving each other and yourself a break from child care on vacation. If both parents are constantly watching children, your vacation won't seem like much of a departure from time at home.

Before you arrive, get information from your destination on spa services, golf outings, wine tastings, or whatever you enjoy. Talk with your spouse about the things you'd like to do while away, and make a plan that allows each parent to have some alone time engaging in a favorite activity.

Traveling alone with your child? Bring your favorite books or DVDs, headphones, and iPod or other music player to enjoy while he is napping. Ask your resort about supervised group activities your child can enjoy while you take a walk on the beach or enjoy a spa service. Make the most of your vacation for your child, but don't forget to engage in activities you enjoy.

## Get Fit for Your Vacation

It's hard to enjoy a vacation when you're tired, run down, or out of shape. Even if your vacation isn't adventurous or physically demanding, with kids involved, chances are you'll be more active than you are at home. A trip to Disney World will require literally miles of walking. Your children and you will enjoy your vacation all the more if you're physically able to fully participate in activities available to you. Plus, experts agree that getting fit is one of the best things a family can do together!

### Fun Family Fitness

Think about your vacation. How much time do you have before you leave? If the answer is weeks, make a list of the activities you'll be doing while away. What can you do to get ready for them? For example, zip lining is a fun and exciting activity that requires upper body strength (see Chapter 14 for more information about zip lining). Imagine how much easier it will be if you and your children are ready for the challenge! Chin-ups, pull-ups, and pushups are the best exercises to strengthen the upper body. You can purchase a pull-up bar at any sporting goods store for less than $20. Hold a family contest to see who can do the most for their weight and age.

Will your vacation include a lot of walking? Every night before or after dinner, take a walk together. A few times a week, drive to your local park and walk as much as your schedule allows. Play a game of catch in the yard, or organize a family game of red rover. Even a game of duck duck goose can be exercise for everyone getting into the game. Whether you use your vacation as an excuse to become a fit family or you want to instill a sense of confidence in your children, encouraging fitness will result in more than just a great vacation—it will help change the course of their lives.

# To Pack or Not to Pack? That Is the Question

Suitcases. Roller bags. Carry-on bags. Toiletry bags. Daughter's celebrity-of-the-moment backpack. Son's Marvel Comics duffle. Baggage seems to be never-ending, and so are the expenses. Airlines, to combat skyrocketing fuel prices are cutting corners and sticking it to customers like never before. This includes charging you for checked baggage. You may have to pay up to $25 a bag depending on the airline—did you budget an extra $100 for everyone's extra bag? Probably not. Most people don't.

But of more importance is the fact that more stuff means more hassle. Schlepping a ton of bags through an airport—even everyone's carry-on—is agonizing. Just try keeping up with all your carry-ons and checked luggage when you land. Even if you have chosen a drive destination, make your life easier and your vacation less stressful by limiting what you take on vacation.

## Packing Tips

Never pack your suitcase by taking clothes from closet or dresser and putting them directly into your suitcase. Put all of your clothing and shoes on your bed first. Based on the number of days you'll be traveling and the activities in which you'll engage, put enough clothes on the bed so that you have lots of choices. Mix and match your separates so they can be interchanged to create a new outfit for each day. Don't bring a shirt that doesn't go with anything else. Plan each day's clothing including underwear. Construct outfits—not a makeshift wardrobe. Pack your outfits according to the day from back to front. Put the clothes you'll wear last in the bottom of the suitcase, and the clothes you'll wear soonest at the top. Atop those clothes, place any toiletries (snuggly wrapped in zip-top bags to protect your clothes) for easy transfer to the bathroom counter. Packing this way, you won't even have to unpack your suitcase when you get there!

## 💼 Travel Tip

Before you pack, have a fashion show. Decide if the outfit you have on is really necessary. If it isn't, leave it at home.

Women should never leave home without a black dress or something that can be worn to a nice dinner. Instead of bringing several evening outfits, bring a few in neutral colors and pack scarves or wraps to dress them up in different ways. The right jewelry and blazer or scarf can make the same dress look completely different from day to day.

### All the Right Shoes

Shoes are the biggest culprit of over-packing. Try to choose clothes that can be worn with the same pairs of shoes. Sometimes packing too many shoes can't be avoided, as in the case of going to a dude ranch or beach, right? Au contraire! At a dude ranch, you'll need three items of footwear: cowboy boots, one pair of comfortable shoes, and flip-flops or other such easy-on, easy-off footwear. You can wear your comfy shoes on the plane and at the ranch when you're not wrangling, and the flip-flops are for roaming around indoors or trips to and from the steam room if your dude ranch has one.

Packing for the beach is even easier. Tennis shoes for outdoor activities and flip-flops are nearly all you need. Mom may want to bring an extra pair of nice heels to go with that black dress, but packing five or six pairs of shoes to choose from is unwise if you want to avoid baggage fees and an aching back.

In addition to packing all the right shoes, choose the right shoes for the journey. Don't wear shoes that are difficult to remove, or have a lot of laces. Mules (like Crocs or clogs) or flip-flops are ideal for traveling. They can easily come off in the car on long car trips. Moreover they can be removed without event in the security line at the airport.

## ▣ Travel Tip

Even companies like Victoria's Secret carry a line of workout pants that are great for traveling and cost less than $30. Their yoga pants sit high enough in the waist to provide coverage and their drawstring "sweat pants," which look more like casual leisure attire, could not be more suitable for cramped flights or hours in the car. Best of all, such items are inexpensive to replace if your airline loses your luggage or the clothes become damaged.

### Get Great Travel Clothes

Packing secrets abound. There are cubes to separate clothes. You can vacuum pack your sweaters. But the best way to make traveling easier on you is to take fewer things and pack wisely. This starts with shopping wisely. Places like Target and Wal-Mart aren't just for the budget conscious anymore. Both retailers have partnered with famous designers to bring quality, attractive clothing to the masses. Target can boast an impressive workout clothing section. And guess what—workout clothes make the best traveling clothes. They fold easily and don't take up much space. They are comfortable. They usually won't wrinkle. They are the quintessentially perfect packing clothes, and most can be worn with tennis shoes or flip-flops.

What if your family vacation requires a plethora of clothing and luggage, say in the case of a ski vacation? In that case, weather-appropriate clothes and equipment will have to be accounted for. If you've planned far enough in advance, consider shipping your clothes to arrive before you do. Via UPS, ground transportation far enough in advance is reasonable and may be cheaper than checked luggage fees.

CHAPTER 6

# Mountains of Fun

A s the leaves change during the autumn months, the mountains explode with color and light. Treetops sweater the mountains in every conceivable green during spring and summer. And wintertime often turns the mountains into magical sugar forests. With the right information and planning, families can easily plan a mountain vacation that's mountains of fun!

## Planning Your Trip to the Mountains

The biggest challenge to planning a mountain vacation is deciding when and which set of mountains to visit. What activities will you most enjoy as a family? Once you decide on activities, you can plan when to travel and to which mountain range. Your atlas is a wonderful tool to help you and your family decide where to take your next mountain vacation.

### When to Visit the Mountains

If you're planning a last-minute trip to a mountainous region, use the seasons as your activity guide. Cold weather means mountain ranges will be largely covered in snow. Summertime brings activities like hiking, a family sport everyone can do together with minimal expense. Springtime in the mountains is all about wildflowers bursting and birds flying everywhere you look. It's the ultimate time for traversing easy trails and enjoying breathtaking views. Bring binoculars for bird watching and a picnic basket filled with plenty of goodies for the trip.

## 🧳 Travel Tip

When driving through the mountains, stop often to take in brilliant vistas. Pick a spot with a great view, and enjoy a family picnic together.

Timing is crucial to planning the perfect foliage vacation. Leaves change according to the weather throughout the year leading up to autumn. Get to the mountains too early and the leaves will still be green. Get there too late and you'll have missed the color. Mountain lodging accommodations begin to fill up as the leaves start to turn, so start looking for lodging two months out before planning your foliage vacation, unless you are planning a last-minute foliage getaway.

Shortlist a few mountain destinations and decide if you will need to fly or if the destination can be reached economically by vehicle. Online, pair the activities your family loves or is interested in with the mountain or town name or mountain range in a search engine. Then you'll be able to decide which mountain community best fits your family and budget.

### Getting Around on Your Mountain Vacation

The mountain lifestyle is laid back and unhurried, so driving is the preferred mode of transportation. On mountain roads, allow an hour of travel time for every forty miles.

Once you've decided which mountain to visit, check for an area calendar of events. Marathons and other special events can be fun to watch but can turn an afternoon of mountain driving into a day-long traffic jam. Make sure your vehicle has a full tank of gas before embarking on a trip through mountain roads. Gas stations in mountain areas are few and far between.

With so many mountain destinations, entire books have been written about single mountain towns alone! This overview is designed to help you understand the geography of the mountain ranges and the variety of activities available. You might also want to reference Chapter 14, to see what's happening in a mountain community near you.

## ≡ Fast Fact

The Weather Channel and Weather.com are excellent sources for finding out when to plan your foliage viewing vacation (*www.weather.com*).

# Mountains in the Northeastern United States

The Appalachian Mountains are a 1,500-mile range extending from central Alabama through New England and into the Canadian provinces of Newfoundland, New Brunswick, and Quebec. Budget-friendly mountains in the Northeastern Appalachian chain include Pennsylvania's Pocono Mountains and Vermont's Green Mountains.

## The Poconos, Pennsylvania

In the Pocono Mountains there are seven ski areas that provide skiing, snowboarding, snowshoeing, and even dog sledding during the winter months, while in warmer months host camping, hiking, horseback riding, and massive indoor water parks. In the Poconos parents can enjoy a variety of spas while kids frolic at water parks, ski schools, kids' camps, or in the care of accredited child care providers available at most Poconos resorts. For families who really want to get up close and personal with the great outdoors, there are more than twenty campgrounds throughout the Poconos. The Poconos have their own tourism clearing house and website (*www.800poconos.com*).

Perhaps the most noteworthy kid-friendly resort in the Poconos is Split Rock Resort. (*www.splitrockresort.com*). Activities at Split Rock include pools, a lakefront swimming lagoon, indoor and outdoor tennis and basketball courts, video arcade, and eight-lane bowling alley. Split Rock has its own movie theater and ice cream parlor. Another amenity offered at Spilt Rock that has kids giving a resounding "thumbs up" is H2Oooohh, a 53,000-square-foot indoor water park. While mom and dad are enjoying a round of golf or spa treatment, kids can try out body slides, raft rides, a multilevel splash playground, and there's an activity pool for the youngest visitors. Or, maybe parents will want to boogie board or surf in the FlowRider water wave.

### LODGING IN THE POCONO MOUNTAINS

- **Woodloch Resort** (Hawley, Pennsylvania), supervised camps and clubs just for kids (*www.woodloch.com*)
- **Great Wolf Lodge** (Scot Run, Pennsylvania), family adventure including indoor water park, rustic family suites (*www.greatwolf.com/poconos/waterpark*)
- **Split Rock Resort** (Lake Harmony, Pennsylvania), numerous recreational activities, 53,000-square-foot indoor water park, golf, and spa (*www.splitrockresort.com*)

## Vermont

The Green Mountains of Vermont encompass 223 mountains over 2,000 feet in elevation. Vermont is famous for mountain bike trails, skiing, and fall foliage. Swimming, camping, kayaking, rock climbing, and canoeing are also popular, along with carriage, sleigh, and hay rides. Vermont has an extensive family vacation planning website with maps and details about each of the eleven regions of the state (*www.vermontvacation.com*).

### Stowe, Vermont

Stowe Mountain Resort in Northern Vermont is home to the Ben and Jerry's ice cream factory where families can take a tour and sample the products. The Alpine Slide at Stowe Mountain Resort is always a hit with kids, though they must be four feet tall to drive their own sled. Fly fishing has become a popular outdoor recreation choice in Stowe, and guides are available. In nearby Smugglers Notch, visitors can explore Smugglers Cave, the Hunter and His Dog, and the Great Spring.

### LODGING IN STOWE, VERMONT

- **Stowe Mountain Lodge** (Stowe, Vermont), Alpine-styled family-friendly lodge (*www.stowemountainlodge.com*)
- **Stoweflake Resort and Spa** (Stowe, Vermont), spa for parents, outdoor activities and recreation (*www.stoweflake.com*)
- **Smugglers' Notch Resort** (Stowe, Vermont), voted number one for family programs by *SKI* magazine readers (*www.Smuggs.com*)
- **Mt. Mansfield Hostel** (Stowe, Vermont), bunkhouse that sleeps ten to twelve people in bunk-style lodging and is extremely reasonable. From November through April, the Stone Hut is only accessible by foot, or chair lift during ski season (802-253-4010)
- **Greenview Cottage** (Stowe, Vermont), bed and breakfast in restored historic accommodations (*www.smuggsvacationhomes.com*)
- **Nye's Green Valley Farm** (Jeffersonville, Vermont), classic New England 200-year-old inn with petting zoo of sheep, goats, and llamas in adjacent pasture (*www.nyesgreenvalleyfarm.com*)
- **Sterling Ridge Log Cabin Resort** (Sterling Ridge, Vermont), two trout-stocked ponds, complimentary canoes, and playground for small children (*www.sterlingridgeresort.com*)

### Killington, Vermont

Killington is in close proximity to Manhattan and other urban areas, so the atmosphere is young. Multiple cross-country ski trails make Killington a great place for youngsters and their parents, since activities like snowshoeing and skiing are doable for all ages. Killington has many dedicated kids' programs, so parents can ski or mountain bike.

### LODGING IN KILLINGTON, VERMONT

- **Summit Lodge & Resort** (Killington, Vermont), representative of traditional Vermont inns, in-house dining and rustic lodging (*www.summitlodgevermont.com*)
- **Mountain Meadows Lodge** (Killington, Vermont), located in the middle of a cross-country ski area featuring a barn with sheep, Shetland pony, goats, and potbellied pig (*www.mountainmeadowslodge.com*)

# Mountains in the Southeastern United States

North Carolina's Blue Ridge Mountains, Georgia's Cumberland Plateau, and Tennessee, North Carolina, and Virginia's Great Smoky Mountains are also part of the Appalachian chain of mountains that stretch from north to south along the eastern part of the United States.

## North Georgia Mountains

The North Georgia Mountains are one of the top mountain destinations in the country. Family and budget friendly, there is much to see and do in the North Georgia Mountains, from festivals to dining, site seeing, and mountain culture. Thanks to the chambers of commerce in nearly every small township, families have an abundance of resources in the mountain community. Multiple state parks offer hiking trails, fishing, swimming, and areas for picnicking. Southern charm can be found in places like Alpine Helen, which offer guests everything from quaint shops to tubing down a nearby river. Places like Tallulah Gorge and Falls are huge attractions—only the mighty Grand Canyon is deeper in the United States. For more information visit: *www.georgiastate parks.org.*

## LODGING IN THE NORTH GEORGIA MOUNTAINS

- **Majestic Mountain Getaways** specializes in family cabins and homes for mountain getaways. (*www.majesticmountain getaways.com*)
- **Brasstown Valley Resort and Spa** (Young Harris, Georgia), centrally located with several family-oriented programs and a Mountaineer's Club featuring specialized activities just for kids. No additional charge for kids staying with parents. Dorm-style lodging at this resort costs as little as $15 per night per person. (*www.brasstownvalley.com*)
- **Glen-Ella Springs Inn & Meeting Place** (Clarkesville, Georgia), built in 1875 offering multiple mountain activities like whitewater rafting, horseback riding, biking, and hiking. Family night featuring surround-sound movies on a flat-screen television. Room charges include full hot breakfasts. (*www.glenella.com*)

## Blue Ridge Mountains

Spectacular vistas reveal themselves on a drive through the Blue Ridge Mountains on the famed Blue Ridge Parkway. Attractions like Grandfather Mountain, Tweetsie Railroad, and the Biltmore Estate are popular family destinations. Places like the Daniel Boone Inn, which serves authentic country mountain cuisine, are visited by multiple generations, as they introduce them to young family members year after year. North Carolina's waterfalls are a sight to behold; hundreds are nestled throughout the mountainous landscape. Native American villages, historical reenactments like award-winning "Unto These Hills," and places like Chimney Rock and Blowing Rock are part of what makes these mountains so alluring. On the Virginia side of the Blue Ridge Parkway, the Natural Bridge and the outdoor market in vibrant Roanoke are must-see spots, along with Mabry Mill, one of the most photographed sites along the historic road. Historic Floyd County is a haven for artists and musicians, and is one of the most popular stops on The Crooked Road's heritage music trail.

### LODGING IN THE BLUE RIDGE MOUNTAINS

- **Earthshine Mountain Lodge** (Transylvania County, North Carolina) eighty-three-acre and nearly two-century-old farm with *Little House on the Prairie*–style lofts and on-site babysitters (*www.earthshinemtnlodge.com*)
- **Best Western** (Downtown Asheville) affordable rates within walking distance to shops and a host of family-friendly restaurants (*www.bestwestern.com*)
- **High Hampton Inn** (Cashiers, North Carolina) historic lodge with family-friendly meals, incredible on-site activities, and acres of grounds for families to explore (*www.highhamptoninn.com*)
- **Natural Bridge Hotel** (Natural Bridge, Virginia) charming hotel and conference center a few miles from historic Lexington with easy access to the historic Natural Bridge just across the street (*www.naturalbridgeva.com*)
- **Hotel Roanoke** (Roanoke, Virginia) Tudor-style historic hotel with multiple dining options, was the centerpiece of Roanoke in the 1800s (*www.hotelroanoke.com*)
- **Hotel Floyd** (Floyd, Virginia) cozy, eco-friendly hotel built entirely from sustainable materials is inviting and within walking distance from the famed Floyd Country Store (*www.hotelfloyd.com*)

## Great Smoky Mountains

The Great Smoky Mountains are located along Tennessee, Virginia, and the most western tip of North Carolina. Otherwise known as "The Smokies," according to Friends of The Smokies more visitors come to this mountain area annually than any other national park in America.

The Great Smoky Mountains feature places like Gatlinburg, which offer dozens of restaurants, attractions like Dollywood, and the Fort Fun Family Entertainment Center.

## ☂ Rainy Day Fun

Gatlinburg's Fort Fun Family Entertainment Center features rain-or-shine laser tag in a 2,700-square-foot lighted arena with music, and a 3-D special effects theater! For more information visit: *www.smoky mountainfun.com.*

Lookout Mountain (*www.lookoutmountain.com*) near Chattanooga, Tennessee, offers views of the Chattanooga Valley; tours of Rock City, America's deepest cave and largest underground waterfall, Ruby Falls; and the Incline Railway, the world's steepest passenger railway.

Another popular mountain activity and lodging destination is the Nantahala Outdoor Center (NOC) because of its driving proximity to Tennessee, Georgia, and North Carolina. The NOC offers a canoe and kayak paddling school and world-class whitewater rafting on nine rivers, group programs, rope courses, fly fishing, hiking, and biking. (*www.noc.com*)

### LODGING IN THE GREAT SMOKY MOUNTAINS

- **Gatlinburg Vacations**, rustic cabins, hotel accommodations and multiple family and kids-stay-free specials (*www .gatlinburg.com*)
- **Great Smokies Vacation Rentals**, near the Fontana Lake and Dam and Bryson City area (*www.greatsmokies.com*)
- **Carolina Mountain Vacations**, fully equipped kitchens in privately owned cabins, personal advance arrival grocery shopping, no two alike (*www.carolinamountainvacations .com*)

# Mountains in the Central United States

More than one hundred mountain ranges make up the Rocky Mountains, also known as "The Rockies," which extend from the Mexican border to the western United States, into Canada and even eastern Alaska! That's a lot of mountain vacations. Colorado's Mt. Elbert at 14,433 feet tall, is the highest point in the Rockies.

### Colorado

Winter skiing or summer explorations. Autumn foliage or spring wildflower trails. Any time of year, Colorado is beautiful and affordable. Colorado is home to Pike's Peak, the most visited mountain in North America, and second in recorded mountain visitors worldwide to Mount Fuji in Japan. It's near Colorado Springs and the spectacular Garden of the Gods. Aspen Mountain in picturesque Aspen, Colorado, offers free, guided nature walks courtesy of the Aspen Center for Environmental Studies along with free yoga. For kids who love reading and writing, the Aspen Writers' Foundation's Scribes & Scribblers camps for kids welcomes children ages eight to fifteen. And the Aspen Music Festival & School classical concerts are for the whole family. The Aspen Chamber Resort Association is a terrific resource for all things Aspen and is available online (*www.aspenchamber.org*).

### Big Sky Mountains

Idaho's Payette River Mountains are where high, high mountains meet beautiful rivers. McCall, on the shores of scenic Payette Lake in Cascade, and Idaho's, Tamarack, welcome families with an adventurous spirit and love of the great outdoors. Idaho, a state teeming with outdoor recreation, is fast becoming the destination to beat for outdoor family fun. Activities are reasonable and aplenty. The Payette River Mountains have their own activity planner website (*www.visitsouthwestidaho.org*).

Boise, Idaho's capital city, offers a wide array of activities and attractions including vibrant art and cultural scenes and their very own museum district. The city's greenbelt links seven parks along the riverfront and the foothills of the Rocky Mountains, just steps away, provide activities like hiking and biking. The Boise River is one of Idaho's favorite fishing, swimming, and rafting destinations. (*www.boise.org*)

Glacier National Park in Montana has 800 miles of trails. About twenty-five miles from the western town of Whitefish, Montana, Glacier National Park is easily accessible by daily Amtrak trains and car. Hiking families could visit Montana every year for the rest of their lives and never hike the same trail twice in Glacier National Park.

Neighboring Swan Mountains are just outside of town in the Whitefish Range. Fishing in Whitefish is a family affair. With multiple outfitters offering all sorts of activity options, the whole family can learn to fly fish (*www.bigskyfishing.com*). Whitefish's Duck Inn is just on the outskirts of town and is affordable on many levels. Despite being affordable, the Duck Inn features flat-screen televisions installed above gas fireplaces and whirlpool tubs. Here guests feel right at home. The Inn provides the makings so that you can fix your own breakfast, with choices like waffles, fresh pastries, cereal, tasty oatmeal, and the best coffee Montana has to offer.

Wyoming's Grand Tetons shoot up to the sky like mighty anvils. Grey and looming, they hold a full court press in the land of mountains, and many naturalists have called them the most striking of mountain ranges. At family-friendly places like Grand Targhee Resort in Alta, Wyoming, chairlifts and snow caterpillars transport guests for an up-close and personal meet and greet with the mighty Tetons. In the summer months, the lifts continue to run, since the only thing that can surpass seeing the Grand Tetons with its base covered in snow, is the Grand Tetons pocketed in a swath of wildflowers.

## LODGING IN THE MOUNTAINS OF THE CENTRAL UNITED STATES

- **Limelight Lodge** (Aspen, Colorado), family-owned and operated for more than forty years, with affordable accommodations up to two-bed, two-bath condos with kitchens, fireplaces, and balconies for traveling with a large family or friends as a group (*www.limelightlodge.com*)
- **Aloft** (Denver, Colorado), hip, modern hotel close to the airport, great home base for families staying in Denver planning on day trips to outlying sites near the city (*www.starwoodhotels.com/alofthotels*)
- **Gateway Canyons** (Gateway, Colorado), western experience resort located south of Grand Junction, Colorado, in the midst of vast canyons and cottonwoods (*www.gatewaycanyons.com*)
- **Steamboat Resorts** (Steamboat Springs, Colorado), multiple resorts to choose from of all sizes and locations throughout Colorado (*www.steamboatresorts.com*)
- **Redfish Lake Lodge** (Stanley, Idaho), watercraft activities, outdoor tours, and family dining (*www.redfishlake.com*)
- **Extended Stay Resort** (Boise, Idaho), situated within Boise's largest entertainment center, family suites available (*http://homewoodsuites1.hilton.com*)
- **The Duck Inn** (Whitefish, Montana), close to downtown and major roads, family-owned, near Amtrak train to Glacier National Park (*www.duckinn.com*)
- **Grand Targhee** (Alta, Wyoming), flawless views of the Grand Tetons, very family oriented with trails, chair lift, and horseback riding on property (*www.grandtarghee.com*)

# Mountains in the Northwestern United States

The Sierra Nevada range of eastern California stretches for 400 miles. The highest point of the Sierra Nevada Mountains is Mt. Whitney, which tops out at 14,494 feet. Families have been coming to the Sierra Nevada Mountains for generations. Places like Lake Tahoe, which has a thriving lake scene, have been a magnet for families for decades. The Cascades Mountain range stretches from northeastern California across Oregon and Washington including the peaks of Mt. Hood, Mt. Rainier, and Mt. St. Helens. The Coast Range is named for the mountains running along the coast of the Pacific Ocean, also in California, Oregon, and Washington. This range also extends to the western border of British Columbia, Canada, and the southern tip of Alaska.

## LaConner, Washington

LaConner, Washington, can be found in the middle of striking Skagit Valley, a historic village on the Swinomish Channel. LaConner is halfway between Vancouver, British Columbia, and Seattle and features museums, art galleries, restaurants, and shops. In the spring, guests come here for blooming tulips, and the arrival of snow geese and trumpeter swans offer a great reason to visit LaConner in the winter months. Lodging in LaConner includes a waterfront lodge, bed and breakfast, and a quaint inn. Families can take a chartered tour of magnificent Puget Sound directly from the Channel Lodge's private boat dock and through Deception Pass where whale watching adventures await. Harbor seals, porpoises, and orca pods can also be spotted. There are eight local wineries and several farms where visitors can taste the fruits of Washington State.

## Skamania Lodge, Washington

Skamania Lodge is not far from Portland, Oregon. Skamania is located in the middle of the Columbia River National Scenic Area and is an all-season destination perfect for soft-adventure families. Skamania allows guests to customize adventure escapes with their "Adventure à la Carte" packages. These packages include a choice of length of stay, forest or river-view accommodations, and recreation including a Columbia River Gorge escape and sternwheeler cruises on the Columbia River. Nearby waterfall tours and water sports in the spring and summer are on the menu. The Skamania also has a spa called Waterleaf Spa and Fitness Center for moms and dads to enjoy. (*www.skamania.com*)

## Suncadia

Suncadia is a nearly 7,000-acre resort destination near Roslyn, Washington, on the Cle Elum River with 80 percent of the resort designed to be open space. Suncadia draws families from Seattle, which is just eighty miles from the resort, and all over the Pacific Northwest. Suncadia is situated on the sunny side of the Cascade Mountains with fifty miles of trails for hiking and biking, golf, a lake, and both indoor and outdoor pools. Waterslides, seasonal festivals, and requisite mountain activities make Suncadia an instant favorite for kids. Suncadia is also a certified Built Green Community. (*www.suncadiaresort.com*)

## Oregon

The Resort at the Mountain on Mt. Hood is in Welches, Oregon, at the mountain's western base. Activities like fly fishing, golf, croquet, snow skiing in cold-weather months, and tennis in warm months are available for families to enjoy.

**LODGING IN THE NORTHWESTERN MOUNTAINS**
- **LaConner Channel Lodge** and **LaConner Country Inn** (LaConner, Washington), waterfront lodging on the Swinomish Channel in Skagit Valley, specials and packages (*www.laconnerlodging.com*)

- **Skamania Lodge** (near Portland, Oregon), summer concert series, packages for the whole family, soft-adventure tours and activities (*www.skamania.com*)
- **Suncadia** (Roslyn, Washington), family-oriented riverside lodging not far from Seattle in the Cascade Mountains (*www.suncadiaresort.com*)
- **Resort at the Mountain** (Welches, Oregon), numerous activities for the whole family including planned picnics and berry-picking, kids' games with book reading and trout farms (*www.theresort.com*)

## Things to Do on Your Mountain Vacation

The mountains are "all inclusive" in that most mountain destinations offer the same or very similar activities, many of which are free, like hiking for example. A mountain vacation is perfect for being spontaneous or planning ahead. You can hop in the car and see what your mountain vacation presents when you get there, or lay the groundwork for activities like fishing, rafting, or biking before you leave. If your family enjoys biking, bring the bikes along and enjoy the thousands of miles of bike trails many mountain destinations offer.

### ≡ Fast Fact

Festivals are a big part of most mountain communities. Foliage festivals, mountain arts and crafts fairs, antique auctions, and art and music festivals occur often in the mountains. Residents gather throughout the year for everything from jug band concerts to chamber music.

Outdoor activities are wildly popular in mountain communities, because the mountains are nature's amusement park. Just a few outdoor activities to enjoy in the mountains include hiking, biking, rafting, fishing, canoeing, kayaking, and zip lining.

Most mountains have a thriving population of arts and crafts masters. Pottery is a prevalent mountain art and many potters allow tourists to watch them work. Sometimes driving around a mountain town is the best way to find a favorite potter. To find a list of potters in the mountains where you're going, search online using the combination "pottery" and the mountain range you're visiting.

Some of the world's best antiquing is scattered throughout mountain towns. Mountain antique stores can be charming inns and old hotels, shacks along the road, stand-alone buildings, and converted apple orchards or vineyards. You can find one-of-a-kind quilts and furniture dating back generations.

From one-of-a-kind Native American wood workings and paintings to the delicate hand blown glass factories, you could outfit your whole house in affordable mountain artifacts. Many mountain arts and crafts can be found in historic homes and buildings. Paradise Inn, a guest lodge built in Mt. Rainier National Park nearly a century ago, is home to a fourteen-foot grandfather clock built by German carpenter Hans Fraehnke in 1919!

## Make Safety a Priority on Mountain Vacations

Mountain ranges are expansive areas with dense forestation, so cell phone signals in mountainous regions are unreliable. Stay with your vehicle in the event of an accident or emergency. Try to call for help, but if your phone is unable to transmit a signal, flag down a motorist and ask for help. Your vehicle will be the primary point of contact for emergency response personnel like a forest ranger, for example. Motorists who leave vehicles in search of help in vast mountain ranges can easily become lost.

The mountain ecosystem is a delicate balance of reservoirs and streams that feed into drinking water and soil. Make sure kids don't litter and always clean up after camping or picnicking.

# CHAPTER 7

# Water, Water Everywhere

Sandcastles. Cotton candy on the boardwalk. Flying a kite as you ran down the shoreline. Asking five thousand times, "are we there yet?" Who could forget your parents telling you to watch out for the undertow? And how about when you got closer to the beach, smelling that ocean breeze for the first time since the summer before? Paddling down a river or taking a ride in someone's boat on a pristine lake. There are so many reasons to love water-related vacations, and as many options to choose from. If you have a water destination like a major river or ocean in your backyard or at least within drive time, which is typically five hours or less, you probably already have a favorite place to enjoy water activities. But if not, there are several worth traveling to—whether it takes a couple of days to drive there, or even if you have to fly.

## Planning Your Beach, River, or Lake Vacation

Many of America's beaches are geared toward family vacations and are budget friendly. Restaurants cater to families, and activities to keep everyone busy are plentiful. Plus, when families vacation at the beach, kids get to do something at which they excel—play. It sounds simple, but unstructured play is a crucial part of a child's development. Experts agree that lack of play is to blame for the massive increase in a variety of childhood problems from attention deficit disorder to youth obesity. On beach vacations, kids get to play in the earth's natural sandbox and run through the waves. Parents get to channel their inner child right along with them. A vacation at the beach isn't likely to include a barrage of structured assignments like soccer games. The only assignment when you vacation at a family beach is to relax and have fun!

The same goes for river and lake vacations, although without a vast beach at your fingertips, a little more planning on your part will be necessary to secure activities to keep the kids busy. River vacations can be some of your most memorable family vacations. Fly fishing, tubing, kayaking, and rafting are just a few activities the whole family can enjoy.

There are so many rivers to choose from across the country. It will usually be more economical to choose a river outfitter closest to your family's home to minimize gas costs.

## ▇ Travel Tip

River activities can be dangerous if you don't have the right equipment or navigational knowledge. Unless your family members are experienced river rats, it's almost always better to let a river outfitter help you plan your journey and provide your family's equipment.

Lake life is all about gathering with family and enjoying activities and amenities that lakes generously provide. Waterskiing, enjoying nature, boating, and just plain hanging out are a few pastimes your family would enjoy on a lake vacation. Chances are you have a lake nearby that your family enjoys. If you think life on your local lake is fun, try vacationing at a lake destination that offers all the amenities you and your family will love.

# Water Destinations in the Northeastern United States

Water vacation destinations of the northeast are usually family-friendly, as families have flocked to their shores to escape city heat for generations. The biggest limitation to planning a water vacation in the northeast is the weather—you're limited by the seasons if your family likes to swim or participate in water sports. It's too cold even in the spring and fall to do either. But during the warm summer months, families crowd the beaches and other water destinations to enjoy most of the same activities you'd find in Florida or other warm-weather water destinations.

## New Jersey Shore

The "Jersey Shore," as the residents and frequent visitors call it, is a fairly large cross section of towns on over 127 miles of coastline from Sandy Hook to Cape May. If you've never been to the area, figuring out where to stay can be challenging because there are so many choices. The New Jersey Shore website (*www.newjerseyshore.com*) includes a compass feature via the site mascot, Darwin the Dolphin, that allows visitors to more easily discover what areas of the Jersey Shore they want to visit and how far apart they are. Food recommendations, lodging options, and easy-to-read maps are also part of this comprehensive site. The Virtual New Jersey Shore website (*www.virtualnjshore.com*) has a "locals" events calendar and many other searchable categories of information.

The Jersey Shore has been a time-honored destination for families due to the activities it offers and multiple affordable lodging choices. Wildwoods at the Jersey Shore in Cape May County is a resort community with attractions, shopping, dining, and historic sites. The beach is flanked by a thriving boardwalk scene that features amusement rides with seven roller coasters and kids rides. The area is also known for its mid-century architecture or "Doo Wop" style of the fifties and sixties. See *www.wildwoodsnj.com.*

## Ocean City, Maryland

Ocean City, Maryland, has been called "the Myrtle Beach of Maryland" and for good reason. It is all about families vacationing together. There are multiple value accommodations in Ocean City and the population swells in the summer months when the beaches pulse with kids at play. One of the major attractions is the Ocean City Boardwalk, which features street performers, inexpensive food, and access to the beach. Rides and a convenient tram make it easy to explore the area along the boardwalk.

## ☂ Rainy Day Fun

The Ocean City Boardwalk is lined with video game arcades. When the weather calls for rain, kids and parents can spend hours trying their luck at the latest video game challenges.

One of the most popular things to do when visiting Ocean City, Maryland, is to make the short drive to Assateague Island to view the Assateague Island wild ponies. Since the seventeenth century, the ponies have meandered around the island. The island is part of the Assateague Island National Seashore, and between Maryland and Virginia there are about 300 wild ponies. Free summer concerts on the beach are always popular events, along with the Family Beach Olympics. The Family Beach Olympics include sandcastle building competitions and traditional games like tug-of-war and relay races.

## Raft Maine

Raft Maine is an association of Maine's seven professional whitewater rafting outfitters. These folks adhere to safety standards set by Maine's Department of Inland Fisheries and Wildlife. River trips include the Upper Kennebec River, the Penobscot River's West Branch, and the lower Dead River. Families of all ages with or without rafting experience can join in the fun on trips through Raft Maine. There are also recreational floats, inflatable kayaks, easy lake kayaking, and canoeing trips. Other supplemental activities families can schedule through Raft Maine include biking, hiking, rock climbing, fishing, moose and wildlife safaris, ATV tours, and even paintball. (*www.raftmaine.com*)

## Cape Cod

New England's historic Cape Cod is located in Massachusetts. Shopping is a favorite activity for regulars to Cape Cod, matched by outdoor activities like bicycling, whale watching, boating, festivals, and coastal recreation. Cape Cod is also known throughout the world for its numerous historic sites and landmarks.

Incredible dining is also a trademark of Cape Cod, where some of the best seafood anywhere can be had year round. Many lodging choices and restaurants throughout Cape Cod are located in and on historic properties.

For families who consider "Fido" to be their child, pet-friendly Lamb and Lion Inn in Barnstable, Massachusetts, was the "Gold Winner" for Best Mid-Cape bed and breakfast inn by *Cape Cod Life* and voted "One of the Top 15 Best Overall Inns in America" by *Arrington's Bed and Breakfast Journal*. The Sea Gull Motel, which has been owned and operated by the same family for more than seven decades, offers affordable lodging right on Cape Cod Bay. It's only open for the tourism season starting in May of each year. Reservations for each season can be made beginning in April. A private beach and close proximity to many local activities keep families coming back year after year.

The Cape Cod Travel Guide, available on the Cape Cod Chamber website includes Martha's Vineyard, Nantucket, and Cape Cod travel resources including hotels, motels, resorts, and vacation rentals. The guide also features restaurants and shops and coastal and other activities. This section of the site also features breaking news about new lodging properties and dining establishments and holiday events and activities. The Cape Cod Chamber of Commerce is a great resource for planning a vacation to Cape Cod, Massachusetts. (*www.capecod chamber.org*)

### WATER DESTINATION LODGING IN THE NORTHEAST

- **Ocean Place** (Jersey Shore, Long Branch, New Jersey), near major attractions and New Jersey's famous boardwalk (*www.oceanplace.com*)
- **Spinnaker Motel** (Ocean City, Maryland), beachfront lodging with apartment features offering hot deals regularly (*www.ococean.com*)
- **Inn by the River** (West Forks, Maine), rustic, classic Maine family lodging on the Kennebec River (*www.innbytheriver.com*)
- **Lamb and Lion** (Barnstable, Massachusetts), charming pet-friendly inn with all the amenities one could want on a historic vacation. (*www.lambandlion.com*)
- **Sea Gull Motel** (North Truro, Massachusetts), situated on more than 150 feet of private beach near the sand dunes of Truro in the middle of the National Seashore. (*www.cape codtravel.com/seagullmotel*)

# Water Destinations in the Southeastern United States

The summer months bring about great vacation deals for families traveling to the southeast, because this is the time when snowbirds (people who live in northern states and vacation in the southeast) return to their northern dwellings. In the Carolinas, however, wintertime is only a few degrees warmer than the northeastern beaches, and swimming and other such water sports will be limited. However, more and more southeastern water destinations are marketing themselves as great off-season destinations. Thanks to development of family entertainment complexes, nature centers, and educational activities, more families are vacationing at water destinations despite the weather!

## Florida's Paradise Coast

In places like Florida's Paradise Coast, the weather is warm all year long. The Everglades, Marco Island, and Naples make up Florida's Paradise Coast. Thanks to its location on the southwestern side of the state, the area is blessed with a tropical climate. The Everglades ecosystem and the Ten Thousand Islands is a marvel of nature and hence is a big draw for tourists, with numerous fishing charters and boat rentals available. The Paradise Coast website (*www.paradisecoast.com*) offers extensive information on vacationing on this stretch of Florida.

By simply driving around this area, you can often see wildlife, including alligators, raccoons, butterflies, and birds. Sightseeing boats take families to see mangrove estuaries leading to the Gulf of Mexico where it's possible to view dolphins, manatees, sea turtles, and birds. Families can kayak or take a guided boat tour of the Cocohatchee River at the Cocohatchee Nature Center. And fast-moving airboat rides allow passengers to closely see alligators and wild boar in the Everglades National Park.

Many beachfront resorts of all shapes and sizes are family-friendly, and family dining options are plentiful. Naples and the surrounding areas are home (or second homes) to some of the world's wealthiest individuals, which makes consignment shopping in Naples like treasure hunting—designer wear and home interior design furnishings can be had for a fraction of their original cost. Naples is a small city with multiple public access points to pristine beaches, within walking distance from downtown where shops and many dining options abound. Naples is also an arts-friendly community. There is always something to see at the museums, along with frequent arts and community events. Naples Zoo at Caribbean Gardens features a Primate Expedition Cruise that coasts by cage-free primates.

On the Paradise Coast, available lodging includes multibedroom suites complete with kitchens so families can stock up on supplies from nearby grocers. Many resorts have formal kids' programs and child care. The Ritz-Carlton Naples Beach Resort and The Ritz-Carlton Golf Resort feature an eco-themed program just for kids called Nature's Wonders in their nature center, equipped with aquariums. Other resorts that have dedicated kids' programs include:

- **Naples Beach Hotel & Golf Club** (*www.naplesbeachhotel.com*)
- **Marco Island Marriott Beach Resort Golf Club & Spa** (*www.marriott.com*)
- **Naples Grande Beach Resort** (*www. naplesgranderesort.com*)
- **Marco Beach Ocean Resort** (*www.marcoresort.com*)

## South Carolina's Grand Strand

The resorts and innumerable activities are what make Myrtle Beach and the surrounding areas known as the "Grand Strand" so family-friendly. Water parks, family entertainment, hundreds of affordable dining options, and affordable lodging have drawn families to Myrtle Beach in droves for decades. It's estimated that there are more than 12,000 vacation rental options on the Grand Strand.

The Sands Resorts offer oceanfront restaurants and lounges, Sands Waterpark, lazy rivers and indoor and outdoor pools, the Atlantis Spa, a children's program, and evening child care. At the Sands, kids eat breakfast free and enjoy free summer recreation including bicycles, paddle boats, kayaks, table tennis, and volleyball. All kids' programs are supervised by experienced staff and counselors. Evening child care service offers nightly themed activities and games under the supervision of professional counselors. The SportsZone, an indoor sports facility, offers league play, birthday parties, arcade games, food, private baseball and softball instruction, and sports camps. The KidZone Summer Sports program provides supervised activities while parents catch up on a round of golf or a quiet day at the beach.

Families who enjoy camping will also find many options in the area, and places like Lakewood Camping Resort will be glad to have you. Lakewood is not just a camper hook-up for your family RV. This campground has two pools and waterslides, a full store with two snack bars, mini-golf, boat rentals, fishing, gem mining, and entertainment. With full hookups for lush campers, Lakewood Camping Resort has recreational activities for all ages year round. They even offer yoga and surfing lessons.

Barefoot and Prince Resorts feature luxury suites and panoramic ocean views. Prince Resort is adjacent to the Cherry Grove Pier and not far from the world-famous Barefoot Landing and attractions like Alligator Adventure.

## North Carolina's Outer Banks

The Cape Hatteras National Seashore, America's first national seashore, is located in the otherworldly beauty of North Carolina's Outer Banks, which are a collection of barrier islands off the Atlantic Coast. The islands are ever changing—shaped by timeless action of tides, storms, currents, and winds. The Cape Hatteras National Seashore is open all year long.

One particular highlight of visiting the Outer Banks is a trip to the Cape Hatteras Lighthouse. Families can actually climb the lighthouse from April to early October. Children must be at least forty-two inches tall, and kids twelve and under have to have an adult go along. In the spring and fall, fishing families flock to beaches and sounds. Pets are welcome at many businesses but not allowed on designated swim beaches in the Hatteras National Park. Horseback riding is permitted anywhere vehicles can go except in area campgrounds.

The Southern portion of the Outer Banks is known as the Crystal Coast. With maritime villages, fresh seafood delivered straight from boat and pristine beaches, the Crystal Coast has been a favorite family beach for generations. Atlantic Beach, Beaufort, Emerald Isle, Harker's Island, and Morehead City make up the Crystal Coast. Part of the area's fun is its checkered past. Edward Teach, also known as Blackbeard, was a frequent guest in the Outer Banks, where he retreated between capturing and sinking many ships off the eastern seaboard. The waters off the Outer Banks are home to thousands of sunken vessels and men of the sea.

## 💼 Travel Tip

Fort Macon State Park in Atlantic Beach is the site of a Civil War skirmish. If you plan to visit Fort Macon, bring a lunch for everyone to enjoy, and after a long hike settle in for a picnic.

Visiting Beaufort is like taking a step back in time. The streets are lined with oaks and there are many waterfront cafés where, if you're lucky, you can catch a glimpse of the wild horses of the Outer Banks running free, their thick manes and fat bellies reflecting the happy life they lead. Bed and breakfasts are the lodging of choice in Beaufort, which is the third-oldest town in North Carolina. The whole coastal area off the coast of the Outer Banks is known as the graveyard of the Atlantic. *Queen Anne's Revenge*, the ship of the notorious pirate, Blackbeard, was wrecked just three miles off the shores of Beaufort.

Emerald Isle is a wholly uncrowded quiet beach with elegant dining and private homes owned by people who have been coming to the Outer Banks for generations. Morehead City is home to a string of fishing charter boats and is an eclectic blend of art galleries and antique stores. The Cape Lookout National Seashore consists of fifty-six miles of largely undeveloped beach on four barrier islands, and they are only accessible by boat.

No matter which town a family chooses for lodging and activities, each has its own unique style, but all have incredible seafood. Recipes in many local restaurants, like crab cakes or she crab soup, have been passed down from generation to generation.

## Wildwater, Ltd., South Carolina

Wildwater, Ltd. is located on the border of Georgia and South Carolina on the Chattooga River. Families with kids as young as four years old can choose from fifteen different river trips on five separate rivers, from half-day up to multiple-day trips. Taking a Jeep Tour and staying at Falling Waters Resort in a yurt is one of the most fun things to do at Wildwater, Ltd. Falling Waters is located above Fontana Lake in the Nantahala River Mountains. A yurt is a circular canvas sleeping structure with a see-through dome roof that gets you close to nature without having to sleep on the ground in a tent. For more information visit *www.wildwater rafting.com.*

## Nantahala Family Outdoor Center, Western North Carolina

Nantahala Outdoor Center, also known as the NOC, is located in western North Carolina near Tennessee. The NOC offers half-day rafting, lake, and all sorts of other mountain water and land activities. A total adventure resort, the NOC has on-site dining and lots of lodging. Beginners and outdoor enthusiasts are all welcome here. NOC is known for its paddling school workshops including the full-day introduction to whitewater, which is available to children age eight and older accompanying an adult. Affordable cabins with full kitchens for two to twenty guests, bunkhouse lodging that can sleep up to sixty-six guests, and platform tent camping are available. Nearby Nantahala Inn also has ten motel rooms and satellite TV, and more upscale cabins that include full kitchens and hot tubs. (*www.noc.com*)

**WATER DESTINATION LODGING IN THE SOUTHEAST**

- Oceanana Family Resort (Atlantic Beach, North Carolina), oceanfront lodging, near attractions and restaurants (*www.oceanana-resort.com*)
- **Watercolor Inn and Resort** (Santa Rosa Beach, Florida), vast resort with multiple family activities (*www.watercolorresort.com*)
- **The Lemon Tree Inn** (Naples, Florida), charming family motel near downtown Naples and beaches (*www.lemontreeinn.com*)
- **Mountain Aire Cottages and Motel** (Clayton, Georgia), cozy cottages in rustic atmosphere with space for everyone (*www.mountainairecottages.com*)
- **Caribbean Resort and Villas** (Myrtle Beach, South Carolina), family destination lodging with packages that include tickets to kid-friendly area attractions (*www.caribbeanresort.com*)

# Water Destinations in the Central United States

Middle America might not have any oceans to enjoy, but there's plenty of river and lake fun to be had! Though in many lake communities it pays to have a boat, there are several lake destinations that bill themselves as water-destination vacations. And there are numerous river vacation outfitters who pack fun activities into every minute of a thrilling trip down river.

## ROW Adventures, Idaho

Idaho's ROW Adventures has been around since 1979. Their early focus was on whitewater rafting in Idaho, Montana, and Oregon. Since then, the company has evolved to become an adventure travel company offering trips to a variety of destinations worldwide. Though they've branched out, rafting is still something they do well—*Outside* magazine recognized their Owyhee Expeditionary Kayak Trip as their 2009 "Trip of the Year: North America." Families with kids five and older are welcome on ROW Adventures "Family Magic Rafting" vacations. On these journeys through the Salmon River Canyons on the Main Salmon River in Idaho, a "River Jester" entertains children with nature hikes and other fun activities; camping includes wonderful meals and stargazing. ROW Adventures guides provide information about the canyon, and rafters get to visit several points of interest on the trip. You won't need to schlep your camping gear—with ROW Adventures a cargo boat will raft ahead of your party and arrange camp, which even includes your tent! Row Adventures also owns and operates the River Dance Lodge in central Idaho for families who prefer soft beds and private baths at the day's end. (*www.rowadventures.com*)

### River Expeditions, West Virginia

Families touring with River Expeditions, West Virginia, spend the day paddling two of the most beautiful rivers in the country, the New River and the Gauley River, home of the famous Gauley Run. Children age six and up can participate. (*www.raftinginfo.com*) Other activity tours in West Virginia include mountain biking, rock climbing, horseback riding, and on-site camping.

### The Lodge at Whitefish Lake, Montana

One of the most pristine lakes in the country can be found in the Montana town of Whitefish. Whitefish Lake is located at the base of Big Mountain. On a clear day, the lake becomes a canvas ready to accept the reflection of the mountain and surrounding landscape. It creates a work of art that will take your breath away. Whitefish Lake stretches for seven miles and is approximately a half-mile wide. The lake's water is crystal clear, making it perfect for catching fresh trout. In the warm summer months Whitefish Lake is very popular. People can be found boating, canoeing, and kayaking between its shores.

The Lodge at Whitefish Lake was inspired by grand old lodges from days gone by, and it has achieved its goal of creating that ambience. In the Flathead Valley, the Lodge at Whitefish Lake is engulfed by the mountains and hence has a nestled quality that feels cozy despite the fact that it is a full-service resort. The Lodge is a five-minute drive to Whitefish's charming western downtown and just thirty minutes to awe-inspiring Glacier National Park. (*www .lodgeatwhitefishlake.com*)

### Bear Lake, Utah and Idaho

Bear Lake, Idaho, has been called the "Caribbean of the Rockies" thanks to its turquoise waters. Situated on the Idaho and Utah border, families who come here are swimmers, boaters, and sailors. The requisite lake sports apply here, including waterskiing and fishing. It's also a great destination for moms and dads to relax—there are two miles of beach space to choose from. On the website, *www .bearlake.org*, you'll find a hot deals page that offers great lodging options for families on a budget. The lake is located in the Bear Lake valley, which is busy with visitors during all seasons. Fishing at Bear Lake can include catching mackinaw and cutthroat trout.

### The Great Lakes Region

Ever wonder why people from Michigan rave about places like Alpena? See for yourself as you stroll down the uncrowded beaches or take a bike ride on historic Mackinac Island. Alpena is a water vacation destination to be sure, and though its body of water is a lake rather than an ocean, the little waves are soothing reminders of why water vacations are so calming. Parents love the local wine and beer that comes from local wine and brewing companies, numerous cafés and shopping. For kids, the activities are endless—water fun includes fishing, sailing, snorkeling, and canoeing and kayaking.

Land fun includes ice-skating, hockey, and geocaching. This hot activity features treasure hunting using a GPS device rather

than a map to find caches, many of which are hidden in the surrounding Alpena area. (*www.nmg-geocaching.org*) Alpena is also
home to fine dining with some of the region's best freshly caught
seafood. (*www.alpenacvb.com*)

Ohio's Lake Erie is home to numerous vacation spots. The Lake
Erie Guide is the key to planning a vacation at this popular family
destination. (*www.thelakeerieguide.com*) There is so much do to at
this water destination. Activities can include water and beach fun
on more than 800 miles of shoreline, cruises and fishing charters,
museums, and enjoying the arts. The famous Walleye festival in
Port Clinton takes place over the Memorial Day holiday weekend.

**WATER DESTINATION LODGING IN THE CENTRAL
UNITED STATES**

- **Shilo Inn** (Coeur d'Alene, Idaho), value-focused, kid-friendly
  packages include "popcorn, pizza, and a movie night"
  (*www.shiloinns.com*)
- **The Resort at Glade Springs** (Daniels, West Virginia), golf,
  activities for kids, and a spa for parents; near numerous outdoor activities outfitters (*www.gladesprings.com*)
- **South Beach Resort Hotel and Marina** (Marblehead, Ohio),
  suites, three heated pools, waterfront lodging with a dedicated children's activity center (*www.sbresort.com*)
- **Thunder Bay Resort** (Hillman, Michigan), all-season destination in Northern Michigan famous for sleigh rides and wilderness experience (*www.thunderbayresort.com*)

# Water Destinations in the Northwestern
# United States

In photographs the coastal regions of the Northwestern United
States often look misty, chilly, and green with moss-covered forests.
In colder months Northwestern coastal towns are brimming with
beautiful sights and scenic vistas, and are still a wonderful choice

for family vacations thanks to activities like whale watching and stunning natural beauty. And in the summer months spectacular ocean, lake, and river beaches welcome families for fun in the sun. Though popular with people who love water vacations, most Northwestern beaches remain sparsely populated compared to their busy Southeastern counterparts.

### California's Half Moon Bay

Half Moon Bay is a coastal town about forty minutes south of San Francisco. The great thing about Half Moon Bay is even if the weather doesn't cooperate, there is so much for a traveling family to do, you'll never want for fun experiences.

Half Moon Bay also has a lot of choices for lodging, from the usual coastal resorts to homelike inns that you might find in a mountain town. And no matter what time of year it is, there is always something to do here. Dining in Half Moon Bay includes the ultra fancy to the ultra casual, but both carry the same quality of cuisine—a burger at a family restaurant in Half Moon Bay will be just as tasty as a steak at a fine restaurant. Visits to amazing nearby farms complete with petting zoos, ponies, trains, and hay rides are a great way to spend a day between the two-dozen beaches Half Moon Bay has to offer.

### 👥 Just for Parents

Besides the family-friendly beach, Half Moon Bay is known for its culinary and wine establishments. Wine tastings abound in the area, and because Half Moon Bay has multiple child-care options, moms and dads can sneak off for adult imbibing.

If you happen to visit Half Moon Bay between December and March, be sure to take the kids whale watching. Gray whales number in the tens of thousands as they swim south from the Arctic to mate and nurse their young in warm, shallow water off Baja, California. What an awesome sight for young eyes! Frolicking in the tide pools at Half Moon Bay is wildly popular with kids, and the charming seaside town of Half Moon Bay is always a hit with everyone in the family. Many places in Half Moon Bay also welcome pets, so bring Fido along for the ride! (*www.visithalfmoonbay.org*)

## San Juan Islands, Washington

Not far from Seattle is one of America's best-kept secrets for fun family vacations, but word is getting around! The San Juan Islands are accessible via the Washington State Ferry. Riding the ferry to and from these amazing natural destinations is worth going to any one of the San Juan Islands. The view is a breathtaking array of water and landscapes. Incredible food, family-friendly lodging, and fun activities await you.

The beauty of the San Juan Islands—prairies, trees, pastures, and island waters—will leave you breathless. Orcas Island is the largest island in the San Juan Islands and is a combination of farms, lakes, and magnificent mountains, featuring arts, outdoor activities, and a bustling downtown. And the Inn at Ship Bay on Orcas Island features some of the finest dining in the northwestern United States and charming lodging with stunning views of Ship Bay. Lopez Island is for families who love the outdoors, especially from atop a bicycle. San Juan Island features breathtaking beaches and shoreline rock formations and is home to Friday and Roche Harbors. Friday Harbor on San Juan Island can boast incredible terrain best viewed from a moped or scootcar from Susie's Mopeds, in business for more than twenty years. (*www.susiesmopeds.com*)

**WATER DESTINATION LODGING IN THE NORTHWEST**
- **Hampton Inn and Suites** (Crescent City, California), spectacular views with babysitting services on a crescent-shaped beach in Northern California (*www.hamptoninn.com*)

- **Bird Rock Hotel** (Friday Harbor, San Juan Islands, Washington), relaxed, yet contemporary style hotel with spacious rooms convenient to downtown and ferry (*www.birdrock hotel.com*)
- **Inn at Ship Bay** (Orcas Island, Washington), comfortable rooms and spectacular waterfront dining with incomparable views of Ship Bay (*www.innatshipbay.com*)

# CHAPTER 8

# America's Coolest Family-Friendly Cities

The beach and the mountains are obvious choices for family vacations. A quaint bed and breakfast in the country always sounds good. But did you know that America's cities are some of the best places to take a family vacation? That's right! Cities are full of culture, great food, nightlife for the whole family, and incredible entertainment. Special family packages and last-minute deals abound in America's coolest cities, along with museums, historic attractions, and even amusement parks. A trip to an urban destination is a great way to travel together.

## Planning Your Trip to America's Coolest Cities

Traveling to one of America's coolest cities is one of the best vacations you can take with your family. Museums, historic sites, and attractions beckon along with world-class dining and unique lodging, Traveling to a city also allows kids to experience urban culture that's often completely different from their own.

Flying into a city can be expensive, and a pain to boot, so be open to alternative ways to get to the metropolitan area you've chosen. For example, a flight to New York's LaGuardia airport might be cheap, but the cab fare to Manhattan will cost a minimum of $40, and another $40 minimum to get back to the airport. With gratuity and toll costs, your cab fare to and from the airport alone will easily exceed $100.

If you live near an urban area, you can probably find a train that regularly, perhaps even daily, makes the trek into the city. Such cities make for great day trips. Most major cities have Amtrak service to and from a central station. Families who have Amtrak stations in or near their hometowns can hop on a train to a major metropolitan area and easily find themselves in the thick of the city without having to fly or drive.

If your town doesn't offer Amtrak service, look into the closest city near you. Calculate the drive and check the Amtrak website at *www.amtrak.com* to see how far away the nearest Amtrak train is to your town, and if it travels to your city destination. Even if you drive to another town and take the train into the city, you'll save big on airfare and cab fare to and from the airport once you land.

When it comes to dining, cities often have their own flair or culinary specialty. Chicago and New York have great pizza. Boston and Seattle have amazing seafood. Nashville has incredible country soul food, and Las Vegas, well, Las Vegas has everything! Although it can be difficult to shop for groceries on an urban vacation, it can be done. City corner markets and local delis have everything you need to make unforgettable sandwiches or bagels that will save your family a lot of money over the course of your trip. Save dining out for special meals that reflect the unique nature of the city you're visiting.

Lodging in urban areas is usually aplenty, but can be expensive. It's a good idea to select family-friendly hotels that market themselves to families with children. Look for special deals where kids under a certain age can stay with you for free. Keep your eyes peeled for weekend packages and last-minute getaways.

# City Vacations in the Northeastern United States

New York City, Philadelphia, and Boston are three of the most exciting and historic cities in the world. Manhattan, the most exuberant part of New York City, has often been called "the capital of the world." In Boston, families can try some of the planet's best seafood among some of the country's richest history. And of all the sites related to the founding of America, just traveling through Philadelphia is practically an education.

## New York City

New York City is made up of five boroughs including Manhattan, Brooklyn, Queens, the Bronx, and Staten Island. Manhattan is a tiny island that packs a whopping number of restaurants, theaters, and other live entertainment. Manhattan is where most people stay when visiting New York City, because it's near all of the major attractions and central to activities a visiting family would enjoy on vacation there. The best way to get around in New York City is by subway or bus. Manhattan is a grid of streets running east-west and avenues running north-south, so navigating the city isn't confusing. But attractions are spread out, so be sure to budget enough money in your trip to take taxis when necessary, especially if you need to hail a cab to transport your family back to your hotel at night.

### *Family-Friendly Activities*

Chelsea Piers is a huge sports complex on the West Side Highway in Manhattan. Chelsea Piers is nearly thirty acres created from four historic piers. The complex is now a massive recreation center on the waterfront of Manhattan's Hudson River in an area of the city called Chelsea, hence the name. Chelsea Piers includes a golf club, health club, sky rink, field house, and maritime center. See *www.chelseapiers.com.*

Enjoying a Broadway show is something every family should do together while in New York City. Formerly, it seemed impossible to get tickets to Broadway shows. But now there are a variety of shows appropriate for families, and the additional choices have made seeing a show on Broadway easier than in previous years, Broadway.com is a website and clearing house that has a plethora of information about Broadway shows and tickets, and includes show synopses. On this site families can read about a show that interests them and determine if the show is something the family would like to see. (*www.broadway.com*)

## 🧳 Travel Tip

Plan to visit New York City during the workweek. Tickets to shows are easier to get and restaurants aren't as crowded.

The Statue of Liberty is a short ferry ride from Manhattan, and families who appreciate history won't want to miss the Statue of Liberty and Ellis Island, which was restored into a museum. There, families can take guided walking tours, watch documentary films and theatrical productions, and take part in workshops. Ellis Island is part of the Statue of Liberty National Monument, which was presented to the United States by France as a symbol of freedom and was dedicated in 1886. Visit Ellis Island and the Statue of Liberty during the workweek to reduce the time waiting in line. Another great place to spend time while in New York City is Central Park. In the park families can visit the zoo, take long walks to see the statuary scattered throughout the park, go ice skating during the winter months, and go to free concerts put on by international performers. (*www.centralparknyc.org*)

Going to the movies in New York City is always fun, especially if you're seeing a film at Bryant Park. The Bryant Park Summer Film Festival showcases films outdoors with Manhattan skyscrapers in the background. With a wedge of cheese and some crackers, a bottle of wine for parents, and a jar of Martinelli's apple juice for the kids, families can enjoy free movies on Mondays through June, July, and August.

## 🧳 Travel Tip

The art galleries in Manhattan's SoHo (which stands for "South of Houston" Street) display some of the finest art in the country. Wandering in and out of the galleries is free, and SoHo is accessible by subway.

A visit to the Empire State Building is almost a rite of passage when visiting New York City. What a view, and what a story. Take time to review the building's rich history when you visit. The American Museum of Natural History and the Metropolitan Museum of Art are two of the world's most famous museums, both located in Manhattan. And no child should leave New York without a trip to FAO Schwartz, the colossal toy store located on Fifth Avenue in Midtown Manhattan.

### Family-Friendly Lodging

The Gem Hotel family in Manhattan provides lodging without the frills. Rooms are not large, but space is used wisely to house comfortable beds and smart storage, like putting dresser drawers in the bed frame. Gem Hotels are known for cleanliness and streamlined décor. Gem Hotels are located in Chelsea on the West side of Manhattan near downtown, in Midtown West near Times Square, and in SoHo near the East side of downtown Manhattan. (*www.thegemhotel.com*)

Families who like to spread out can check out the Grand Hyatt New York in Midtown Manhattan. Its close proximity to Grand Central Station, Times Square, Midtown, and all transportation mediums make this hotel a perfect location for families, especially those who are new to visiting Manhattan. (*www.grand newyork.hyatt.com*)

### Family-Friendly Dining

When it comes to fine, cheap, filling, and family dining, nobody does it like New York City. Virtually every kind of cuisine and culinary culture can be found in Manhattan, starting with Chinatown. In Chinatown visitors can sample authentic Chinese cuisine in tiny restaurants at more than reasonable prices. (*www .explorechinatown.com*) Just around the corner and across the street from Chinatown is Manhattan's Little Italy. Authentic Italian restaurants are packed together by the hundreds in this radius of just a few blocks. (*www.littleitalynyc.com*)

## Boston

Boston is the capital of Massachusetts and is the most recognized city in New England. Thanks to its starring role in the American Revolution, Boston is all about history. The dynamic city is full of historic sites, which are preserved under the umbrella of Boston National Historical Park.

Using public transportation in Boston, also known as the "T," is essential to staying within budget. Parking in Boston is difficult and when you can actually find a space, parking fees can add up. Therefore staying on budget in Boston requires getting to know the public transit system. For finding the best hotel for the activities you want to try, click to Boston's Convention and Visitors Bureau website at *www.bostonusa.com*.

### Family-Friendly Activities

The Boston Children's Museum is a great family destination in Boston. There are exhibits for kids of all ages up to tweens. The Museum of Science is the largest science museum in the Northeast with nearly 500 interactive exhibits that include information about everything from astronomy to medicine to natural history.

A Discovery Center caters to preschool-aged kids, and the Planetarium is fun for the whole family.

## 🧳 Travel Tip

Parents who love art and art history will enjoy the Museum of Fine Arts, while kids will love the family activity books that go with the self-guided tours. There is also a Children's Room for kids aged six to twelve that features museum collection workshops every week.

There is seafood aplenty in Boston, and not just for eating! The New England Aquarium is the best place for families to see thousands of species of marine life. Sea lion feeding time is not to be missed.

Kids will love seeing Boston via Boston Duck Tours. Each "DUCK" is a World War II-style amphibious landing craft. "ConDUCKtors" narrate the tours as you travel all around Boston until it's time for "Splashdown" when your duck goes right from street into the Charles River for more touring by water. (*www.boston ducktours.com*)

The Freedom Trail is part of the National Park Service. It's a tour marked with a red line throughout historic Boston. It meanders for about three miles along numerous historic sites and is free to the public. Freedom Trail sites include:

- Boston Common
- Massachusetts State House
- Old Corner Bookstore
- Old South Meeting House
- Old State House
- Boston Massacre Site
- Faneuil Hall
- Paul Revere House
- Park Street Church

- Granary Burying Ground
- King's Chapel
- Site of the First Public School
- Franklin Statue
- Old North Church
- Copp's Hill Burial Ground
- *USS Constitution*
- Bunker Hill Monument

Visitors to Boston's Freedom Trail can walk, go by trolley, or take guided tours. Plan to spend at least an entire afternoon for the tour, or, take the day and plan for stops along the way for lunch, coffee or hot chocolate, and an afternoon snack.

### Family-Friendly Lodging

The Colonnade Hotel is convenient to everything in Boston and has both a front and back entrance to busy streets, making getting to a restaurant or nearby activity easy. Legal Seafood restaurant is right down the street, as are several museums and local attractions. It's welcoming to families and business travelers. (*www.colonnadehotel.com*)

The Seaport Hotel and World Trade Center in Boston is a destination in itself. The hotel is in a picturesque location with easy access to activities including the Freedom Trail, Children's Museum, Newbury Street, and the North End. (*www.seaportboston.com*)

### Family-Friendly Dining

Legal Seafood (*www.legalseafoods.com*) is known for their friendliness toward kids, and their Long Wharf location is a great family dining destination because of its close proximity to many family activities such as Quincy Market, the New England Aquarium, and Rowe's Wharf. Long Wharf is the pier-side section of Old Boston where kids can learn about Boston's seafaring history. Touring vessels, famed Duck Tours, and Old Town Trolleys stop at Long Wharf so families can recharge their batteries at Legal Seafood. Don't leave Boston without trying the New England clam chowder!

## ☂ Rainy Day Fun

When the weather is uncooperative on your trip to Boston, parents can take the kids to an IMAX movie at the Mugar Omni Theater in the Boston Museum of Science. It's near Long Wharf, the films are usually educational, and seeing a movie on the five-story dome screen is always a treat for the kids.

Vinny T's is family-friendly because it provides great value and good food, and kids love it. You'll be able to split one pasta dish among three kids at Vinny T's. The Italian restaurant serves its dishes family style, which can really shave dollars off your budget. After dinner families can play "Italian bingo" for gift certificates. (*www.vinnytsofboston.com*)

### Philadelphia

Philadelphia, otherwise known as "The City of Brotherly Love," is full of incredible food, history, and culture. It's a city different from all others in America. Philadelphia is the keeper of America's history and home to places and historic items from America's founding. Independence National Historical Park is the hub of all the fuss. This is the location of the signing of the Declaration of Independence and the Liberty Bell among many other cool sites. A family city with tight-knit neighborhoods and family-owned restaurants, some of the country's best and most reasonably priced cuisine can be found in Philadelphia.

### *Family-Friendly Activities*

Philadelphia has a major museum scene. There is a museum to tempt practically everyone's taste, including:

- The Franklin Institute Science Museum, home of Benjamin Franklin National Memorial
- The Academy of Natural Sciences
- The University of Pennsylvania Museum of Archaeology and Anthropology
- National Constitution Center
- The Atwater Kent Museum of Philadelphia History
- The National Museum of American Jewish History
- The African American Museum in Philadelphia
- The Historical Society of Pennsylvania
- Philadelphia Museum of Art

America's first Please Touch Museum for kids under age seven is located in Philadelphia. The Please Touch Museum has nearly 40,000 square feet of kid-friendly exhibits and is home to the 100-year-old, fully restored Woodside Park Dentzel Carousel. There is family-friendly dining on-site. Information on museums and other activities in Philadelphia can be found at GoPhila.com. (*www.gophila.com*)

### Family-Friendly Lodging

The Comfort Inn Downtown/Historic Area is located on Penn's Landing with Delaware River and Center City views. Families staying here are within walking distance of major historic sites including the Liberty Bell Center, Independence Hall, Elfreth's Alley, Betsy Ross House, Penn's Landing, and Old City neighborhood. (*www.comfortinn.com*)

Best Western Independence Park Hotel is located within a Victorian building, also at Penn's Landing within walking distance of relevant historic sites including Franklin Court, Society Hill, and Independence Mall. Best Western Independence Park Hotel serves a daily European complimentary breakfast and offers weekend packages. (*www.independenceparkhotel.com*)

### *Family-Friendly Dining*

Philadelphia is famous for its cheese steaks, and there are several places to grab one on the go, and on the cheap. Dalessandro's has been serving these delicious sandwiches since 1960, piled high with beef, fried onions, and American cheese on fresh hoagie rolls. Fans pile in to get their fix, so there may be a wait for lunch, but it's worth it. (*www.dalessandros.com*)

Philadelphia is also known for its authentic Italian restaurants. South Philadelphia's best Italian food can be found at Ralph's. The restaurant has satisfied some of the pickiest taste buds since 1900. Five generations of the same family have operated Ralph's, serving all the Italian favorites. (*www.ralphsrestaurant.com*)

# City Vacations in the Southeastern United States

Washington, D.C., is one of America's great family destinations—who can argue with educational travel when kids are tagging along! This vibrant city is jam-packed with dozens of family-friendly attractions. And guess what—many of them are free! Washington, D.C., is all about fun and education, plus great food and experiences everyone can enjoy together.

## Washington, D.C.—A Capital Place for Families

Washington, D.C., has it all, from traditional sightseeing to new attractions that thrill and inspire visitors from around the world. In Washington, D.C., public transportation is crucial if you want to save money on your tour of the Nation's Capital. Taxi fares are expensive and can eat a hole in your budget very quickly.

### *Family-Friendly Activities*

The best way to get to know the nation's capital is to take one of the several walking tours of the city. Many themed tours are planned for children and families. Washington Walks features "White House Un-Tour," tales of FDR's presidency and the Great Depression in "In Fala's Footsteps," and the "Good Night, Mr. Lincoln" tour. (*www.washingtonwalks.com*) DC by Foot offers free one-hour walking tours that provide basic information on Washington's national treasures. (*www.dcbyfoot.com*) Narrated sightseeing tours are also available. (*www.washington.org*)

What better way to inspire kids to become enthralled in books and reading than a visit to the Library of Congress. High-tech, interactive kiosks and experiences make the Library more than just a library. Kids can see books from Thomas Jefferson's library, artifacts including "America's Birth Certificate," and other significant objects. (*www.loc.gov*)

Madame Tussauds Wax Museum is located in the Penn Quarter/Chinatown neighborhood of Washington, D.C. This Madame Tussauds is all about Washington, D.C., and visitors love to have their photos made near the replica of the Oval Office, with Franklin D. Roosevelt or Winston Churchill. (*www.madametussaudsdc.com*)

## ☂ Rainy Day Fun

> The National Air and Space Museum tells the story of the history of air travel. Kids have a chance to be a pilot in the cockpit of an airplane replica in the midst of a simulated takeoff. (*www.nasm.si.edu*)

The National Museum of Natural History is a nature education destination for families. New exhibitions to the museum include The Soils Exhibition and Butterflies and Plants, featuring a 1,400 square-foot Butterfly Pavilion with live butterflies and plants. (*www.mnh.si.edu*)

Visitors to Washington, D.C., during spring will witness a most dazzling display of natural firecrackers. Thousands of cherry trees, gifts from Japan in 1912, are literally exploding with color through the spring, so much so that The National Cherry Blossom Festival was created in its honor. They're all around the Jefferson Memorial along the Tidal Basin and the Washington Monument. The festival draws thousands from around the world. (*www.national cherryblossomfestival.org*)

In the hour-long Operation Spy program at the International Spy Museum, which debuted last year, participants who are age twelve or older can take on the role of U.S. intelligence officers. They're on an international mission to locate a missing nuclear device on the verge of being sold to a rogue nation. Participants take part in an intrigue-filled live-action adventure based on an actual case drawn from the files of U.S. intelligence. Challenged to "feel, think, and act" like real intelligence officers, they uncover layers of deception to reveal a world of double agents and corrupt officials. Participants leave Operation Spy either congratulated on their success or aware of their failure, and conscious of the real challenges of participating in the "great game" of espionage. (*www.spymuseum.org*)

### Family-Friendly Lodging

Your hotel location is critical to getting around, but with so many areas to visit, where do you stay? The Washington Convention and Visitors Bureau keeps an updated list of hotels to choose from for quick reference. (*www.washington.org*) L'Enfant Plaza Hotel is located directly above a major Metrorail (subway train) station that connects you to everything in Washington, which makes it a great home base for families visiting the city. Guests who stay at L'Enfant Plaza Hotel have many resources under one roof including a dedicated coffee bar and three different restaurants. Kids love the veggie pizza on the room service menu. Be advised that valet parking is standard at just about every hotel in Washington, D.C., and it is expensive—it can be as high as $30 a day. Be sure to budget for parking if you're driving to D.C.

L'Enfant Plaza Hotel has a positive pet policy. You can bring your pet to Washington, and in fact L'Enfant Plaza Hotel would

love to have him. Washington is a pet-friendly destination. (*www*
*.lenfantplazahotel.com*)

### Family Dining

Old Glory Barbeque has a massive barbecue pit and open
kitchen making for lots of eye candy for little ones who'll be hungry
and tired after a day of sightseeing. Located on M Street in George-
town, Old Glory serves a variety of barbeque styles from various
areas of America. Families can join the restaurant's e-mail club and
receive a free entrée. (*www.oldglorybbq.com*)

Families looking to try delicious dishes from the other side of
the Atlantic might want to try ICI, which means "here" in French.
Incredible dishes like Croque Monsieur and cassoulet are served
up along with pastries and breads that are baked twice daily on
site. Kids love the crispy Parmesan rolls served at brunch. ICI
Urban Bistro is located in Hotel Sofitel Lafayette Square. (*www*
*.iciurbanbistro.com*)

## City Vacations in the Central United States

Chicago, also known as the "Windy City" and "Chi-Town," has been
a family-friendly city for decades, with numerous sites and activities to keep everybody entertained. Sporting events and parks are
frequent and everywhere when good weather permits.

Nashville is a thriving city in Northwestern Tennessee. Nashville is all about music, art, and history. It is a vibrant city with a
flourishing culinary scene and regional cuisine that has become
well known by chefs internationally. One of the best things about a
visit to Nashville is the amazing entertainment available for families
of all shapes and sizes.

### Chicago

During milder months when good weather blesses the city
with a little sunshine, Chicago swells with the hustle and bustle of

people coming outdoors to enjoy the many pastimes its residents engage in.

### Family-Friendly Activities

The Chicago waterfront is a destination in itself and features amazing dining including several cultural restaurants that feature ethnic food. Chicago is known for its great food, especially pizza.

## ≡ Fast Fact

There are hundreds of parks and numerous beaches where visitors can kick back and relax, especially those families accompanying family members in Chicago on business.

There are several museums to choose from, and other educational destinations like the Adler Planetarium and the Shedd Aquarium. New visitors to Chicago can opt to take tours of the city. Chicago Tours offers a multitude of tours of areas that are of interest to your family. Tours traverse the city to showcase places like Grant Park, Soldier Field, Adler Planetarium, Art Institute of Chicago, Orchestra Hall, the Shedd Aquarium, and the Museum of Natural History. Don't miss the Sears Tower and Skydeck, Chicago's answer to Manhattan's Empire State Building tour. (*www .ChicagoTours.us*)

For families with small kids, Chicago's LEGOLAND Discovery Centre is the perfect antidote to boredom. The center contains life-sized LEGOs where kids can build and test creations, enjoy rides, and expend energy in the soft play center. (*www.legoland discoverycenter.com*) The Kohl Children's Museum is an interactive museum for children with nearly twenty exhibits. (*www .kohlchildrensmuseum.org*) Chicago's Brookfield Zoo has thousands of animals. (*www.brookfieldzoo.org*) The Lincoln Park Zoo has well over a thousand animals, and a train and carousel rides.

(*www.lpzoo.org*) Chicago's Navy Pier has acres of parks, dining, attractions, and great shopping. (*www.navypier.com*)

### Family-Friendly Lodging

The Holiday Inn Hotel and Suites in downtown Chicago is in the business district, and is close to attractions, shopping, dining, and entertainment. (*www.ichotelsgroup.com*) Guests at the Best Western Grant Park Hotel can walk to the Shed Aquarium and other attractions. At the Best Western Grant Park Hotel kids who are aged seventeen or younger stay free with parents. (*www.bwgrantparkhotel.com*)

### Family-Friendly Dining

Chicago is known for its great pizza. For more than thirty years the family members at Giordano's Pizza have sent pizza lovers into a new dimension. Giordano's stuffed pizza is world famous. They also offer thin crust pizza, sandwiches, and appetizers appropriate for the whole family at reasonable prices. (*www.Giordanos.com*)

The Chicago Pizza and Oven Grinder Company is known for its delectable pizza pot pies, made with homemade sauces and Sicilian dough. Another popular must-try item at the Chicago Pizza and Oven Grinder Company is the authentic oven grinder, a hot baked sandwich made out of Italian bread, stuffed with meat, cheese, and toppings. (*www.chicagopizzaandovengrinder.com*)

## Nashville, Tennessee

Nashville is a booming music-business town. The world's most talented and successful musicians come to Nashville to record music, so the entertainment in Nashville is some of the best in the world. Though originally known for country music, all genres of musicians come to Nashville to further careers and work with the hundreds of producers, directors, and songwriters who make their homes there. The result is world-class cuisine mixed with country flavors for an eclectic experience the whole family will love.

### Family-Friendly Activities

At places like the world-famous Bluebird Café, you can see the next "it" star to burst onto the music scene. Artists like Faith Hill and many others were discovered at the Bluebird Café. (*www .bluebirdcafe.com*)

The Country Music Hall of Fame and Museum is a shrine to country music legends including Hank Williams and Patsy Cline, George Strait, and Alabama, among many others. At the Country Music Hall of Fame and Museum, visitors can watch interactive interviews with people like Dolly Parton and see some of the original pages on which their songs were written. The historic RCA Studio B was where the great Elvis Presley, Chet Atkins, Dolly Parton, Eddy Arnold, and the Everly Brothers made records many years ago. The studio has been frozen in time, and wandering through the original instruments and studio space with songs from long-dead recording artists playing, the space eerily comes to life. (*www.countrymusichalloffame.com*) Nearby Ryman Auditorium is a national landmark, which was a church until it became the home for the Grand Ole Opry in 1943. Artists within and outside the genre of country music have played here. (*www.ryman.com*)

The Frist Center for the Visual Arts is located in what used to be a massive United States Post Office. Nashville's interactive Adventure Science Center is a children's facility encompassing the Sudekum Planetarium. The Cheekwood Botanical Garden & Museum of Art was formerly the private estate of the Check family, founders of Maxwell House Coffee. The more than fifty acres of the estate includes botanical gardens, sculptures, and an art museum. History buffs visiting Nashville can visit The Hermitage, which was President Andrew Jackson's home, and Belle Meade Plantation, the location of English Derby winner Iroquois and now a thoroughbred stud farm. Seabiscuit, War Admiral, and Smarty Jones are all horses whose lineage can be traced back to Belle Meade Plantation.

Within the massive Gaylord Opryland Resort is a destination that parents, especially music-loving parents, will love, the historic

650 AM WSM Studio. The 650 AM WSM Studio is the broadcast home of the station that delivered country music and the Grand Ole Opry to America for nearly a century. (*www.visitmusiccity.com*)

### Family-Friendly Lodging

Gaylord Opryland Resort is a family destination in Nashville that is so large it's almost like another planet. Delta River Flatboats cruise throughout the "river" within the complex, containing waterfalls and gardens with thousands of species of plants on nine acres. Every kind of food imaginable is at the ready at Gaylord Opryland Resort. More than twenty different places to eat, from sushi to barbecue, are available to families at all hours of the day and night.

There are many activities to keep kids entertained, including Gaylord Opryland Resort's daycare, La Petite Academy Kid's Station, where kids can stay for a short while or play all day. The Resort has a world-class spa for parents to enjoy while the kids tire themselves out having fun doing all the kid-friendly activities Gaylord Opryland Resort has to offer. (*www.gaylordhotels.com*)

### Family-Friendly Dining

Families who want to enjoy great dining with regional flair and be entertained will love the Wildhorse Saloon. At the Wildhorse Saloon, you can do the two-step between servings of barbecue, fried pickles, and ice cold beer. The Wildhorse Saloon is a multistory restaurant, bar, and concert hall in the heart of Nashville near Printers Alley, where some of the city's best nightlife can be found, and where up-and-coming and established stars can be seen. (*www.WildhorseSaloon.com*)

The Loveless Café is a half-century-old café that features amazingly good country cooking. The Loveless Café is patronized by celebrities and world travelers for the incredible local food like country ham and red-eye gravy, southern-fried chicken, and made-from-scratch biscuits with homemade preserves, which are created in the Loveless Café's kitchen. (*www.lovelesscafe.com*)

# City Vacations in the Western United States

San Francisco is famous for its landmarks and steep hills. It is a beautiful city, but not the place for rollerblading. Its steep hills throughout the city make just getting around a work out.

Seattle is nature's urban destination. All about being earth friendly, and near multiple nature day trips, Seattle is the perfect destination for families who enjoy the activities in a city but want to take day trips to natural destinations.

## San Francisco

Visitors to San Francisco can take in sites like the Golden Gate Bridge, Alcatraz Island, and Chinatown. Fisherman's Wharf is San Francisco's main boardwalk, and places like Baker Beach present incredible views of the Golden Gate Bridge; it's a charming local beach where, well, the locals go! Golden Gate Park is all about the active lifestyle. Walking trails, rental boats, and botanical conservatories, along with thousands of trees, make it a natural oasis. At Stowe Lake, visitors to the lake can rent pedal and rowboats, and for kids who love model boats, Spreckles Lake is a must-see. San Francisco's Japanese Tea Garden is the oldest Japanese garden in the United States, featuring five acres of sculptures, bridges, ponds, and a teahouse serving tea and cookies. Best of all, there's no charge to enter Golden Gate Park. Only the exhibitions charge an entrance fee.

Transportation in San Francisco, especially riding on the cable cars, is more than just a way to get around. It's a rite of passage in this town! Movies have been filmed around San Francisco cable cars. The San Francisco Cable Car website is home to the first online interactive cable car. Families can visit the site to learn all about the cable cars, fares, locations, and hours. There's even such a thing as "cable car etiquette" for riders who are new to this mode of transit. (*www.sfcablecar.com*)

### Family Lodging

Many hotels now provide an evening wine service for adults. The family-friendly Best Western Tuscan Inn At Fisherman's Wharf in San Francisco serves complimentary hot chocolate at night. (*www.tuscaninn.com*)

The Argonaut Hotel is all about pleasing those kids (and parents!). Cribs are free and kids get to choose a toy from the hotel's treasure chest when families check in. (*www.ArgonautHotel.com*)

The Palace Hotel, albeit more pricey than its cousins in Fisherman's Wharf, is worth it if you budget for the additional cost and adults want time for themselves. This historic property offers family-friendly room service, holiday tea, and Santa Claus in the lobby at Christmas with presents for kids aged five through ten. There's even a gingerbread class, and child care with advance reservations. (*www.sfpalace.com*)

### Family Dining

There are hundreds of places for hungry families to dine in San Francisco. But it's the uncommon places not exactly serving full meals that really shine. Scharffen Berger Chocolate Maker in the East Bay has free public tours of the factory. Families can learn how their chocolate is produced and enjoy a chocolate tasting. Best of all, the public tours are free of charge. Kids must be at least age ten and no flip-flops or open-toed shoes are allowed. (*www .scharffenberger.com*)

Charles Chocolates Factory Store & Chocolate Bar, also in the East Bay, offers free tours as well, after which guests can pay $10 for an unforgettable chocolate tasting. The tours are available Wednesday through Sunday. (*www.charleschocolates.com*)

### Activities

Kids age three and under are admitted free to the Aquarium of the Bay in San Francisco's Fisherman's Wharf. Here 20,000 marine animals float by as visitors meander through 300 feet of see-through tunnels, and guests can touch sharks and rays. Just a few steps away is Pier 39 at Fisherman's Wharf. Pier 39 is a festival marketplace that features more than 100 stores, restaurants, and attractions for the whole family. Starring sea lions, street performers, and live entertainment, Pier 39 is quite a show. Kids love the Riptide Arcade, which can boast 10,000 square feet of video, prize, and virtual reality games, and an Old West shooting gallery.

The Presidio of San Francisco, a former military post, is now a national park and recreation center. Beautiful views, history, and architecture make visiting the Presidio worthwhile during your trip to San Francisco. If anyone in your family has been in the military, make this a must see on your list. Best of all, entrance to this park and most of its programs are free.

Another incredible historic attraction in San Francisco is the submarine USS *Pampanito* at Fisherman's Wharf. It's an authentic World War II submarine that has been almost perfectly restored.

## 👥 Just for Parents

If your hotel offers child care, the Winchester Mystery House in nearby Silicon Valley is great fun for lovers of bizarre architecture. The historic 160-room Victorian mansion, former home of rifle heiress Sarah Winchester, is an impressive way to spend the afternoon.

The Children's Program at the San Francisco Zoo is supported by the education department and fosters a true awareness of wildlife for kids. Programs exist for toddlers to tweens, and feature activities including wildlife crafts and games, talking with zookeepers, tours of the zoo, and animal encounters. The zoo sponsors the Junior Keeper Club for young people who may be interested in careers with animals. The programs provide a snack. (*www.sfzoo.org*)

The Rooftop at Yerba Buena Gardens has a playground and carousel, museum, and other fun activities to keep kids more than occupied; this family-friendly activity destination keeps kids engaged. Here the Children's Garden & Carousel is more than 100,000 square feet of nature including grassy spots to have a picnic, beautiful gardens, and streams in the heart of the city. The nearly century-old amusement park carousel ran at Playland at the Beach from 1912 to 1972 before it was restored by the City of San Francisco and installed at Yerba Buena Gardens. Two rides are just $3, quite a bargain for memories that will last a lifetime—be sure to bring your camera! (*www.yerbabuenagardens.com*)

## Rainy Day Fun

Yerba Buena Gardens has an ice skating and bowling center that is the perfect place to go if the weather decides not to cooperate on your visit to San Francisco. The centers offer public skating and bowling daily.

Alcatraz Island, infamous in its history as a federal penitentiary, can sell out, so interested families should book these tours early. There is no food available on Alcatraz, so make sure kids get something to eat before embarking on your tour. Besides the historic aspect of Alcatraz, the island is a bird sanctuary where avian lovers gather to watch the thousands of seabirds. (*www.nps.gov/alca*)

To get to Angel Island State Park, visitors must take a ferry from the city (it's only accessible by boat). Once there, families can rent bikes or hike along one of many trails on the island to see captivating ruins and the untamed splendor of nature. (*www.angelisland.org*)

At Golden Gate Park, families can enjoy walking trails, rent boats, and meander among hundreds of thousands of trees. Dutch windmills and tulips placed around the park are meant to reproduce the way the landscape looks in Holland.

## Seattle

Seattle is known for many things, chief among them great coffee, the birth of grunge music, frequent rain, and an amazing outdoor lifestyle. Walking and bicycling are two of the city's most popular ways to get around, though the city is large and spread out. Outdoor enthusiasts and novices alike take full advantage of water sports in neighboring sounds. The Cascade and Olympic Mountains are close to Seattle making them great day-trip destinations. Seattle is also home to incredible cuisine, especially seafood like salmon, due to its close proximity to cold-water fishing in the Northwestern United States.

### Family-Friendly Activities

Pike's Place Market is a popular place to eat, and it's also a great place to see. Don't miss the fish throwers and a cup of chowder or crab soup at any one of the restaurants. Gourmet markets make Pike's Place Market the perfect place to outfit your family's lunch stash. Puget Sound is a beautiful destination adjacent to Seattle that plays host to water sports including kayaking, canoeing, and sailing. (*www.GoNorthWest.com*)

Seattle's Space Needle is more than 600 feet tall and was a symbol for Seattle's World's Fair in 1962. Visitors can visit the renovated structure and get an incredible view of Seattle. For a special treat families can eat at SkyCity, a restaurant located at the site. Visitors to the Space Needle can enjoy a 360-degree unhindered view of the city on the O Deck.

Right next to the Space Needle is a mecca of science adventures called the Pacific Science Center, an educational entertainment center for kids of all ages including an Imax Theater. (*www.pacsci.org*)

### Family-Friendly Lodging

Inn at the Market is a boutique hotel close to attractions and restaurants like Pike's Place Market and downtown Seattle.

(*www.innatthemarket.com*) For families who want to stay near the university, Seattle's Watertown Hotel is within walking distance to dining and an easy drive to the rest of the city's attractions. (*www.watertownseattle.com*)

# City Vacations in the Southwestern United States

Paris, France, may be the city of lights, but Las Vegas does a pretty good job of lighting up the skyline here in the United States. Las Vegas isn't just for gamblers anymore. Families flock to Las Vegas for all sorts of activities, and with hundreds of free activities for families, it's easy to see why.

## Family-Friendly Activities in Las Vegas

There are hundreds of free attractions in Las Vegas. The Aquarium at the Silverton Hotel has a saltwater aquarium of more than 100,000 gallons. Primm Valley Resort & Casino features the Bonnie & Clyde getaway car, the shirt Clyde died in, Barrow family photos, and handmade items manufactured by Clyde. The Conservatory at The Bellagio was created by more than 100 horticulturalists and is a sight to behold. Also at the Bellagio, the fountains are works of art and a show in themselves as they display each evening to music. The Ethel M. Chocolate Factory is about seven miles from the Las Vegas Strip but offers free admission so visitors can see how the candy is made and, of course, taste it!

At the Fremont Street Experience, visitors can see what a $70 million light canopy looks like and listen to a nearly 600,000-watt sound system. Like lions? Then don't miss the lion habitat at MGM Grand. These incredible creatures can be seen chasing balls, licking paws, or chilling out right before your eyes.

The Marjorie Barrick Museum displays western culture and desert life including the history of ancient Mexico. If you didn't get enough chocolate at Ethel M. Chocolate Factory, M&M's World should be your next stop. The replica of the Eiffel Tower at the Paris Hotel in Las Vegas provides an incredible view, and if you budget accordingly, you can enjoy dinner in the tower's restaurant, the meal of course is not free, but seeing the tower is.

The Mirage spouts out fun just after dusk when its volcano "erupts," while the wildlife Habitat at the Flamingo features the creatures up close and personal. (*www.vegas.com*)

An all-day pass at the Adventuredome Theme Park is your ticket to hours of family fun. This five-acre indoor theme park is a wonder to behold, with its gravity-defying roller coasters, games, and amusements like SpongeBob's four-dimensional theme ride for younger kids. Junior rides, family fun rides, and rides best suited for fearless teens make it a great one-stop shop for family entertainment while in Las Vegas. (*www.adventuredome.com*)

### Family-Friendly Lodging in Las Vegas

Kids-eat-free specials are common offers from Las Vegas hoteliers. And many Vegas hotels can help arrange for child care so parents can gamble or have dinner in one of hundreds of internationally renowned restaurants.

At the Circus Circus home page there is a special link to "hot deals" where families can check in for last-minute offers, specials, and discounts. (*www.circuscircus.com*) The Excalibur Hotel and Casino is a fairy-tale-themed property with a giant "castle" to captivate young guests. This property also has a hot deals section on its home page. (*www.excaliburcasino.com*) Bally's Las Vegas is usually reasonable as well. This property is classic Las Vegas with many stay-and-play packages that include activities for everyone. (*www.ballyslasvegas.com*)

# CHAPTER 9

# A Taste of the Past— Historic Destinations

C owboys and Indians. Ghost stories. Shoot-outs. War battle-grounds. All of these make traveling to historic destinations perfect for family fun. They combine fun with education. From the Old West to the haunted inns of New England, America is full of adventures and lore from ages past. Traveling with your family to any of these destinations is a history lesson that they're sure to remember.

## Historic Destinations in the Northeastern United States

New England is positively full of American history. You can't step on a cobblestone street without practically standing on something historic! From the Salem Witch Museum in Salem, Massachusetts, to New London, Connecticut's Ancient Burial Ground, you could spend weeks in this area and never know everything there is to know about its history. There are many New England towns to choose from, and in each one of them there are unique sites and museums.

The entire town of Salem, Massachusetts (*www.salem.org*), is a historic destination with many things to see, places to stay, and fantastic dining, but the Salem Witch Museum is one of the most popular tourist sites. The Salem Witch Museum, the most visited museum in Salem, chronicles the Salem witch hunts and trials that took place in 1692. Hundreds of accused were imprisoned and approximately twenty people were executed before the trials ended. (*www.salemwitchmuseum.com*)

## 💼 Travel Tip

While walking around Salem you will notice a red line painted on certain sidewalks. This red line is the Heritage Trail. The red line connects all of the city's historical sites including the Witch Trial Memorial, Old Burying Point Cemetery, and more. There are four red line loops through the city to help you explore. You can find maps marking the red line in the Salem Visitor Guide and in the information kiosks throughout Salem.

Visiting the *Mayflower II* at Plimoth Plantation in Plymouth, Massachusetts, is a step back in time to the 1600s when the real *Mayflower* (yes, *the Mayflower*) crossed the ocean to land on Plymouth Rock. Every detail of the *Mayflower II* ship has been meticulously recreated, even down to the cramped passenger quarters. The ship you'll see was featured in the PBS series *Colonial House* and feature film *The New World*.

Often guests will encounter people onboard outfitted in period costume who are portraying some of the Mayflower pilgrims. Plimoth Plantation has three other exhibits including the Wampanoag home site, 1627 English Village, and Crafts Center. (*www.plimoth.org*)

In a 1999 *New York Times* article, the director of New York State's Antiquarian and Landmarks Society, William Hosley, referred to graveyards as outdoor art museums. Ye Antientist Burial Ground, also known as The Ancient Burial Ground in New London, Connecticut, is like an outdoor art museum from hundreds of years ago. It's one of the first graveyards in New England, circa 1652. It can be found between Hempstead and Huntington. Experts agree that these gravestones are like works of art, and they can recognize many of the individual stone carvers.

Museums of Old York in York, Maine, make up nine historic buildings. They include a colonial tavern, jail (dungeons and cells are still on site), riverside estate, and an old warehouse once owned by patriot John Hancock. Over 300 years of New England's legacy are interred on these grounds. And antique lovers will swoon over the Bulman Bedhangings. They are the only complete set of eighteenth-century American crewelwork bed curtains in existence. (*www.oldyork.org*) For more information or to find more New England historic sites, visit the New England visitors bureau website at *www.visitnewengland.com*.

### LODGING NEAR HISTORIC DESTINATIONS OF THE NORTHEAST

- **York Microtel** (York, Maine), new hotel property near beaches and historic York, and convenient to airport and shopping (*www.yorkmicrotel.com*)
- **Bunker Hill Bed and Breakfast** (Charlestown, Massachusetts), near Boston's Freedom trail and waterfront area; includes free breakfast and snacks, pets welcome, and no room tax (*www.bunkerhillbedandbreakfast.com*)
- **Salem Waterfront Hotel** (Salem, Massachusetts), Reader's Choice Award for "Best North Shore Hotel waterside in historic district" (*www.salemwaterfronthotel.com*)

# Historic Destinations in the Southeastern United States

The southern United States is full of history and destinations that market themselves as historic vacation destinations. They include numerous civil war battlegrounds and Native American historical sites along with Colonial Williamsburg. Many families choose to visit these destinations because each represents a unique way to educate kids about history that's fun and entertaining. Kids can better understand their past by walking in the steps of their fore-fathers in many locations across the country, well preserved and brought to life in museums and tours.

## Civil War Battlegrounds

The Civil War was one of America's bloodiest and most controversial times in its history. It left behind stories and sites that are frozen in time for visitors to see and learn from. Civil War battle-grounds cut a swath from North to South over hundreds of miles, and many pertinent sites have been preserved or restored for the general public to see and explore.

Does your family have a desire to tour some of America's greatest Civil War sites, but you're not sure where to start? Check out the Civil War Discovery Trail. This site connects over 600 Civil War sites. (*www.civilwardiscoverytrail.org*)

In Virginia's Orange County, Montpelier is world famous as President James Madison's lifelong home. Madison was the fourth president of the United States and is known as the "Father of the Constitution."

## 💼 Travel Tip

Montpelier hosts a popular wine festival each spring that includes activities for the entire family with live music, cooking classes, and children's entertainment and rides. Wine tastings go on all day.

Just a mile from Montpelier, freedman George Gilmore and his wife Polly set up a farm and cabin that still stands. They lived on or near the land dating back to 1870. Gilmore built his cabin from the remains of a deserted Confederate camp. The couple had five children and the Gilmore family farmed the property until 1920. The trail to the Gilmore cabin is located on the grounds of

Montpelier and is free with purchase of house admission. (*www* *.montpelier.org*)

Bentonville Battlefield State Historic Site is in Four Oaks, North Carolina, and the Bentonville Visitor Center features a fiber-optic exhibit that details the conflict that took place on March 19, 1865, including major battlefield maneuvers of both Northern and Southern armies. The Harper House at Bentonville Battlefield was a functioning Civil War field hospital. Visitors to the site can tour a Confederate mass grave and Harper family cemetery, and walk a trail leading to a Union XX Corps earthworks. (*www.nchistoricsites* *.org/bentonvi*)

The Battle at Gettysburg was the site of the bloodiest battle of the Civil War, with an estimated 51,000 deaths. Here President Abraham Lincoln gave his address that would go down in history. (*www.Gettysburg.com*)

The Confederates saw their last victory at Chickamauga Battle-field in the Campaign for Chattanooga in Georgia and Tennessee. The area was the "gateway to the deep south" and was the nation's first national military park, created in 1890. The park is over 5,000 acres and can boast monuments, historical tablets, exhibits, and trails. (*www.nps.gov/CHCH*)

## Colonial Williamsburg

A visit to Colonial Williamsburg is like a hands-on history les-son. Featuring buildings from 1699 to 1780, Colonial Williamsburg was Virginia's capital in Colonial times.

In Colonial Williamsburg's "Revolutionary City," families can watch a dramatic street theater program about colonial times between the years 1774–1781 as if they were really there.

Colonial Williamsburg also has evening entertainment that includes concerts, films, dramatized witch trials, and ghost walks. Kids who love animals will flock to Colonial Williamsburg's Rare Breeds program, which breeds and cares for animals that would have been living at Williamsburg more than two centuries ago.

Colonial Williamsburg also features educational, fun tours and events that allow visitors to see what it was like in colonial times:

- "Crime and Punishment" is a walking tour that reveals what English law was really like.
- "A Pirating" is a recreation of the 1727 trial of accused pirates John Vidal and Martha Farley.
- The "In Defense of Our Liberty" event allows guests to "enlist" as a new recruit in the Continental Army and get a firsthand glimpse into life as an eighteenth-century combatant.
- "Cry Witch" is a popular drama, whereby guests help settle on guilt or innocence for "The Virginia Witch." (*www.colonial williamsburg.com*)

## Just for Parents

One of the best things for families visiting Colonial Williamsburg is the Colonial Kids Club, an on-site summer program that includes four or eight hours of supervised activities with other kids. The club includes lunch, so parents can sneak off for a whole day of spa services, shopping, golfing, or just to reconnect with each other in the romantic setting of Colonial Williamsburg.

### Savannah, Georgia

Historic Savannah, Georgia, attracts thousands of visitors to its sites every year. Many Savannah cemeteries are stunning examples of historical architecture all on their own. One of the best ways to see this historic destination is by carriage ride or walking tour, as well as the many "hop-on/hop-off" tours that stop at historic landmarks. Savannah was laid out in a grid of open squares, which still entice lovers of history and architecture to visit year after year. Savannah's many squares are scattered throughout numerous historic neighborhoods.

Savannah has many museums and historic landmarks relevant to United States history. The old Central of Georgia Railway Passenger Station dates back to the mid 1800s and is home to the Savannah History Museum and visitor's center. Savannah is also home to the Museum of Black History, which preserves African American history and culture, Ralph Mark Gilbert Civil Rights Museum, Roundhouse Railroad Museum, and Owens-Thomas House.

## ≡ Fast Fact

War memorials are prevalent in Savannah. There are a multitude of monuments to people who fought in the Civil, Spanish American, and Vietnam Wars. One of the largest Confederate monuments stands in Savannah's Forsyth Park, where soldiers drilled before marching off to war. The Vietnam Veterans Memorial, dedicated in 1991, is in Emmet Park and is a beautiful reflecting pool surrounded by marble blocks inscribed with names of local soldiers killed in the war.

Savannah is home to some of the country's best home cooking, serving the region's southern delicacies. Grits, biscuits and gravy, pies, and seafood dishes are among some of the recipes that are served in Savannah kitchens. (*www.visit-historic-savannah.com*)

### LODGING NEAR HISTORIC DESTINATIONS OF THE SOUTHEAST

- **America's Best Value Inn** (Savannah, Georgia), very reasonable value hotel near Savannah's attractions and local transportation (*www.americasbestvalueinn.com*)
- **Crowne Plaza Williamsburg Hotel** (Williamsburg, Virginia), at Fort Macgruder, pet friendly and located in close proximity to historic Williamsburg (*www.cpwilliamsburghotel.com*)
- **Inn on Poplar Hill** (Orange, Virginia, near Historic Montpelier), bed and breakfast with historic tours and packages (*www.innonpoplarhill.com*)

# Historic Destinations in the West and Central United States

Virtually every western state has its own Old West attractions. A good place to start your search for a historic destination is the Spirit of the Old West website. (*www.thespiritoftheoldwest.com*) The American Old West has a life of its own, full of adventures and lore.

There are many places with colorful names like Tombstone, Arizona. Tombstone's nickname is the "town too tough to die." Tourists can't get enough of the shoot-outs, stagecoaches, and Old West Main Street. Tours of Tombstone are available by stagecoach and wagon, which adds to the experience. The "Gunfight at the O.K. Corral" was real, and your family can take a tour of the site where this famous gunfight took place.

## Just for Parents

After the kids see the main attractions, parents who love historic architecture will relish St. Paul's Episcopal Church (1882), the decadent Crystal Palace Saloon, and Tombstone Epitaph building, where Arizona's oldest continuously published newspaper is still printed.

The Arkansas Fort Smith National Historic Site on the Arkansas River is home to what remains of the 1817 fort. Here visitors can see the courtroom, which has been restored, of infamous "Hangin' Judge" Isaac C. Parker. The frontier jail at the fort was awarded the moniker of "Hell on the Border" right near Judge Parker's gallows, also restored. (*www.fortsmith.org*)

## Historic Native American Destinations

America has hundreds of Native American sites that can take children back to a time of traditional medicine, craft, woodworking, and storytelling. The importance of educating coming generations can't be understated. The story of Native American peoples is the study of how America came to be. Many vacation companies, recognizing the value of history in education have organized tours of Native American sites, ancient villages, and recorded battles. And in an effort to preserve tribal customs and structures, many conservationist and archeological groups have organized in order to maintain Native American history.

Native American Nations is an online research site that provides copious information on the American Indians, including tribal history. On this site, you and your family can research various tribes to see in which ones you have an interest. Perhaps there are tribal sites near your home. Maybe a Native American historic destination is a weekend drive away. Pick a Native American tribe or history that interests your family, and learn about them. Then when you visit your selected site it will all the more rewarding, and you'll appreciate the people who first inhabited that land. (*www.nanations.com*)

At Oconaluftee Indian Village in Cherokee, North Carolina, guests take a step back to Cherokee life in 1759 to see authentic dwellings, traditional medicine, and chores like hulling canoes, crafting masks and pottery, basket weaving, and beadwork. Here nighttime brings storytelling that enraptures all who listen. The Village also hosts live reenactments, interactive demonstrations, "Hands-On Cherokee" arts and crafts classes, Villager outfit rentals for children, and evening storytelling performances.

Native American touring company, Go Native America (*www*
*.gonativeamerica.com*), offers guided and self-guided tours that can last one day, one weekend, or two weeks. Their special family program allows families to get acquainted with Native American culture on their own using the Go Native American guidebook. The self-guided tour called Native Edventure Trails is designed to be completed in a day, but the planned tour's route is also flexible. Participants visiting at least three out of five listed stops are

awarded prizes by tribal representatives. The guide book for the family self-guided tours is available online for children of varying ages. Along with tours, Go Native America offers lodging, buffalo dinner, and many other options.

One of the more well-known tours Go Native America offers is the *Dances with Wolves* tour. The movie showcased the Native American Lakota tribe in South Dakota. The tour takes participants to sites including the location of the film's winter scenes, and provides the background behind the movie.

The Little Big Horn tour takes guests to the site where Crazy Horse crossed the Little Bighorn River to converge with Custer, and describes the battle that unfolded afterwards. Guests can also take a ride on horseback on the actual Little Bighorn Battlefield. On such hallowed ground, the ride offers participants a look inside what the celebrated Lakota warriors saw on horseback in 1876.

Horse lovers love Go Native America's Wild Mustangs tour. When the army planned to kill Cheyenne and Crow Indian pony herds in an effort to stunt Native American nations, the ponies survived thanks to warriors who set them free in the Prior Mountains. The amazing descendents of the herds continue to roam free.

The Road to Wounded Knee tour is a sacred journey. Wounded Knee is where a massacre of 300 Native American men, women, and children took place in 1890. They were shot down as they surrendered; one can only wonder how it could have happened. Tour guides flank the tour with facts about the tragic event.

### LODGING NEAR HISTORIC DESTINATIONS IN THE CENTRAL AND WESTERN UNITED STATES

- **River Cove Cabins** (Murphy, North Carolina, near Cherokee), rustic riverfront cabins with kitchenettes, front porches, and rockers (*www.rivercovecabin.com*)
- **Holiday Inn Express** (Rapid City, South Dakota), convenient to Wounded Knee with reasonable rates and is receptive to children (*www.holidayinnexpress.com*)

- **Boothill Inn and Suites** (Billings, Montana, near Little Big Horn), about an hour from the Little Big Horn battlefield at the base of Billings's historic rimrocks (*www.boothillinn.com*)

# Ghost Towns and Ghost Stories for the Road

Most ghost towns have little left standing but their original foundations. Often with only ruins remaining, they're not a destination in themselves, but great places to visit if you're traveling to a nearby resort or town with lodging and additional activities. But ghost towns are just as fun to visit as cities brimming with activity and residents if you can infuse great area lodging and dining into the trip.

Legends of America, a terrific resource for all things ghostly and legendary, says that a true ghost town is one that has been abandoned entirely. (*www.legendsofamerica.com*) Another resource, GhostTowns.com provides photos and information for families thinking about taking a tour of America's ghostly architectural remains. (*www.ghosttowns.com*) Finally, families who want to set up tours of historic and ghostly places can look into scheduling tours with touring companies like Trusted Tours. Outfitters like these can handle all of the details and recommend lodging so your family isn't stranded in the middle of nowhere! (*www.trustedtours.com*)

## Ghost Towns

Places like the mill town of Gillette, Arizona, the site of multiple unsolved robberies, are now just ghost towns. The ruins of the Burfind Hotel is the only evidence that anything happened in Gillette.

Mineral Park, Arizona, was a thriving mining camp. Thieves killed in a gunfight had buried a box full of gold and jewelry on the side of the road—naturally it was never found, adding to the lore and intrigue of Mineral Park. A graveyard and minimal buildings are all that remain of the area. It's now a privately owned mining site.

## Ghost Stories to Tell on the Road

Traveling to historic destinations provides an opportunity to learn about the past. And part of the fun can be the journey, especially if your trip includes telling ghost stories along the way! Your local library is full of books that recount legendary ghost stories, and you can even make up your own. Here are a few to get you started.

### Boots Berry

The lovely Green Mountain Inn in Stowe, Vermont, is home to Boots Berry, a local hero who lived there more than a hundred years ago. Born in Room 302 in 1840, Berry was the son of an Inn chambermaid and later worked as caretaker for the stagecoach horses. Berry once stopped a runaway coach, and saved a little girl from falling from the Inn's roof. The last act cost him his life when he fell to his death from the roof over the room where he was born. People say sometimes they can still hear Berry tap dancing on the roof, and he has also been heard entering Room 302.

### Maco Lights

The Mystery of the Maco Lights has been told to the children of North Carolina for more than a century. Maco Station is in Brunswick County in southern North Carolina near Wilmington, itself a city of spirits and lore. A railroad crossing just outside of town is the site of a mysterious light resulting from an accident in 1867 in which a man died.

Joe Baldwin was a railroad man, and the railroad was his life. A conductor for the Atlantic Coast Line Railroad, Joe Baldwin rode in the last car on the train. Late one night Joe made a horrific discovery —his car had separated from the rest of the train, and another train wasn't far behind. He ran as fast as he could to display a lantern on the rear platform. He waved his arm wildly, the lantern swaying with the movement of his arm. But the engineer driving the train behind him didn't see Joe's frantic signal. Moments later, the trains collided, severing Joe's head from his body.

A witness said Joe's light was hurtled away from the accident just before it happened. When the lantern hit the ground, it rolled time and again until finally coming to a stop upright. Soon after, Joe's light began to appear by the track. It's reported that even president Grover Cleveland in 1889 claimed to see Joe's lantern light, joining the list of thousands of people who have seen it as well.

### Key West Lighthouse

Key West's Lighthouse and Keeper's Quarters Museum is the restored home of a lighthouse constructed way back in 1847 to help ships navigate the deadly reefs of the lower Keys. It was powered by fifteen oil lamps with reflectors each more than a foot wide.

Lighthouse keepers climbed eighty-eight steps every day to clean and fuel the lighthouse lamps. One lighthouse keeper, Barbara Mabrity, took over the job when her husband died in 1832. For almost forty years Barbara tended to the lamps in the lighthouse. In 1846, a hurricane came and damaged the light station. Barbara and her family retreated to the safety of the lighthouse tower, but six of her children perished in the storm. Then, when Barbara was eighty-two years old during the Civil War, she made statements against the Union, which at the time was in control over Key West and the lighthouse. She was fired as a result. Today you can still walk up eighty-eight iron steps to the lighthouse deck and look out onto Key West and the path of the hurricane.

## CHAPTER 10

# National Parks

 ew sights can compare to America's national parks. The first
national park was Yellowstone National Park established by
President Ulysses S. Grant in 1872. The National Park Service
was soon to follow in 1916 thanks to President Woodrow Wilson.
Today, the National Park Service cares for 391 areas and more
than 84 million acres. They include national parks, monuments,
battlefields, military parks, historical parks, historic sites, lake-
shores, seashores, recreation areas, scenic rivers, and trails. All
of America's national parks can be found on the National Parks
System website at *www.nps.gov*.

## Planning Your Vacation to a National Park

Like most mountain destinations, many national parks provide the
same opportunities to be active. Each park has unique qualities
that make it different from other parks. But most parks offer similar
activities. These are a few things you can expect to find available at
a national park or nearby:

- Hiking
- Biking
- Camping
- Sightseeing

- Wildlife watching
- Eco-tours
- Photography
- Horseback riding

America's national parks help children learn to appreciate nature and history. Kids can learn about the ecosystem of the great outdoors, and appreciate the steps they need to take to preserve nature for future generations. Many parks include incredible geological sites in the form of rock formations, canyons, trails, and water. Some feature ancient burial sites and homes of people who lived hundreds of years ago. Wildlife is abundant.

There's so much information available for children through the National Park Service, it's easy for kids to learn in advance about the park you're planning to visit. The National Park Service has a whole bounty of information on their website, including the National Park Junior Ranger program. A small fee for the child's educational booklet is usually about $3. By completing program activities listed for their age group (such as writing about their favorite area of a park, writing a poem, or possibly attending a Ranger-led activity), kids can receive an official Junior Ranger patch modeled after the National Park Service patch.

## ═══ Fast Fact

The National Park Service also has an online Junior Ranger program called WebRangers featuring more than fifty games, pictures of parks, and stories about visits with fellow WebRangers.

It's difficult to recommend lodging and dining choices in national parks. Most National parks have very few choices, and many have no lodging or dining except for vending machines. Also, many national parks span areas larger than some states.

It's important to carefully review the national park your family is interested in visiting. If you're planning to see a specific section of a large national park, then that will dictate in which state you'll stay and which area of the state you can make your home base. It can take days to travel through some of America's largest national parks, and travelers can waste most of a vacation if they don't plan carefully. The best thing to do is to look into which national parks you want to visit and plan around the closest city in that area. Information on all of the U.S. national parks is available online at the same website, managed by the National Parks Service at *www.nps.gov.*

# National Parks in the Northeastern United States

National parks of the Northeast may not be as spread out as national parks of the central United States, but they are just as exciting. And because the Northeast includes so many urban destinations, great dining and convenient lodging make these national parks great targets for family vacation fun. Plus, many of these parks are educational or historic in nature, and can help kids better understand America's rich history.

## Ellis Island and the Statue of Liberty, New York

In the late 1800s Ellis Island was the portal of immigration to America. It operated as such until the 1950s and it's estimated that nearly half of America's population can trace their relatives through Ellis Island. Several years after it closed, Ellis Island was restored into a museum. Bringing your family to Ellis Island is a journey into history and is a great way to educate kids about America's vibrancy and diversity. Transportation to Ellis Island is available only by ferry.

On Ellis Island, visitors can take advantage of walking tours guided by knowledgeable park rangers or volunteers, or you can purchase audio tours. The park offers free educational documentary films, theatrical productions, additional tours, and workshops.

## 📼 Travel Tip

Visitors to Ellis Island have to pass through security before departing on the ferry, so get to the ferry early. As part of these security screenings, oversize bags (including large backpacks) are not allowed on the ferry or anywhere in the park.

The Statue of Liberty National Monument was given to the United States by France as a symbol of freedom and was dedicated in 1886. Visitors can climb into the crown of the Statue of Liberty for an incredible view of Manhattan. However, the hike includes nearly 400 steps, and kids have to be a minimum of four feet tall to walk into the crown. The busiest season for Ellis Island and the Statue of Liberty is summer, so if you can plan to visit in the fall or spring, your wait can be significantly shorter.

### Independence National Historical Park, Philadelphia, Pennsylvania

Certainly the Liberty Bell will be the highlight of your visit to Independence National Historical Park and Independence Hall. But the Liberty Bell isn't the only attraction in this fun national park that spans more than fifty acres across twenty city blocks. The Independence National Historic Park is situated in Philadelphia's vibrant historic district.

This park has preserved several works of art that were used in establishing the United States of America. Just a few of the sites that played an important role in the founding of our nation are First Bank of the United States, Second Bank of the United States, Old City Hall, and Congress Hall.

The Independence National Historical Park also educates visitors about Benjamin Franklin through the preservation of Franklin

Court, the location of Benjamin Franklin's former home. Kids can especially benefit from the many educational activities and programs at Independence National Historical Park. As archaeologists looking for artifacts, and by compiling their own journal from the 1700s, kids can learn about American history in a fun, hands-on way.

## ≡ Fast Fact

No visit to Independence National Historical Park would be complete without a visit to the Liberty Bell. This symbol of freedom weighs more than 2,000 pounds and displays the words "Proclaim Liberty."

At Independence Hall, visitors can see where the Declaration of Independence and U.S. Constitution were signed. Timed tour tickets are distributed to reduce long wait times.

# National Parks in the Southeastern United States

Many of the national parks in the Southeast are dedicated to historic events such as the Civil War. But did you know some of the Southeast's national parks are home to some of the of the country's oldest artifacts? At many of these locations, demonstrations and dwellings help educate kids (and parents too) about the rich history of the Southeast and the people who came before them.

### Russell Cave National Monument, Alabama

This amazing monument marks the place where prehistoric people lived for more than 10,000 years. Located in Bridgeport, Alabama, visitors to Russell Cave can see both real artifacts and replicas from the cave, view photos, and read about the early North American cave dwellers who lived there from 6500 B.C. to A.D. 1650.

Tools and weapons were an important part of early human life—they were used for defense and to obtain food. At Russell Cave, you can watch demonstrations that feature the kinds of tools and weapons the Russell cave dwellers used, including spears and materials they used to make fire. Kids can see how hard it was to exist many years ago by taking a turn at a pump drill and corn grinder. The North Alabama Birding and Nature Trail are popular with families who love to experience nature, and the trail is perfect for hiking and seeing flora and fauna. Be aware that the terrain is somewhat steep and only partially paved.

### The Tennessee Civil War National Heritage Area

The Tennessee Civil War National Heritage Area in Murfreesboro, Tennessee, encompasses all the story of the Civil War including emancipation and the Reconstruction, a story that includes national battlefields, homes of historic significance, museums, burial grounds, religious buildings, and even towns that are linked to Tennessee's Civil War heritage. Tennessee has four Civil War national battlefield parks and was the state President Andrew Johnson called home.

# National Parks in the Central United States

Most national parks in the Central United States are vast, sprawling vistas made up of unforgettable landscapes that stretch for miles and miles. Some central United States national parks are bigger than some states! To plan a visit to one of these parks requires research, but it's well worth the effort. A visit to one of these parks means educating your family about surrounding cities and towns and understanding the lay of the land—literally! If you're not careful, you can plan a trip to a national park in Utah, and discover that you need to fly into Montana to get the best deal. Research the park you want to see, and look into surrounding destinations for lodging and transportation options.

## The Ozarks, Arkansas

In the Ozarks, nature meets history in a breathtaking combination of incomparable views and cool attractions. The colossal twin lakes of Lake Norfork and Bull Shoals Lake and Ozark mountain rivers make possible all sorts of warm-weather water activities, and ancient bluffs serve as perfect models for incredible photography. Underground caverns add a layer of mystery to the Ozarks, and museums and railways provide a hearty helping of nostalgia. All of these coupled with historic sites and charming mountain towns make the Ozarks an ideal national park for a family vacation.

## ═ Fast Fact

The Eureka Springs & North Arkansas Railway thrills families with a railroad show that includes a vintage collection of authentic railroad memorabilia. The railway exhibit re-creates turn-of-the-century railroad life showing how rail service helped the first visitors reach Eureka Springs way back in 1883.

Unlike many other national parks, in the Ozarks water sports abound. Float trips, water skiing, wake boarding, canoeing, sailing, even spear fishing and scuba diving are common activities. Rafting on level-one and level-two rapids attracts rafting families, while calmer waters welcome families who like float trips down cool streams on duckies and novice kayaks.

Aside from Mother Nature's attractions, history is a draw to the Ozarks. The Arkansas Air Museum holds historic aircraft, but this museum's aircraft are an exception to those of the typical aircraft museum. Most of the aircraft on display at the Arkansas Air Museum can still fly. The museum features famous racing planes from the roaring twenties and thirties as well as an early airliner. The museum keeps the planes in flying condition.

Horseback riding is another popular activity in the Ozark Mountain Region. Exploring the Ozarks on horseback allows visitors to leave the modern world behind and experience the area in the way their forefathers did: up winding mountain trails on the course of a wilderness. It's best to explore the Ozark Mountains on horseback through a reputable ranch or equestrian outfitter. Several are scattered through the Ozark Mountain Region, and many provide both horses and lodging.

Experienced mountain and road bikers flock to the Ozarks for challenging road and mountain biking. Along scenic byways and mountain trails, riders are treated to ascending and descending twists and turns. The Buffalo National Forest historic roads, used at one time to get to homesteads, are now beautiful bike trails. These and other trails are mapped. Bikers visiting the Ozarks should obtain a bike map and stick to well-marked trails. (*www .ozarkmountainregion.com*)

### Scott's Bluff, Nebraska

Nearly a thousand feet above the North Platte River is the natural landmark Scotts Bluff. Located in Nebraska, the park encompasses 3,000 acres of extraordinary land formations. The land formations are a stark contrast to the flat prairie that surrounds them.

Scotts Bluff National Monument is home to the biggest collection of William Henry Jackson paintings, a collection that includes his sketches, paintings, and photographs. Jackson observed and documented westward expansion and American Indian life in his work. For westward travelers, seeing Scotts Bluff for the first time on their long journey from the east signaled the end of the Great American Desert and beginning of the Rocky Mountains.

Kids visiting Scott's Bluff National Monument can hike to the summit and participate in guided walks with park rangers. On summer weekends at Scotts Bluff, they can see what life was like as a child traveling on the Oregon Trail. There are several outdoor activities at Scott's Bluff, but visitors can also drive around the park via the historic Summit Road or ride the Summit Shuttle, a guided tour, to the top of the monument. The hike to the summit on the Saddle Rock Trail is just over one and one half miles. From the summit, visitors can walk a little further to the North Overlook Trail where they can see the Badlands area, the town of Scottsbluff, and the North Platte River Valley. Just a little farther and visitors can take the South Overlook Trail to get a bird's-eye view of the Oregon Trail and Mitchell Pass. Scotts Bluff also features the Oregon Trail Museum and Visitor Center, which is itself a national historic structure.

### The Badlands, North Dakota

The Badlands of Theodore Roosevelt National Park in North Dakota have been called "The Land God Forgot" and is one of the most mystifying and scenic places on the planet. Craggy terrain and remarkable rock formations make it a feast for the eyes. Theodore Roosevelt said, "This broken country has been called always, by Indians, French voyagers, and American trappers alike, the Bad Lands." The more than 70,000-acre park is North Dakota's top tourist attraction, partly because of the long list of animals that can be seen in the park.

The park is divided into three different sections including the South Unit, North Unit, and the Elkhorn Ranch Unit, a remotely primordial unit. The South Unit is a thirty-six-mile scenic drive on which visitors can see elk, prairie dogs, and wild horses in addition to other animals. The old west town of Medora is also located in the South Unit of the park. Western theme musicals and a visit to Teddy Roosevelt's cabin are just two of the attractions. Visitors to the park shouldn't leave without touring the incredible twenty-seven-room Chateau De Mores constructed in 1884.

The North Unit is along a fifteen-mile scenic drive. The River Bend Overlook is an astounding panoramic view. About 300 buffalo roam freely in the South Unit and there are about 100 in the North Unit. Buffalo in these areas have even been known to hold up traffic as they meander across roadways. Despite their size, however, buffalo are able to run up to thirty-five miles an hour.

# National Parks in the Northwestern United States

Once-in-a-lifetime memories are created during vacations to national parks of the great northwestern United States. People come from all over the world to see places like Glacier National Park. These parks are also vast, expansive empires of woodlands, lakes, rivers, mountains, and valleys. Safety is of paramount importance when visiting these parks; hikers have become lost, for days at a time, on what look like perfectly safe trails. Get to know the park you're visiting and always educate your family on the area. Research is an important component in your visit to a northwestern national park.

### Glacier National Park

Glacier National Park is located in glorious Montana, where winter weather can affect access to all areas of the park. So the best time of year to visit is in the spring and summer months when the weather is warmer and activities like hiking, camping, and mountain biking are all the rage. Glacier National Park, a majestic 1.4 million acres, was once home to the Blackfoot and Kootenai Indian tribes. There are several spiritual sites in the park that are considered sacred.

Glacier National Park can claim fifty glaciers and more than 200 lakes and streams. Hikers have 730 miles of trails to explore. Going-to-the-Sun Road is how visitors access and traverse the park from east to west. The drive is breathtaking and is in itself a reason to travel to Glacier.

Wildflowers, wildlife, and thick forest awaits you at Glacier, and don't be surprised if you're minding your own business hiking and a deer simply trots by unfazed. Other animals like big horn sheep, mountain goats, elk, and black bear are frequent residents, along with grizzly bear, moose and wolves. A whole host of other animals live and prosper in the park, including birds like the bald eagle.

The nature trails in Glacier National Park are legendary. There are several self-guided walks. They include Trail of the Cedars, Huckleberry Mountain, Hidden Lake, Sun Point, and Swiftcurrent Nature Trails. Trail of the Cedars is handicapped accessible. Campers can camp at a limited number of campsites in the park, but camping families should be advised that Glacier National Park is true wilderness. Caution when camping is essential. It is easy to get lost, so staying on marked trails is always a good idea.

Everywhere you look at Glacier National Park is awe-inspiring, but make a special effort to visit Two Medicine while in the park. The view is simply heart-stopping, the mountain reflection on the glass lake unreal. Most people find after visiting Montana that they can't narrow their favorite places down to one. At Glacier this is doubly true.

## Kenai Fjords, Alaska

The Ice Age may appear to be a thing of the past. But in Alaska in the Kenai Fjords National Park, the Ice Age seems to linger in the form of unfathomably large glaciers that seem to go beyond the heavens. Despite the chilled environment, many species of animals thrive under these conditions. Families who want a once-in-a-lifetime vacation should consider a visit to the Kenai Fjords. Kenai Fjords seems uninhabitable but resident animals include ice worms, bears, fish, whales, and sea lions.

Visitors to the Exit Glacier, the only part of Kenai Fjords accessible by road, can walk along trails, see an active glacier up close, or opt for a guided walk led by a Kenai Fjords park ranger. Here in Kenai Fjords, visitors can learn how glaciers, a vital part of earth's ecosystem, reshape the landscape and how subsequently the plants around them reclaim rocky landscapes when a glacier retreats. Exit Glacier is open year round and has a nature center with information and maps of the Exit Glacier area.

## ≡ Fast Fact

Kenai Fjords is bear country. Brown and black bears can be found in the park, but black bears are more likely to be seen. Salmonberries are a favorite food of black bears, and thickets of them are scattered throughout. Black bear sightings are recorded nearly each day on the Harding Icefield Trail. A bear's main interest is getting something to eat, second only to protecting a cub. It's illegal to feed bears and to leave food or garbage that attracts bears.

An eight-mile walk will land you at Harding Icefield. The trail begins on the floor of the valley winding through cottonwood and alder forests. Hikers will meander through meadows carpeted with heather and ascend far above the line of the trees until the Icefield comes into view. The whole horizon is occupied by ice and snow that extends as far as human eyes can see. Though the trail is strenuous and takes approximately a day to complete, families with older children in good shape can handle the elevation and rocky sections. Some scrambling in the first few hours may be necessary.

Kayaking and fishing for salmon, halibut, rockfish, and lingcod are popular, but a fishing license is required.

### Yosemite National Park

Yosemite National Park, in Yosemite California, is almost 95 percent designated wilderness. The park is 1,169 square miles and was designated a World Heritage Site in 1984. Yosemite is famous for granite cliffs, waterfalls, streams, massive sequoia groves, and a complex biological diversity. There are more than 400 species of fish, amphibians, reptiles, birds, and mammals in Yosemite. More than 3.5 million visitors come to the park each year!

There are several popular campgrounds. Families who plan to camp in Yosemite should make reservations as far in advance as possible. Seven are reserved campgrounds and others are first-come first-serve. During the warm months, first-come first-serve campgrounds can be full by noon.

Yosemite National Park's giant sequoias are like nature's fire-fighters, because the bark is fire resistant, a good thing since fire helps open the sequoia cone to scatter seeds, and fire clears forest debris from mineral soil providing nutrient-rich seed beds. Water-falls, meadows, cliffs and unusual rock formations are just a few reasons the Yosemite Valley is vehicle accessible annually. Another attraction families won't want to miss is the Mariposa Grove.

## Yellowstone National Park

Yellowstone National Park is America's first national park. It was established way back in 1872. The park encompasses an enormous 2 million-plus acres in the states of Wyoming, Montana, and Idaho. That's larger than some states. Yellowstone is so large that one visitor center just wouldn't be enough to accommodate the thousands of visitors to the park each year. Yellowstone has nine visitor centers, seven campgrounds, and more than 400 campsites.

There are more than 10,000 thermal features and more than 300 geysers, including the world-famous Old Faithful, located within Yellowstone National Park.

Yellowstone has a gigantic petrified forest—one of the largest in the world. Scattered throughout the park are 290 waterfalls including the more than 300-foot Lower Falls of the Yellowstone River. Yellowstone Lake has an area of more than 100 square miles.

Nearly 100 other mammals call Yellowstone National Park home, including the gray wolf.

Family activities at Yellowstone include horseback riding and llama packing. Xanterra Parks & Resorts (*www.xanterra.com*) can organize a one- or two-hour riding adventure and wagon rides that end with a steak dinner at a cookout site.

## ≡ Fast Fact

In 1988 wildfires spread and damaged nearly 1 million acres, about 36 percent of Yellowstone National Park. Five major fires burned into Yellowstone from public lands nearby. The North Fork Fire, which was the largest, began thanks to someone's carelessness in discarding a cigarette. Nearly half a million acres burned in that one fire. Never smoke when visiting a national park.

# National Parks in the Southwestern United States

United States National Parks of the Southwest present some of the most unique natural sites on earth. Rock formations in every color of the rainbow jut out from mighty rivers and hang over green spring valleys. Hot sands by day become cold-weather destinations by night. A seemingly uninhabitable environment for animals, wildlife actually thrives in this desert atmosphere thanks to adapting for millions of years to the harsh conditions. A southwestern national park vacation is full of adventure!

### Grand Canyon

President Theodore Roosevelt was one of the very first elected officials to take action to preserve America's most beautiful natural resources. Of the Grand Canyon he said, "Leave it as it is. You cannot improve on it. The ages have been at work on it, and man can only mar it. What you can do is to keep it for your children, your children's children, and for all who come after you, as one of the great sights which every American should see." (*www.theodoreroosevelt.org*) Roosevelt called on Americans to keep the great wonder of the Grand Canyon as it was—pure and unspoiled.

Since then Grand Canyon National Park has become a World Heritage Site. Encompassing more than a million acres on the Colorado Plateau in northwestern Arizona, the Grand Canyon is famous for three out of four eras of geological time, diverse fossils, geologic rock formations, and multiple caves. The Canyon has been carved by the Colorado River and averages 4,000 feet deep, and at its deepest point is a massive 6,000 feet deep. At its widest the Grand Canyon is fifteen miles! The Grand Canyon is home to nearly 2,000 types of plants, almost 400 kinds of birds, nearly 100 mammals, 47 reptiles, 9 amphibian species, and 17 species of fish.

Due to its massive size, one of the best ways to see the Grand Canyon is by air, and both fixed-wing and helicopter daily tours of the Grand Canyon are available. Bus tours and ranger-guided hikes are also available to families within the park. Daily tours can include desert-view, sunrise, and sunset tours among many others. The Grand Canyon Chamber of Commerce maintains the latest listings of air, bus, and guided tour operators. (*www.grandcanyon chamber.com*).

The Grand Canyon Field Institute offers guided educational tours. Expert instructors from the Grand Canyon Field Institute lead tours that cover the geology, ecology, history, and archaeology of the park. Guests can take these tours by mule, on horseback, and even by wagon.

The Grand Canyon Field Institute and Xanterra South Rim offer "Learning and Lodging" programs that allow families to combine guided trips into the Canyon with an expert instructor, lodging, and meals. For families who enjoy traveling by train, all aboard the Grand Canyon Railway. The Railway leaves from Williams, Arizona, to the Grand Canyon carrying more than 200,000 people annually. (*www.grandcanyon.org*)

## The Red Rocks of Sedona, Arizona

Though not a designated national park, the red rocks of Sedona are one of world's most breathtaking natural wonders. Canyons that look as if they were painted red, hence their nickname "painted rocks," are nestled against giant rocks that create a startling contrast to the bluest sky.

Sedona is at the opening of spectacular Oak Creek Canyon and was named by Theodore Carl Schnebly for his wife, Sedona. Sedona has much for families to do, from Jeep Tours to hiking to UFO stores and art centers. (*www.VisitSedona.com*)

## The Great Sand Dunes National Park and Preserve

On the northeastern side of Colorado is the Great Sand Dunes National Park and Preserve. These sand dunes are taller than any other sand dunes in North America. There are nearly forty square miles of sand dunes that jut upwards nearly 800 feet above the valley. The Great Sand Dunes are quite a sight to behold, born from wind and rain erosion of the San Juan and Sangre de Cristo Mountains that circle the San Luis Valley. The Great Sand Dunes are like sculptures that are constantly changing, although they sustain an amazingly firm structure thanks to the moisture they receive from rain and snow. It's the surface layers of dry sand that change patterns with the blowing wind.

Great Sand Dunes National Monument has only been a National Park and Preserve since 2004.

Park visitors can enjoy nature walks and lectures on topics like geology, plant life, animals, and the history of the Great Sand Dunes. Besides the dunes themselves, there are other things to see in the Great Sand Dunes National Park. The elevation is too high in the dunes for poisonous snakes, but as the elevation begins to decrease rattlesnakes can be found south of the boundary of the park. Visitors may see graceful deer and elk both in the park boundaries and on park roads, along with pronghorn antelope. It's important to drive carefully (and slowly) to avoid a collision with any of the animals.

Guests should be aware of weather, lightning specifically. Barren dunes are prone to lightning strikes and summer is the most common season for thunderstorms. Always wear shoes in the Great Sand Dunes, as the surface of the dunes can exceed more than 100°F. It's also important to watch out for holes, as falling into a hole in these deep sands can make it impossible to extract yourself. Kids can dig, but not more than a little over a foot in a downward direction. Visitors should bring plenty of water to avoid dehydration, and wear clothing that prevents wind burn from the sand; blown sand can be painful and dangerous. Plan to hike the dunes in morning or evening hours when it's more likely to be calm and cool, and check the forecast if you are heading into the backcountry. Afternoons, especially in spring, are sometimes windy and can be uncomfortable on the sand. Shade is a scarcity, so people with pets need to make their visit to the Great Sand Dunes a short one.

## ≡ Fast Fact

The Great Sand Dunes formed in this spot because winds blowing in opposite directions meet causing sand to fall. Water from the Sangre de Cristo River held the sand in place over many thousands of years, forming the dunes you see here today. Every day they change because this process continues all the time.

Nearby is Medano Creek, which, depending on precipitation, flows at the dunes' base. When the creek is wet, kids love playing in the wet sand. It's the perfect place for a sandcastle building contest or for sliding downward on the dunes. There is a footwash near the restroom.

It's a good idea to bring plenty of food and water for a picnic while you're visiting the Great Sand Dunes, as the park is off the beaten path. Just remember not to feed any animals.

The Montville Nature Trail is a hike that is less than a mile at the start of the Mosca Pass Trailhead Parking Area. Some visitors climb the high dune, which isn't the tallest dune in the park. There aren't any trails to the summit, so hikers are advised to take a zig-zag approach to the ridge lines. One of the star attractions at the Great Sand Dunes is the "Star Dune" jutting nearly 800 feet, with three arms, thanks to compound wind patterns—star dunes make great photo subjects. Sunset and sunrise at the Great Sand Dunes National Park, like most of America's national parks, are a sight to behold.

# CHAPTER 11

# Eco-Travel

As the distance between cultures and countries grows ever smaller, destinations once off limits to families have become almost commonplace. Places that used to be considered too expensive are now within reach for families who plan carefully. Even ecologically friendly travel, better known by its abbreviated monikers "eco-travel," "green travel," "sustainable tourism," and "ecotourism," has become routine to frequent travelers. The rewards of choosing an earth-friendly vacation are many. Ecotourism destinations are usually pristine, lush, and many are unspeakably beautiful to behold. Visiting an eco-friendly destination means your family's travel dollars will benefit the environment and often aid local residents of that area.

## Planning Your Eco-Vacation

Many organizations exist for the sole purpose to promote earth-friendly travel. A few moments online will reveal hundreds of eco-vacation operators, touring companies, and organizations heralding the latest way to leave the lightest footprint. Whether you chose paint-by-number eco-vacations or design your own, become familiar with your ecotourism options, costs (which can be considerable), and safety.

Becoming a green traveler is all about choices your family makes before you leave home and while you're on vacation. Those choices differentiate the responsible traveler. Eco-travel is also an opportunity to educate your children about being good stewards of the planet, even while on vacation. The first step toward planning an eco-vacation is to get educated about ecotourism. There are many resources to help you become acquainted with taking an eco-vacation.

## Earthwatch Institute

The Earthwatch Institute can boast 120 projects in more than 55 countries researching climate change, marine biology, endangered species, and traditional cultures. At this organization it's all about sustainable environment, so it's a great resource to learn about eco-travel. Got teenagers or tweens in the family? This site in particular is perfect for them because through the Earthwatch Institute teens can participate in Earthwatch's Teen Teams expeditions. In this program, high school juniors and seniors can work with local partners and scientists in the field to learn how to safeguard endangered resources. Earthwatch is the largest environmental volunteer nonprofit organization and contains a wealth of family-friendly information on green travel. And you never know, besides being a great resource for your eco-travel planning, your teen might become inspired to be an Earthwatch volunteer! What a great item to put on a college application. For more information visit, *www.earthwatch.org.*

## The Ocean Conservancy

More than half a million members and volunteers advocate on behalf of the world's oceans through the Ocean Conservancy. The science-based group has already changed the world through promoting healthy ocean ecosystems and opposing fishing and other practices that harm or threaten ocean and human life. Kids can go online to the Ocean Conservancy's website to learn about, vote for, and help save their favorite fish. The Ocean Conservancy magazine is full of enough information about ocean conservation and animals to keep your family busy discussing all the ways you can leave the lightest footprint on your vacation. *(www.ocean conservancy.org)*

## 📛 Travel Tip

Tell tour operators and reservationists that you are a responsible consumer. Ask questions about their environmental policy, percentage of local employees, and how their destination benefits the local community.

### The International Ecotourism Society

The International Ecotourism Society (TIES) is a 501(c)(3) nonprofit organization and the oldest and largest ecotourism organization in the world. TIES has members in more than ninety countries and is a resource for finding the latest and greatest in eco-travel referrals for you and your family. Though you can save money researching and booking your eco-vacation yourself, sometimes, and particularly for first-time eco-traveling families, it's a good idea to ask an expert for help. Members of organizations like TIES are usually required to follow responsible ecotourism guidelines in order to be a member, a list of whom can be found on the TIES website: *www.ecotourism.org.*

### EarthEcho International

The earth's oceans offer numerous opportunities for engaging in sustainable travel. EarthEcho International was founded by the grandson and granddaughter of legendary oceanographer Jacques Cousteau. Philippe and Alexandra Cousteau have followed in their family's footsteps, and have continued the quest to preserve the planet's oceans and freshwater systems. Considering a water vacation? Your family can begin learning online about preserving the planet's water systems and how conservation is relevant to their daily life at *www.EarthEcho.org*. Then together everyone can follow those important lessons with real-world ecological practices.

Are you ready to start planning your earth-friendly vacation? The world awaits you, but how do you start planning? An easy way to begin is to discuss what type of eco-vacation you're interested in taking. Are the nutrient-rich waters of Washington State calling you? Perhaps you've always wanted to see the California redwoods. Maybe interacting with vibrant sea creatures is more your style. How about a rafting trip through the Amazon? You'll have to research your area of the world to determine the closest eco-destination near your home, but here are a few destinations to get you started.

## Destination: SEE Turtles Baja Ocean Adventure

The Sea Turtle Ecological Expeditions (SEE Turtles) is a conservation tourism campaign by the Ocean Conservancy. Through the campaign people are linked with sea turtle sites in ways that directly support efforts to protect the turtles. There is no telling how many hundreds of thousands of sea turtles the Ocean Conservancy's efforts have helped save.

Sea turtles survived the dinosaurs (they've been on Earth for 100 million-plus years). Now six species of sea turtles are on the brink of extinction. Sea turtles drown or are killed when they're caught in fishing gear. Development along the coasts destroys nesting sites. Lights from houses and other buildings attract hatchlings away from the ocean instead of toward the sea where they belong. When sea turtles ingest pollution like plastic bags, which can be mistaken for jellyfish, they often die. And even with all we know about these magnificent creatures, sea turtles are still hunted for meat and shells in some countries.

Saving the sea turtle may seem impossible under such odds. But that's where ecotourism comes into play. All you have to do to help is go on vacation. Eco-travel supports communities that protect sea turtles. SEE Turtles' partners include Baja California, Mexico; Costa Rica; and Trinidad—travel there in the SEE Turtles program, and your vacation dollars will go right to the very conservation efforts that protect endangered sea turtles and support those local businesses.

## ☰ Fast Fact

Leatherback sea turtles are found as far south as Chile and as far north as Alaska. Their entire lives are spent at sea, except when moms come ashore to lay eggs. Hatchlings emerge, shake off the sand and try to make it to the ocean—they're drawn to the horizon. If they make it, and many of them don't, their lives are spent in the open ocean until it is time to come ashore and nest.

What better way for your children to learn the importance of preserving their planet, than to get hands-on experience, and see the sea turtles firsthand!

The Ocean Conservancy's SEE Turtles vacations are trips that should be planned in advance. For starters, it is not a weekend vacation. Plan to be gone for a week including travel time to experience a SEE Turtles adventure. (*www.seeturtles.org*)

## Destination: Crown of the Continent

The Crown of the Continent—termed "North America's Rocky Mountain Majesty" by British Columbian writer David Thomas, is located where the corners of Alberta, British Columbia, and Montana meet, including Waterton-Glacier International Peace Park. This geographic area is one of North America's most diverse, expansive areas. Teeming with unspoiled places and habitats, the

Crown of the Continent offers families 16,000 square miles with an almost unfathomable number of activities, destinations, and reasons to visit.

A map of the Crown of the Continent was developed by National Geographic Society Maps, Center for Sustainable Destinations, and regional organizations—all who collectively serve as the Crown of the Continent Geotourism Council. (*www.crownofthecontinent.net*)

The map is a great resource for planning a vacation to this pristine wilderness. It's community based and includes a highly developed list of resources available to families who want to see this part of the world. Highlights include cultural, environmental, and historical sites and destinations. Best of all, families interested in traveling to these areas can plan their trip almost entirely from the resources located in the map.

## ☂ Rainy Day Fun

Rain is a part of the earth—and in places like the Crown of the Continent, there is still so much to do in the way of museums and historic sites, your family will always find things to do. Refer to the history key on your map to locate attractions your family would like to see.

History seekers will find in the Crown of the Continent, five tribal and First Nation reserves and two World Heritage sites: Waterton Glacier International Peace Park which straddles Montana and Alberta's border, and Head-Smashed-In Buffalo Jump adjacent to Fort McLeod, Alberta. An Eden of natural ecosystems, valleys, ancient cedar forests, prairies, and diverse wildlife abound in the Crown of the Continent.

Scattered throughout the map are listings of places to visit including family-friendly towns that contribute to ecotourism. Since the map is organized by region, families can easily determine which areas of the Crown of the Continent to visit.

You don't have to go to Africa to see a wildlife savannah—there's one right in the Crown of the Continent. Moose, bighorn sheep, grizzly bears, elk, lynx, wolves, and bison all share this massive swath of land. The animals are allowed cross borders, roaming freely as nature intended. The map contains extensive information on the types of wildlife found in the region, and how and where visitors can enjoy seeing some of the wildlife in their native habitats. In Canada, salmon runs in the Kootenay River and Head-Smashed-In Buffalo Jump are on polar ends of the spectrum in ecology—both provide lifelong learning for families with young travelers. Lussier Hot Springs in British Columbia, located just inside Whiteswan Provincial Park, were known by the Ktunaxa people as having therapeutic benefits. Winter brings cross-country skiers to the Allison/Chinook lake trails. Montana's National Bison Range and ecological masterpieces like Glacial Lake Missoula and Two Medicine Lake provide breathtaking sites your family will remember all their lives. In the Crown of the Continent, nature puts on her finest show, by which families will be forever touched.

A wealth of ideas for planning an eco-friendly trip and endless resources are available on the Crown of the Continent website. The website also highlights how, by traveling to the Crown of the Continent, tourists help sustain the assets of the region. Useful information such as how to take a shuttle bus, booking passage on Amtrak to Glacier National Park, and finding guided tours is also included. On the website families can order their free copy of the Crown of the Continent map.

# Destination: Mendocino County, California

Mendocino County, California, is becoming one of the most well-traveled wine destinations in the country. But did you also know that Mendocino County is also an eco-destination? It began long ago, when the county was the first in America to ban genetically modified organisms (GMOs).

The highest percentage of organic grapes in America are grown in Mendocino. The county can boast hundreds of family-owned wineries and the oldest organic vineyards. Wine tastings are almost always free of charge. The world's first organic brew pub—the Ukiah Brewing Co.—is located in Mendocino County. Mendocino County even has its own festival to celebrate its commitment to the earth. PURE Mendocino Festivals (August) and Mendocino Bounty (June) provide a platform for showcasing Mendocino's organic food and wine. The cuisine in Mendocino is all about the earth. Organic farms seem everywhere, churning out ingredients year round.

## 💼 Travel Tip

Picnics are a great family activity in Mendocino County. Farmers' markets sell truckloads of local organic cheeses, produce, seafood, meats, and wines.

Whale watching is big business in Mendocino County. Migrating California gray whales, humpback whales, and orcas are in plain view as they travel along the Mendocino Coast between March and April, and September through December. Mendocino County founded three festivals in honor of the whales, which take place in Fort Bragg, Gualala, and Mendocino Village.

Botanical ecology is part of the Mendocino County landscape. Many of the earth's tallest redwood trees call Mendocino home, no surprise since America's highest percentage of certified sustainable forest is located in Mendocino County. The Jackson State Demonstration Forest teaches visitors about sustainable forestry. State parks replete with waterfalls and trails make for spectacular wildflower viewing. Mendocino Coast Botanical Gardens—the only coastal botanical gardens in North America—encompass forty-seven acres. A must visit for bird watchers, on the way down to the ocean, visitors to the botanical gardens can stroll through a fern-filled canyon. Visit Mendocino in September and you'll be able to attend the area's popular wine auction, "Winesong!" hosted by the botanical gardens.

True eco-traveling families will love spending time at the Solar Living Institute. There you can learn how to solar power your home; retrofit the family car to run on bio-fuels, build energy-efficiently, and garden organically. The Institute's festival, SolFest, celebrates solar education with activities that are fun for everyone in the family. (*www.gomendo.com*)

# Destination: Snohomish County and the Olympic Peninsula

Snohomish County is located in the picturesque northwestern United States in Washington State. Near Puget Sound Cascade Mountains not far north from Seattle, Snohomish County is a great home base for exploring this area of the country. Snohomish County, nearby San Juan Islands, and the Olympic Peninsula are known for unparalleled natural beauty. Snohomish County, the Olympic Peninsula, San Juan Islands, and pretty much the entire natural areas of Washington State offer scenery for photo opportunities that families will remember for a lifetime. Bring lots of cameras and make sure your camera's memory card has lots of room!

## Snohomish County

Snohomish County has so much to do for families of all shapes and sizes. Just a few activities families can experience together in Snohomish County include:

- River float trips
- Kayak tours

- Whitewater rafting
- City and country walking trails
- Hiking
- Mountain and street biking
- Snowshoeing and snowmobiling (during the winter months)
- Whale watching
- Camping
- Trail hiking in the forests
- Picnicking
- Lake recreation
- Wildlife watching

One of the perks of visiting Snohomish County is the opportunity families have to learn about the Native American culture and heritage of the area. Snohomish County has several cultural destinations that can help young people better understand the peoples who came before them. Heritage Park is a compilation of many historic buildings that once were Alderwood Manor, a mill community circa 1917. The park includes a house and barn, store, and post office built in 1919, and cottage and water tower from the 1930s. (*www.alderwood.org*)

The Stanwood/Camano Island has nine historic sites dating back to the late nineteenth century, and other historic sites include Floyd Norgaard Cultural Center, Little White Church on the Hill, Camano Pioneer Cemetery, Hevly Cash Store and the Cama Beach Resort. (*www.sahs-fncc.org*)

Aviators and their family members will relish a stop at the Flying Heritage Collection in Everett, Washington. The collection is housed in a whopping hangar that spans more than 50,000 square feet. This assortment of aviation is a private collection of rare finds. The exhibits include warbirds and examples of technology from 1935 to 1945. For more information see *www.flyingheritage.com*.

Art is a big part of life in Snohomish County (*www.Snohomish .org*). Galleries feature local artists, and events offer a chance to snap up great pieces for bargain basement prices. Artwork at the Snohomish galleries includes watercolors, hand-blown glass, and oil paintings, among other media. Art loving families can stop by the historic Monte Cristo and see what's new on the Snohomish County arts scene. The Artists' Garage Sale takes place in June. (*www.artscouncilofsnoco.org*)

## The Olympic Peninsula

Washington State's Olympic Peninsula is truly one of nature's most beautiful playgrounds. Birding, food, wine and outdoor festivals, art and history museums, performing arts, and Olympic coastal gourmet cuisine are all what make this part of the world so special. And there are so many free things to do in the Olympic Peninsula that every member of the family will find something to love!

Olympic National Park has a nominal entrance fee, but that's a small price to pay for almost a million acres of rain forest valleys, fields, glacier-capped peaks, and more than fifty miles of wild coastline.

In what has become an international sensation, Forks, Washington, is the backdrop to the *Twilight* series of books. Thanks to the success of the stories, organized tours have popped up all over the Olympic Peninsula. The Forks Chamber of Commerce can provide free Twilight maps for self-guided tours, and while you're at the Chamber, get a shot of a replica of Bella's truck from the movie. (*www.forkswa.com/twilight.html*)

The Quinault Valley is home to some of the largest trees in the world, including the Western Red Cedar, Douglas Fir, Sitka Spruce, and Mountain Hemlock. The stars of this forest show are the trees, but the trails visitors take to get to the trees are almost as spectacular. Visitors can go to Enchanted Valley, a one-way backpacking trip of about fifteen miles, and even climb inside the Western Red Cedar, which is the biggest tree on earth not located in California. Just five minutes into the trail walk will land you and your family at a Sitka Spruce likely to be more than 1,000 years old! (*www.rain forestgetaways.com*)

The "Magical Misty Tour" is on the Olympic Peninsula Waterfall Trail. The Waterfall Trail provides visitors with views of the Cape Flattery cliffs and Hood Canal fjord plus numerous waterfalls. The waterfalls are accessible by different paths; some can be seen from paved paths that have disabled access, while others can only be reached by kayakers, rafters, or hikers. (*www.olympic peninsulawaterfalltrail.com*)

The lavender fields of Sequim, Washington, provide more than forty different field trips, and families can enjoy a pick-your-own lavender day. And visitors to the area in July can attend the nation's biggest lavender festival. (*www.lavendergrowers.org*)

The tide pools in and around the Olympic Peninsula are brimming with creatures including starfish, sea cucumbers, sea anemones, crabs, and urchins among other delightful sea animals. Families can jaunt over to Salt Creek to see amazing views of Strait of Juan de Fuca, and hang out in Victoria, British Columbia, to find more thriving tide pools and experience the Tongue Point Marine Life Sanctuary. (*www.visitolympicpeninsula.org*) (*www .olympicpeninsula.org*)

## Family-Friendly Lodging

Kalaloch Lodge in Forks, Washington, is all about sleeping as close to nature as possible, but with all of the amenities you and your family love! Kalaloch Lodge has various accommodations to choose from including snug cabins with fireplaces, guest rooms, and suites in the Kalaloch main lodge. The resort restaurant features fresh, regional cuisine paired with amazing views. And Kalaloch Lodge can organize family hikes, beach combing, fishing expeditions, and wildlife watching, as well as help you explore the Olympic Peninsula. The resort also features special "Stay and Play" packages that include lodging, meals for kids, and recreational equipment such as kites. (*www.visitkalaloch.com*)

With the Cascade Mountains and Puget Sound nearby, Tulalip Resort Casino and T Spa is near many outdoor recreation areas, charming small towns, and things to do. Kids and parents can golf together at nearby mini-golf and kayak at spectacular Kayak Point. Tulalip Resort is also on the way to the spectacular San Juan Islands. The Tulalip Resort Casino and T Spa is an earth-inspired resort destination near Seattle with a multitude of things to do for the whole family close by. Parents love the cedar saunas, grotto-style showers, and massage rooms with double-sided fireplaces. And kids are welcome in the spa provided they are accompanied by a parent. Tulalip Resort Casino has nearly 200,000 square feet of gaming and six restaurants, and a concierge who can help parents locate and hire babysitters. Other attractions at the Tulalip Resort Casino include the Tulalip Amphitheatre with 3,000 seats, and nearby Seattle Premium Outlets. The Tulalip Resort Casino has a complimentary, on-demand shuttle service that travels back and forth to the Seattle Premium Outlets. The humongous hotel has almost 400 rooms. (*www.tulalipresort.com*)

## Surprisingly Affordable Eco-Trips of a Lifetime

The earth as we know it is rapidly changing. Now is the time to encourage small children to love the planet, and there's no better way to do that than through ecotourism. Soon, preservation of the earth's resources will be up to them. Eco-travel is one of the best ways to teach your family this important lesson. Eco-travel doesn't have to be expensive or take you across the globe. Local zoos, raptor centers, botanical gardens, and organic farm tours can provide a great education on being environmentally friendly. L.L. Bean's Outdoor Discovery Schools offer paddling courses, tours, and trips starting at just $29. And your state's universities should be able to offer a mountain of resources on how to find local eco-friendly sites in your state. But some families want to step out of the backyard to see the side of the planet featured on the Discovery and Travel Channels. Those eco-trips are, quite simply, out of this world.

### Ariau Amazon Towers

Perhaps the mother lode of eco-travel can be found in the Amazon at the Ariau Amazon Towers. Falling under trips of a lifetime, Ariau Amazon Towers has been named one of a thousand places to see before you die (*www.ariautowers.com*). It's located approximately thirty-five miles northwest of Manaus in Brazil. Alongside the largest freshwater archipelago on earth, Ariau Amazon Towers has 263 rooms. What makes these rooms special is that they are all built at treetop level for unparalleled view of the Amazon rainforest. Tree house rentals are available and a wise idea if you are traveling with another family. Packages at Ariau Amazon Towers are all-inclusive, including several tour options.

## 🧳 Travel Tip

Combination packages are available when booking a trip to Ariau Amazon Towers that include a visit to a nearby city. Such a package allows families to view how other cultures live in urban areas.

One of those tours involves swimming with pink—yes, pink—dolphins. These are some of the few freshwater dolphins in the world. The Jungle Survival Tour teaches participants how to survive in the jungle without modern day resources. Navigating Anavilhanas and the Meeting of the Waters tours will earn you an appreciation for the world's river systems.

### Zegrahm and Eco Expeditions

Marco Polo said he didn't tell half of what he saw, because no one would have believed him. Nowadays, almost nothing is out of reach. Even the snow monkeys and cranes of Japan, Antarctica, and the wilds of Patagonia and India are reachable if you book a trip with Zegrahm and Eco Expeditions. The company organizes trips from Iceland to Greenland, to the Adriatic Sea, and everywhere in between. You can even book passage on their circumnavigation of New Guinea. Tours vary in price from reasonable to expensive, but are doable on a budget with enough advance planning. (*www.zeco.com*)

## Finding an Earth-Friendly Destination Tour Operator

How do you know which websites or green vacation planners really specialize in ecotourism? Look for the signs. Many eco-travel companies or destinations are constantly vying for accolades— look for eco certifications, ratings, and awards when researching your vacation.

And while the web is a great resource, sometimes nothing beats personal contact. Don't be afraid to call or e-mail destinations or tour operators to glean the firsthand knowledge you need to make an informed ecotourism choice.

### Just for Parents

Many ecotourism destinations have activities and fun classes about the environment geared especially for young people. By the same token, at those same destinations, activities like kayaking on rough waters are only appropriate for parents. Find out from your tour operator or concierge about child-friendly and parent-friendly activities when you book your trip.

Eco-travel directly benefits the environment and local peoples. But some adventure travel companies take ecotourism a step further, and reward the planet whether you choose an eco-trip or not. Gap Adventures is a Canadian Travel company with many eco-friendly trips to choose from. Their "Book a Trip, Plant a Tree" tree-planting program funds planting one tree for each person who books a Gap Adventures vacation. (*www.gap adventures.com*)

# CHAPTER 12

# Winter Wonderlands

What is it about big fat snowflakes falling in snowstorms? Or the way snow falls on tall trees in the mountains? For many families who live in cold-weather climates, snow is no big deal. But for families who live in humid, hot-weather climates, a snow-covered vacation is something they look forward to all year long. And many families, despite living in chilly, snow-laden northern states, love to get away for a winter vacation to a nearby resort or ski town for its many winter activities.

## Planning Your Winter Wonderland Vacation

Cold-weather months provide fun family activities that everyone can enjoy together, especially at winter-weather resorts. If there's snow on the ground, there's something fun to do.

- Snowshoeing
- Snowmobiling
- Sledding and tubing
- Cross-country skiing
- Skiing
- Snowboarding
- Dog sledding

- Sleigh rides
- Gondola rides
- Ice skating

These and other activities can be found at most cold-weather resorts, so your decision on where to vacation during the winter months is not limited to resort activities. Families who want to vacation at a resort that offers winter activities can choose from several ski and snowboarding resorts. You don't have to ski or snowboard to enjoy fun in the snow. However, many ski resorts are frequented by serious skiers who can afford the sport and all it entails. Therefore many ski resorts are wildly expensive and some are not well-suited for children. Choose a resort that boasts that it is family-friendly and offers special programs for children, as these are most likely to be less expensive and have more for kids to do.

## Snowmass, Colorado

On the list of ski resorts that cater to families, specifically children, Snowmass near Aspen, Colorado, takes top honors. The Treehouse Kids' Adventure Center is a kids' paradise. Parents can breathe a sigh of relief as they hit the slopes knowing kids want to hang at the Treehouse because it's just more fun. While adults enjoy cruisers, glades, terrain parks, and half-pipes throughout twenty-one lifts and ninety-one trails, kids can learn to ski and relish time in the Treehouse Kids' Adventure Center. For infants ages eight weeks to eighteen months, day care is available in the Butterfly Meadow Room. Toddlers spend their time in the Trout Haven Room and Beaver Lodge, an aquatic-themed indoor play area and forest-themed play area with immediate access to a play yard outdoors. Preschoolers stay in the Fox Den Room, which has a crawl-through tunnel and science and nature themes.

The first floor of the Treehouse Kids' Adventure Center is a 700-square-foot Aspen Climb Room complete with safety netting and built-in discovery places. The Bear Den Room welcomes older preschoolers and features a storytelling and puppet theater, direct access to two magic carpet ski areas, and a loft for napping. The Eagle Peak Room serves several purposes, including ski and snowboard school rentals, Four-Mountain Kids retail store just for kids, and kitchen and lunchroom. (*www.aspensnowmass.com*)

Family-friendly lodging in the Aspen/Snowmass area includes the Silvertree Hotel at Snowmass Village (*www.silvertreehotel.com*) and Aspen's Limelight Lodge. (*www.limelightlodge.com*)

## Stowe, Vermont

The Stowe Adventure Center offers licensed day care for kids six months through six years old at the Cub's Day Care Program. Kids' ski school begins at age three. In the Mountain Adventure program, kids can learn to ski and snowboard; lessons are available for kids age six to twelve. The mountain also offers the Extreme Adventure program for advanced young skiers and snowboarders eleven to fourteen who can ski with peers and guides from the Stowe Ski and Snowboard School.

### 👪 Just for Parents

The Spa at Stowe Mountain Lodge includes Vermont's natural elements and the four seasons in its spa treatments. Parents can enjoy spa treatments with astounding views of surrounding mountains while kids learn to ski at the Adventure Center Ski School.

Family-friendly lodging in Stowe includes the Commodores Inn (*www.commodoresinn.com*) and the Trapp Family Lodge. Vacation planning tips for traveling to Stowe with the kids are available at *www.gostowe.com/KidsZone* and on the Stowe website at *www.stowe.com*.

# Bryce Resort, Virginia

On the website OnTheSnow.com, viewers voted Bryce Resort of Basye, Virginia, in the Shenandoah Valley for Family-Friendliness, receiving near perfect scores in the family-friendly category. Ski school instructors are trained to work with kids, and the resort is family oriented, having been in business for forty years. The small ski area is about two hours from Washington, D.C. Bryce Resort has just five chair lifts and eight ski runs, and a carpet lift escalator to take beginners to the top of the Bunny slope. Bryce Resort is perfect for families looking for an intimate ski vacation. (*www.bryceresort.com*)

Bryce Resort's Ridge Runner's Tubing Park makes it easy for people of all skill levels to enjoy playing in the snow thanks to 800-foot-long tubing lanes. Bryce Resort doesn't have a formal hotel; however, the Sky Chalet Mountain Top Lodge accommodates families and small groups in a rustic six-bedroom lodge. Just five minutes to Bryce Resort, the Sky Chalet includes a continental breakfast room service every morning, and pets are welcome with advanced reservations.

## 💼 Travel Tip

Family-friendly lodging includes Sky Chalet (*www.skychalet.com*), and for added value parents can try the all-you-can-eat prime rib buffet where kids under age five can eat free.

# Alta/Snowbird, Utah

Alta is all about family, all about skiing, and all about good clean fun. The air in Alta seems as if it's been filtered a dozen times and the view is endless. Skiers can enjoy an astounding 4,000 acres of powder by purchasing an AltaSnowbird combination ticket. Memorable terrain from beginner to expert, Alta is the perfect site for family ski vacations. Snowboarding at Alta is not allowed.

Alta Lodge offers the Free Kids' Program whereby kids can make new friends, take the Ski School shuttle in the morning, and enjoy *après-ski* activities at night followed by an exceptional kids' dinner. Children of all ages are welcome, but the program is designed for kids four to twelve years old or for kids where one-on-one supervision isn't required. Kids under the age of four have to be accompanied by a parent or other responsible adult.

The Alf Engen Ski School offers classes and private lessons, and the Children's Ski Adventures is for kids of all skill levels. The Mountain Explorers Package offers two-hour lessons and day-long packages that include lunch. Visitors to Alta, Utah, fly into Salt Lake City. Family-friendly lodging at Alta Snowbird can be found at Alta Lodge, where family dining is part of the fun. (*www.altalodge.com*)

## Beaver Creek, Colorado

Beaver Creek is what people think of when envisioning a winter village paradise, a ski hideaway neatly tucked into the valley or side of a mountain. Covered in snow, Beaver Creek is infused with the special winter magic of an Alpine Village. It exudes charm and everything people love about winter. And against the backdrop of some of Colorado's most beautiful mountains, Beaver Creek is at once enchanting and inviting. Beaver Creek is truly a winter wonderland for snow sport enthusiasts.

### ☰ Fast Fact

Beaver Creek Resort has been called the "consummate kid-friendly resort" thanks to the multitude of kid-friendly activities they provide. All of the family activities at Beaver Creek Resort are complimentary. Beaver Creek even has its own website for kids called "Snow Monsters," which kids can check out on property, at home before travel, and to stay in touch when they get home. See *www.beavercreek.snowmonsters.com*.

A big draw for families to Beaver Creek Resort are programs like Ski with a Ranger, Figure the Skating Series and Kid's Tubing. And activities for kids like Disco Skate Night make it a huge hit for families with children of all ages. (*www.beavercreek .snow.com*)

# Top Family-Friendly Ski and Snowboarding Schools

Many ski resorts offer incomparable skiing. Others offer great *après-ski* activities. Some are great for families, while a few have everything you could want under one roof. But if you're taking your family skiing for the first time, the most important thing to look for is a resort with a great ski school for kids. Having fun on the slopes is secondary only to safety. A child who can't ski is a child who shouldn't be anywhere near the slopes. Finding a good ski school is as easy as deciding which area of the country you want to visit. Hours of operation and seasonal schedules can change daily, so be sure to call ahead for updated schedules and times before you book a flight or reserve lodging.

### Northstar at Lake Tahoe, Nevada

Northstar at Lake Tahoe's Paw Parks is a like a winter ski kingdom constructed just for kids. Everything here is their size, even the moguls, bumps, jumps and hideouts. Ski runs just for kids are adjacent to mainstream ski runs close to where their parents are skiing, making it easy for kids to ski together.

Perfect areas to play in the snow are cordoned off and patrolled by Northstar's ski patrol and mountain safety staff. Child care is available through Minors' Camp for full days or afternoons. A free Mommy, Daddy & Me program is provided every afternoon except Saturdays for parents of young children. (*www.north starattahoe.com*)

## Kid's Mountain of Discovery at Breckenridge Resort, Colorado

Kids from age three to thirteen become incredible skiers at Breckenridge's Kid's Mountain of Discovery. Instructors teach traditional fundamentals of skiing and encourage a passion for the sport. Conventional lessons are specific and take place in designated teaching spaces that are usually restricted. Kid's Mountain of Discovery at Breckenridge Resort gets kids out on the slopes and helps them fall in love with the sport of skiing. (*www.brecken ridge.snow.com*)

## Beaver Creek Children's Ski and Snowboard School, Colorado

"The Ranch" at Beaver Creek is a state-of-the-art children's ski and snowboard school. What makes this ski school different is its promise to "revolutionize the way kids learn to turn." The Ranch is a 4,000-square-foot center on the mountain accessible via the Buckaroo Express Gondola. It's flanked by beginner terrain and customized slopes intended to help kids learn correct body movements. Two-way mirrors in viewing areas let parents watch their kids learn to ski and ride snowboards without getting in the way of the learning process. (*www.beavercreek .snow.com*)

## Snowmass, Colorado

Snowmass is all about the kids. From the Treehouse Kids' Adventure Center to the kid- and family-friendly restaurants and candy shop, child care is widely available and private, and group ski lessons for families and groups of families are easy to come by. Child care at Snowmass begins with kids ages eight and up. Kids' learn-to-ski and snowboard programs include "Grizzlies," which offers on-mountain adventure for kids of all ski levels between five and six years old, while "First Turns" is for first-time skiers and snowboarders ages seven through twelve. Group and private lessons are available for kids of all ages. (*www.aspensnowmass.com*)

# Winter Activities

Leave room in your imagination for anything that might come up, but in the cold-weather months if there's snow on the ground, you'll want to consider taking part in several fun activities that are only possible when there's snow. Most winter activities can be found at popular cold-weather resorts. Some activities are more difficult than others and require physical stamina. For example, ice skating requires a tremendous amount of balance and grace, while tubing is a sport practically everyone can do.

You have to be in pretty good shape in order to go downhill skiing, but anyone can enjoy a sleigh ride. And often people don't realize how strenuous cross-country skiing truly is. It requires cardiac stamina and perseverance, unlike taking a gondola ride on which you simply sit comfortably and revel in the view. Even snowshoeing isn't for the faint-hearted. Picking up snow-covered snow shoes the size of tennis racquets isn't as easy as it looks. The good news is, however, that every one of these activities means fun for the whole family and with a little patience and effort, families can enjoy them all together. No matter which winter sport you engage in, make sure you and your family are wearing helmets. Even a bike helmet will suffice.

## Snowshoeing

Snowshoeing is becoming one of the most popular winter sports around. Besides being fun, it sure does burn calories. Experts estimate snowshoeing burns 600 to 800 calories an hour—that's more calories than jogging, biking, or cross-country skiing. Snowshoeing is also easy on the wallet because it's such an accessible sport— anywhere there's snow, you can snowshoe. You don't have to buy lift tickets or rent skis, poles, or snowboards. Snowshoes are the most reasonably priced winter sport rentals.

Many families are even buying snowshoes and keeping them in the garage with bikes and other family athletic gear to use year after year together on winter vacations. This low-impact sport is great for anyone sufficiently fit to participate, and you choose your own pace. When snowshoeing, you'll work up a sweat but remember to wear warm clothing, gloves, and warm boots.

## Sledding and Tubing

Whether you went sledding as a child or you've never been sledding, this economical sport is fun for everyone. You may be tempted to save a few bucks on a sled rental by grabbing a trash can lid from your hotel room, but that's not a good idea. Check with your resort's activities director to find out if they have sleds for rent; some resorts actually lend sleds to guests as part of the resort package.

Tubing is another popular activity that's become wildly popular with families. Like sledding, riders sit on an inflated tube at the top of a hill and let gravity do the rest. There's not a lot of friction in tubing, so riders can reach high speeds quickly—always remember to wear a helmet, and restrict little ones to small hills and bunny slopes. Whether you're sledding or tubing, don't forget gloves or mittens and cold-weather insulated boots.

## Ice Skating

If your family is planning a cold-weather vacation, see if your community has an ice rink close by where the family can practice. When you arrive at the resort, ask about approved ice skating locations.

Never take your family ice skating anywhere that's not approved for skating, as evidenced by city, town, or resort signage. Ice skates must be the perfect fit in order to prevent falls and injuries. Never go ice skating without a helmet.

## Skiing and Snowboarding

Skiing and snowboarding are two of the most popular winter sports. They're also two of the most difficult. But ski and snowboard schools abound at just about every ski resort internationally. Kids need ski boots that are made just for them, and adults also need boots and equipment made specifically for them. It's not a great idea to share ski equipment other than clothing. If you and your family don't have your own equipment, reasonable rentals are available at most ski and snowboard resorts. The best part of renting ski equipment at resorts is that equipment specialists will fit your boots, skis and poles, and snowboards to your feet. Don't forget your helmets! Most resorts now have helmets for rent and some resorts are beginning to require helmets to use on the slopes. You'll have to buy lift tickets and rent ski gear, which can be expensive, so it's important that families interested in skiing and snowboarding research the cost of their destination and budget for chair lift, equipment, and other fees.

## Snowmobiling

Snowmobiling is one of the most fun things to do on a winter vacation. Young kids can ride with mom and dad and older kids can get their own snowmobiles. Snowmobiles when used appropriately are safe, but unsupervised use can be dangerous. You can usually rent snowmobiles from snowmobiling outfitters, but your resort may also have some available for use. Snowmobiling can be expensive if everyone gets his own, so it's best to double up to save on rental fees. Some snowmobile outfitters will request a deposit that is refundable upon return of the snowmobile, so be sure to budget enough padding in your vacation budget to accommodate for this temporary expense.

# CHAPTER 13

# Camping: America's #1 Vacation

C amping is America's number one vacation. It's also one of the most cost-efficient ways to spend time traveling with your family. It's a great way to bond with your family—especially if your family is as busy as most families are these days. Moms and dads working, kids to soccer, rare dinners together—who has time to bond anymore? Camping is character building; it's all about teamwork and interdependence.

## Sleeping under the Stars

Camping is a great way to develop communication with your kids. Everyone has to work as a team to raise camp. Everyone gets to weigh in on where to make camp, and then where to pitch the tents. Everyone has responsibility, and that's how families learn to work together in their camp.

For example, one family member's job might be to gather firewood. Another family member might be tasked with shaking out sleeping bags in the morning. Someone else might be in charge of getting water from the nearby stream. Another person might be in charge of boiling it. Kids have to learn to entertain themselves without the help of handheld electronics, assuming that mom or dad has insisted such things be left at home. Instead of playing games, kids get to be participants in the game of life, one-on-one with nature.

## 🧳 Travel Tip

In addition to electronic games, leave cell phones at home, except for mom or dad's, which should be used only in the event of an emergency.

### The Cost of Camping and How You Save

To think that camping is less expensive than staying in modest lodging isn't the right way to think. Camping is all about amortization. Say a family of four spends $500 in gear including a tent and sleeping bags, and that the supplies last just five years (although camping supplies are known for being robust.) If that family spends vacations camping instead of staying in hotels, over the course of just two seasons or vacations, the gear will have paid for itself.

The other great thing about the cost of camping is how fun camping is in itself. When families go camping, part of the fun is pitching the tent, getting everything ready, fishing, and all the things that involve nature. There are no tickets to buy, no bar tab to pay. No restaurant gratuity, no valet charge. Usually there's just a reasonable campground fee of around $15 per vehicle.

Because campgrounds are near almost every attraction in the country, camping is a great vacation even if you want to venture away from nature for a night on the town.

### Common Camping Activities

Half of your time camping will be spent, well, camping! Setting up camp, cooking meals, sitting around the campfire and sleeping under the stars will take up a large portion of your time. The other half of your camping trip should include activities the family can do together. These are just a few activities that will likely be available for you and your family to enjoy while camping:

- Hiking
- Fishing
- Wildlife viewing
- Mountain biking
- Boating
- Swimming
- Canoeing

Many activities are easy and don't require much more than walking out of your tent, like hiking, for example, or biking if your family brings bicycles. Other activities like canoeing or kayaking and even fishing may require a guide and/or outfitter. Your campsite or a Chamber of Commerce near your campsite will have information on area activities and the outfitters who provide those services.

## Various Kinds of Campsites

Kampground of America (KOA) is a chain of campgrounds that provides the same level of amenities across the country. The campgrounds are clean, and provide a family-friendly atmosphere. At these and other such campgrounds, you're not necessarily in the woods all alone. You're camping next to your neighbor's tent and have access to a bathhouse; some locations also have a pool and tennis courts. You're still roughing it, but camping at a pre-established campground means you can probably get items you might have forgotten without having to leave the campground.

State parks are a whole different ball game. When camping in a state park, families may not have amenities such as bathhouses or showers. You may have to gather your own firewood. When camping at a state park, families will need to bring everything they need if they don't want to have to leave camp to retrieve something. Camping in state parks is not for beginners or families with small children. Many state parks have a plethora of campsites, but these are not equipped with creature comforts. Camping at most state park campgrounds is roughing it, much more so than at a prepared campground like KOA.

# Camping Dos and Don'ts

Your family camping trip will be memorable—but make sure it's memorable in the right way, for the fun you'll have, not the difficulties you encounter. Remember that while camping is a safe, fun way to vacation, everything involving the outdoors carries a certain level of risk. Anything can happen, but careful planning on your part is the best insurance that it won't.

## ≡ Fast Fact

Watch paths carefully and never, ever pick up a snake in the wild. Nonvenomous snakes and venomous snakes can be nearly impossible to tell apart. When you're far from medical care in a remote campground, snakebite from a venomous serpent can quickly become fatal. Wild animals also carry a multitude of diseases. They may look cute, but don't touch!

Prevent forest fires by cooking foods only in designated areas that are clearly marked. If you plan on cooking while you're camping, check your campground or state website for a list of places where you can cook. Never leave a fire burning. Smokers cause forest fires by dropping lit cigarettes on the ground and tossing them out car windows, so never throw a lit cigarette out of your window or try to extinguish a cigarette on the ground. Smokers are also at risk of serious cardiac and respiratory problems at high altitudes. Don't smoke while camping.

Medical experts agree that parents with babies under the age of six months should abstain from high ascents and activities like camping, even with a child in a backpack. Altitude sickness can include dizziness and headache, weakness, loss of appetite, and nausea as well as impaired judgment, and many campgrounds are in the mountains at high altitudes. Hyperventilating, or taking too many shallow, short breaths can cause you to pass out. If you plan to hike during your camping trip, get fit before you travel to avoid health risks like hyperventilation. When hiking to your campsite, stay on well-marked trails. Use caution in the winter months. Poor judgment is a mainstay of hypothermia because it affects the brain, so victims often don't realize they are slowly freezing to death.

Don't feed the animals. You can run into a veritable zoo of creatures when camping, including bears, snakes, raccoons, and opossums. To animals, it's natural to be outdoors, and when camping you are a guest in their home. Be gracious houseguests (don't litter or smoke), but steer clear of wild animals. Otherwise, the house special on the evening's menu could be you!

Don't drink the water. A cool mountain stream can contain water parasites like *Giardia* that will make your family, especially children and the elderly, extremely sick. Bring lots of bottled water.

## ≡ Fast Fact

Parasites like *Giardia* die after sixty seconds in boiling water. At high altitudes water boils at lower temperatures, but to be safe, boil mountain water for an additional minute and cool before drinking.

## Plan for Everything, Prepare for Anything

Part of your planning process needs to include making a lengthy list of everything you might need on your trip. This will include food, clothing, safety gear, first-aid kits, any prescriptions your family might be taking, and so on. Don't leave anything off your master list no matter how small or insignificant it might seem. Remember simple things like a can opener. All the soup in the world won't feed you when you're camping if you don't have a can opener. The following dos and don'ts list for camping is a good start, but the more you camp, the more you'll want to add to it and make it your own. Before long, your family will be expert campers.

- Don't plan anything too strenuous or complicated the first time you go camping.
- Do expect the unexpected.
- Don't go camping without making sure you know how to pitch your tent and use your gear.
- Do try a camping test run in your backyard or local park.
- Do pitch your tent and set up camp before you leave to go camping to make sure your equipment is working and you know how to use it.
- Do bring copious amounts of light, including LED battery-powered flashlights, lanterns, matches, and plumber's candles.
- Do keep matches and candles in sealed plastic containers to prevent them from getting wet.
- Do bring extra batteries and a flashlight for every family member.
- Do not use gasoline lanterns.
- Do learn how to build a fire before you leave for your camp.
- Do set up camp in the daytime. Try to avoid arriving at camp at dusk or in the dark.
- Do take a family field trip to your local fire department to learn the basics of building a fire and extinguishing it.
- Do bring many pairs of extra socks. Your socks will get dirty and wet, and will require changing frequently.

## Weather

Nothing could be worse on a camping trip than to get caught in a rainstorm. All of your belongings will get soaked and everyone will be miserable. If rain is in the forecast, be wise. Throughout the United States in the camping months of spring and summer, thunderstorms are likely anytime, but they are usually of high intensity and short duration. The key is in knowing when the rainy season occurs for the particular location where your family is interested in camping.

The remedy in a rainy camping situation is to plan rainy day camp activities before you leave home. Have a rainy day contingency plan. Research things to do that are indoors in case it rains. Also research and decide on your outdoor activities. Plan for easily switching activities depending on the weather. If you're camping and you see it's going to rain, step one should be to put anything you don't want to get wet in plastic bags, watertight storage containers, or in your family's car. Modern tents, even moderately priced tents, will have some level of water resistance. Technology for waterproofing camping materials has greatly improved and become more advanced, but nothing beats a solid roof over your heads when it's raining. There's nothing like a deluge of water to put a damper on everyone's spirits, so be sure to seal anything you can't get wet in waterproof containers before it begins to pour.

## Dining under the Stars

A huge part of the fun of camping is dining under the stars. Nothing compares to sitting around the campfire and breaking bread with your family as the soundtrack of nature echoes all around you. Camp food can be food you bring from home or catch in a nearby stream. Fishing is fun for the whole family and can provide delicious meals throughout your whole trip. It's important to know long before your trip what you plan to feed your family while camping, and to be sure you bring enough food to last until it's time to come home. That's where a solid menu plan comes in!

### Menu Planning

Rule number one—always bring an extra day's food for each person even if you think you've packed too much. Camping is an activity that will require reenergizing regularly. Campers need more calories to keep up with hiking and fishing or whatever activities the camping trip might offer.

One night at the family dinner long before you leave to go camping, and before you go shopping for your camping food, sit down with a pen and notebook. Use one page per day for your family's meal planning. Plan out breakfast, lunch, dinner, and snacks in meticulous detail. Don't leave anything to chance. Don't try to snack on the fly when you're camping. Snacking uncontrollably will sap your food supply much faster than you'll realize. When you list the amount of bottled water you think you'll need, double it. Be very liberal with the amount of water you bring along.

## ■ Travel Tip

Making s'mores and enjoying them with your family is one of the great pleasures of camping. A s'more is made of graham crackers, a piece of chocolate bar, and a marshmallow cooked over a fire for a sweet treat of a sandwich. This time-honored ritual doubles as the best dessert many families will ever have!

Unwanted dinner guests are camp party crashers. But there are lots of things you can do to keep wild animals from joining the party. In some national parks in many areas of the country bear safety is a huge issue. Foods should immediately be put away after consumption; any trash has to be completely sealed. Even leftover table scraps should never be left in camp. These attract wild animals on the prowl for food. Campsites that have problems with wildlife will usually have an animal-proof trash can in which you can deposit your trash. If you're camping on your own, put all food including scraps and leftovers in an airtight container in your vehicle.

# Gear Guide

Getting the right camping gear can be tricky. On one hand, you want lots of it. On the other hand, it's heavy, takes up a lot of space in a vehicle, and can be very complicated to erect. How do you know what to buy?

## Tents

A tent can have so many extra features it appears to rival a condo. Stay away from complicated tents. The one thing you want to avoid is misunderstanding how many people a tent truly sleeps. Be wary of slick marketing statements like "sleeps three people" or "three-person tent" because most tents are not as roomy as they appear on the packaging. Plus, until you get into a tent, you really won't know how many people it comfortably sleeps. Many outdoor stores have tents set up on display; try out a couple with as many of your family members as possible.

There are a few key things you need to look for in a tent. A rainfly, or tent covering, helps protect your tent from the elements. Another important consideration for the perfect family tent is height—you don't want a four-foot tent that you can barely stand up in. Don't shortchange yourself on height. For everyone to really be comfortable, a family of four needs a tent that sleeps six people. A good recommendation for a family tent is Cabela's Quad Pole Dome Tent. This tent has just four poles and sleeps five to six people (remember, that means four comfortably.) This tent has a center height of seventy-seven inches, or six feet five inches.

## Don't Forget Something to Sit On

Did you know one of the most important pieces of camping gear next to your tent and sleeping bag is a seat? Every family member will need a place to sit around the campfire or even in their tent if it's large enough. Seating is critical to how comfortable you'll be when camping, but bring chairs that are lightweight and fold easily.

When buying seats, think about how far it will be from your parked car to your campsite. When it comes to seats and most other camping equipment, less is more. Unless you plan to park directly beside your tent, carrying heavy camping equipment long distances is not fun.

### Sleeping Bags

A warm sleeping bag is essential. Even if your family is camping in the summer months, most mountain destinations or campgrounds next to bodies of water get chilly at night. Sleeping bags are made by comfort range of temperature.

## █ Travel Tip

A hammock is a great thing to bring on a camping trip. It's very relaxing and you can also sleep in it above ground. Some manufacturers also make hammocks with mosquito netting just for that purpose.

You don't have to spend a fortune to get a good sleeping bag. Choose one that feels most comfortable to you. Look for sleeping bags that are made for camping. Price them according to where you'll be camping and the seasons. If you know your family will only go camping in the warm summer months, choose a sleeping bag that's thick enough to keep you warm but won't be so hot you can't get any sleep.

### Cookware and Camping Stoves

Cookware and camping stoves are also necessary for a camping trip. Whether you catch fish or bring sandwiches, you may need to boil water or cook meals. That's part of the fun of camping.

Outfitters like Cabela's and Bass Pro Shops can provide one-stop shopping for family camping adventures. They also employ people who can assist you in making the right choices if you and your family are first-time campers.

There are many other cooking accessories and campsite gear options for your family. Visit a store near you that offers camping supplies. Don't buy anything until you're ready and you've decided what kind of camping trip you want to take.

## Keep the Bugs Away

Finally, one of the most important things you will ever need when camping is bug spray. There are many kinds to choose from, and be sure to ask your retail associate in the camping section about what would be best for your area.

Another great option for mosquito bite prevention is Therma-CELL. ThermaCELL is a mosquito repellent that runs on a butane cartridge and effectively produces a 225-square-foot "mosquito-free-zone" in just a few minutes. Mosquitoes hate it and steer clear, but ThermaCELL doesn't harm humans or animals such as household pets.

# Ready, Set, Camp! Prepared Campgrounds

Not every family who enjoys camping enjoys the work that goes into setting up camp. Some families want to show up for a camping vacation to find the camp has already been set up for them—tent and all. In America there are hundreds of camping outfitters who can provide ready-made campgrounds. These outfitting companies set up camp before guests arrive, and clean up and disassemble camp after they leave. Families can choose to be as much of a part of the assembly process as they like. Families new to camping might want to consider using a camping outfitter the first time they go camping to see what it's all about before they go out and buy all of the equipment they'll need to go camping by themselves. Guided camping trips often provide the following amenities:

- Campsite, including tents, sleeping bags, and cookware
- Trail maps and guided hikes or walks
- Boat launches if kayaking or canoeing is part of the camping trip
- Handicapped accessibility
- Clean water for drinking and cooking
- Trash removal
- Accommodations for pets
- Campfires
- Parking

Outdoor enthusiasts flock to places like Northwaters Wilderness Program in Ontario, Canada. This mega-outdoors camp program includes sea kayaking on Lake Superior with the aid of guides who help pitch tents and prepare gourmet meals. (*www.northwaters.com*)

Camping trips run by Colorado River & Trail Expeditions are widely popular with families and even executives who crave challenges but who don't have the time to plan and execute adventure excursions themselves. (*www.crateinc.com*)

Maine's Sebago Lake Family Campground is family-oriented. There are 101 campsites with eight cottages. Swimming, hiking, boating, and exploring the beauty of nature in glorious Maine is on the menu here. (*www.sebagolakecamping.com*)

The Miami Everglades Campground is about twenty-five miles from Miami near the massive mangrove and saw grass forests of the Everglades National Park. This campground features a recreation hall with full-service kitchen, tiki huts, air conditioned cabin camping that sleeps two to six people, sports, and kids' playground. Some of their campsites have patios and picnic tables, and the campground has volleyball and basketball courts. While families are here, they can also enjoy "pick your own" avocados and mangos. (*www.miamicamp.com*)

In North Carolina camping families can stay at Falling Waters Resort in something called a "yurt." Falling Waters is located above Fontana Lake in the Nantahala River Mountains. Their yurts are circular canvas structures that are the next best thing to sleeping on the ground in a tent. These modern buildings sport vinyl-laminated fabric wrapped around Douglas fir lattice walls with Mylar windows, a clear acrylic dome for star gazing, and Plexiglas and wooden doors. More commonly found in the West, these units offered by Falling Waters Resort are the first in Western North Carolina. This campground is conveniently situated near Wildwater's Nantahala Rafting Center, the Great Smoky Mountains Railroad, Fontana Lake, the Tsali Mountain Bike Trail, and the world-famous Appalachian Hiking Trail, so there are lots of activities for families to enjoy away from camp. (*www.falling watersresort.com*) Another easy getaway to a prepared campground in North Carolina is the Nantahala Outdoor Center (also called the NOC). The NOC is located adjacent to the Nantahala River, Appalachian Trail, and Great Smoky Mountains Railroad. A whitewater rafting and outfitter, the NOC has been taking families camping and rafting for thirty-five years. They were recognized as the "Number 1 Vacation with a Splash" by *Good Morning America.* (*www.noc.com*)

## Wilderness Camping

Wilderness camping is when you and your family battle the elements on your own—you bring and set up your own camping equipment, including the tent, campsite, and fire pit. Before you trek out into the wilds, erect a test camp at someplace like a state park close to home or even in your own backyard to be sure your equipment works properly and to ensure you're familiar with assembly and disassembly of your camp on your own.

## Great Wilderness Campground Locations

In the Ozarks State Park Campground in picturesque Arkansas, families will find unspeakably beautiful views and access to restrooms, showers, a trout dock and marina, great hiking trails, and picnicking spots. (*www.ozarkmountainregion.com*)

Pinyon Flats Campground is a National Park Service campground at the Great Sand Dunes in northeastern Colorado and features more than eighty sites. Restrooms with sinks, flush toilets, and dishwashing sink are available at this campground and each site comes with a fire grate and table for picnicking. Only one restroom is outfitted for winter, and each campsite can sleep six people including two tents and cars. Campsites are first come first serve, and the park doesn't accept reservations from individuals. The park does accept group reservations depending on the size of the group and equipment—RV, tent, multiple tents, etc. Nearby Medano Creek flows in spring depending on precipitation, and during these times the campground is far busier.

Pets are allowed but must be kept on leashes. However, the Great Sand Dunes are too hot on mid-summer days to walk pets on the dunes.

One unwelcome resident of the area is the black bear, so food must be stowed in the bear-proof boxes that are provided. You can bring a recreational vehicle, but there aren't any electrical, sewer, or water hookups at the campground.

The Boston Harbor Islands are only forty-five minutes from downtown Boston. Visitors arrive by ferry and can enjoy old roadways to historic foundations and forts, picnicking spots, and trails. There is no drinking water or food resources here, so be sure to bring lots of bottled water and food. Composting toilets are available but pets are not allowed. Grape Island, Bumpkin Island, and Lovells Island allow for overnight camping from June until September. Reservations for camping are necessary, and the park charges a nominal fee for overnight camping. The weather can be cooler than mainland temperatures. (*www.bostonharborislands.com*)

Jellystone Park Camp and Resort in Nashville, Tennessee, has a special host to welcome kids: Yogi Bear! Kids can also enjoy mini golf and pool activities and the campground features bath houses, laundry, game room, and arts and crafts. Surrounding Nashville includes hundreds of fun tourist sites all within a short drive from the campground. (*www.nashvillejellystone.com*)

Tally Lake Campground is located in the Flathead National Forest in the northwest corner of spectacular Montana. It includes basic facilities like water, restrooms, and dedicated campsites. Lake and stream fishing are both fun family activities that can be complimented with swimming, canoeing, and, of course, long hikes among some of America's most beautiful nature trails. Picnic tables and fire pits are available and the campgrounds do allow pets.

Neighboring Glacier National Park Campgrounds offers ten main campgrounds. Glacier National Park includes arguably some of the most memorable vistas on earth, so it's no surprise the campgrounds fill up with families eager to experience the park. Make reservations for these campgrounds long in advance of when you plan to visit. For families who don't have reservations, the campgrounds have kiosks near the entrance that detail available campsites. Each campsite can comfortably sleep eight people and accommodate two cars per campsite. Most of the campgrounds at Glacier National Park Campgrounds have water for drinking and restrooms. No pets are allowed on the trails at Glacier National Park Campground, but they are allowed in the campground provided they remain on a leash, in a cage, or in a vehicle. (*www.nps.gov/glac*)

Southwest Colorado's Mesa Verde National Park in Cortez is a fantastic place to camp for family bonding and a hands-on history lesson! Cliff dwellings of the Ancestral Puebloans are located here and have been preserved for generations to enjoy and learn from. The Puebloans were an ancient civilization that settled Mesa Verde. Visitors can get camping information from the Mesa Verde

National Park (*www.nps.gov/meve*) and from Cortez itself. (*www .cortezchamber.com*)

On the Blue Ridge Parkway in the North Carolina Mountains, visitors can camp along the parkway at any of nine campgrounds with restrooms, drinking water, picnic tables, and grills. Some campgrounds are only open from late spring to early fall for foliage, which is when the leaves change during the fall season. Other campgrounds are open year round. (*www.blueridgeparkway.org*)

### Wilderness Camping Tips

It's hard to set up a tent in the dark—you never know what you're setting it up on top of, and you may assemble it incorrectly because you can't see what you're doing. Allow plenty of time to set up your camp before darkness.

Depending on where you're camping, it may be a good idea to bring some type of defense. This might include a large knife, baseball bat, or other such device that can double as a weapon. In Yellowstone for example, you can obtain bear pepper spray.

## 💼 Travel Tip

Snakes want to be left alone. But they can get aggressive when someone stands on them or when they feel threatened. Snakebite kits may be available for purchase at your local sporting goods store like Bass Pro Shop or Cabela's.

Brings flares in case you get lost, and in an emergency, flares can be used to start a fire. If you're planning on camping in the wilds of Alaska or the Rocky Mountain states, consider purchasing a firearm. In the past several years people have been attacked by wildlife.

# CHAPTER 14

# Adventure Travel

A dventure is everywhere. It may seem to come dressed in exotic locales under the cover of rain forests or African sunsets. But adventure is many colors and wears many hats. There are so many ways to find adventure, and many opportunities for adventure can even be found in your own backyard. Often the beauty of nearby nature provides all the adventure you'll need, and you don't have to traverse the globe to find it.

## Finding Adventure on a Budget

Adventure doesn't have to be expensive, but it often is. You can find adventure without it costing too much, but a little research on your part will be required. Where you live has a lot to do with the number of adventure destinations that are close by.

If you live near the sea, look into wildlife watching. Whale watching has become one of America's favorite pastimes—best of all, it's free unless you go on a tour boat and even then, the fee is reasonable. Hiking can be very adventurous especially if you live near a mountainous place.

Camping is always an adventure—between making your campfire and catching dinner in a nearby stream, camping is probably one of the most exciting and bonding experiences a family can have. If your family has never been camping together because you think it's too adventurous, consider this: camping is America's number one recreational activity. It can't be too difficult or so many people wouldn't love it.

## Saving for Adventurous Activities

Think about activities and budget accordingly. If vacation money is tight, you may have to prolong a vacation to have the time to set aside enough money to partake of certain activities, but they are worth the wait. Many types of adventurous activities seem expensive. But when you weigh your options, you're likely to find they are worth it.

When you think about a helicopter tour of the Grand Canyon costing $150 or more per person, consider the value of watching your children see one of the planet's most incredible sights, and what that will mean to them for the rest of their lives. Steering clear of expensive restaurants for a month can help you save enough money to be able to afford such a tour.

# Zip Lining

Years ago zip lining used to be considered a radical adventure activity, suspended above tropical canopies in faraway, exotic places. Now zip lines have sprouted up all over the place, and riding one is definitely something to try at least once in your lifetime. A zip line is an apparatus consisting of a cable mounted on an incline with a pulley attached. A strapped seat is often attached to the pulley and people sit in it to "zip" down the line to the other side where there is usually a tree house or other such platform. Powered by gravity, riders fling from one end of the zip line to the other, encountering unforgettable views along the way. The only difficult part of zip lining is the climb you may have to endure to get to the starting point at the top of a tall tree or platform. It's also an experience that builds character and promotes courage. If you can conquer your fears in this process, zip lining can be more than just memorable—it can be life-altering.

## The Original Canopy Tour

The Original Canopy Tour Company (*www.canopytour.com*) offers zip lining canopy tours all over the world. It's a good place to start if your adventure travel vacation includes zip lining. More than a million people have zip lined with this company, which began its first tour in lush Costa Rica.

Costa Rica is famous for its zip line tours through a canopy of breathtaking rain forests that showcase hundreds of plants and animals. The Original Canopy Tour Company has a tour in Drake Bay, which is in the Osa Peninsula adjacent to Corcovado National Park. This area is home to one of the last untouched rainforests of its size in Costa Rica. The zip line tour begins as you climb to the top of the tower onto the first platform. Once you ascend, you might think the view from the platform is so beautiful you don't even want to zip line. But you'd be wrong—this platform is only one of several stops on your zip lining experience. The first platform consists of a large viewing station approximately 40 feet above ground. Traverse number one zips you down 200 feet to the next tree, which has several platforms at varying levels. You then zip to the third tree, which has about a 30 foot walkway between two humongous trees. Here you are about 85 feet above ground. It's an experience you and your family will never forget.

## Domestic Zip Line Adventures

In beautiful Colorado, you can have a zip line experience practically all year long. Thanks to the agreeable climate in Salida, Colorado, Captain Zip Line Adventure Tours welcomes families from ages eight to eighty. On Captain Zip Line's adventure, guests traverse more than 2,000 feet on seven cables 150 feet over the magnificent Lost Canyon. Cliff formations and a whole host of wildlife are part of the view. (*www.captainzipline.com*)

New Hampshire's Sky Rider Treetop Canopy Tour was the first treetop canopy tour in New England. This zip line takes zip liners through pine, hemlock, oak, beech, and birch trees. Along the way, you can often see the many kinds of wildlife that live in the trees. There are six zip lines from 80 to 600 feet long. A 60-foot-high-by-75-foot-long suspension bridge allows visitors to experience the majestic Barron Gorge. Sky Rider's famous "Zip #7" is a thirty-five-mile-per-hour free-fall (optional, of course!) At Sky Rider, guests can also do dual zip lines. Treewalk Village provides views of the western White Mountains. After crossing the Burma bridges, a 1,200-foot zip line awaits. At Sky Rider, guests must be age ten or older and between 70 and 240 pounds to partake of the Treetop Canopy Tour and Sky Rider Tour. (*www.visit-newhampshire.com*)

# Helicopter Tours

A helicopter tour is one of the best ways to see a city or natural attraction. The perspective is so unique, that once you take a helicopter tour, you might find yourself to be somewhat alien to tours where your feet touch the ground.

## Grand Canyon Helicopter Tours

The Grand Canyon is one of the best places to take a helicopter tour. Imperial Helicopter Tours takes visitors on an air tour of the North Canyon with views of the Painted Desert and Colorado River. The tour lasts about forty-five minutes. Visit *www.grand canyon.com/grandcanyonhelicoptertours.html* to learn more.

Grand Canyon Helicopter & Sunset Ranch Adventure has the added benefit of culminating at the one-million-acre Grand Canyon West Ranch. Families then pile into a horse-drawn wagon for a picturesque ride through a Joshua tree forest after which you arrive at a Ranch House for dinner and Western-style cowboy entertainment by campfire (*www.heliusa.com*)

## ≡ Fast Fact

The Hoover Dam Helicopter Tour is another helicopter tour of the Grand Canyon. The tour showcases the western part of the Grand Canyon West, the Hoover Dam, and Lake Mead. This helicopter tour might be more expensive than the previous tour, but encompasses more sights. See *www.grandcanyontourcompany.com* for more information.

### Helicopter Tours of Hawaii

Paradise Copters wows guests with Hilo's Fire and Falls Adventure and the Best of O'ahu. Hilo's Fire and Falls Adventure is a forty-five-minute narrated question-and-answer tour via two-way communication with the pilot and passengers. The tour consists of an active volcano, molten lava, tropical rainforests, and majestic waterfalls. Every seat is by a window so everyone gets a bird's-eye view of the tropical rainforests of Puna, Hilo Harbor, and the Waterfalls of North Hilo.

The Best of O'ahu includes a look at the thousand-foot "Sacred Falls" and Ko'olau Mountains, along with the famed North Shore surf breaks. Breathtaking Kaneohe Bay is also on the menu. (*www.paradisecopters.com*)

### Manhattan Sky Helicopter Tour

Manhattan Sky Helicopter Tour gets visitors up close and personal with the capital city of the world—Manhattan. No other way of seeing the city is like this. Sights you'll see by helicopter include the Empire State Building, Statue of Liberty, Ellis Island, Brooklyn Bridge, United Nations, and Central Park among others. On the Manhattan Sky Helicopter Tour, kids two and under can ride free on the lap of paying adults. (*www.allnew yorktours.com*)

### Niagara Falls Helicopter Tour

A Niagara Falls helicopter tour is one your family won't want to miss. And Niagara Helicopters is especially family-friendly. They cater especially to families with children. Niagara Helicopters features "Kids Zone" whereby kids can complete an interactive learning tool before flying, and they have a separate viewing area for kids who just want to see helicopters take off and land.

Every minute on these tours brings a breathtaking view of the majesty of the falls. The tour also points out historic landmarks and wine country before returning to the ground. (*www.niagara-helicopters.com*)

# Houseboating

If you've ever wanted to enjoy a truly unique adventure on the water, consider taking your family houseboating. This popular vacation may not be on everyone's radar, but it ranks just as high for adventure as the rest of its water counterparts. It's always close to many outdoor activities—simply dock your houseboat at a nearby island and go hiking, lay out on the beach, play Frisbee, or build a campfire and sleep under the stars. You'll have everything you need on your houseboat.

### Dining on Your Houseboat Vacation

One of the best things about houseboating is the dining. Sure, you'll need to go grocery shopping for the things you can't catch in the water. But if your family loves fresh seafood, you'll be able to enjoy the freshest meals caught from your own houseboat. On houseboat vacations, fishing is a wonderful family activity that can result in more than just a fun afternoon. From the comfort of your houseboat, you can catch what you eat, and eat what you catch.

You'll need to familiarize yourself with the types of fish available where you're vacationing, which fish are in season, how to recognize them, and how to clean them for cooking. A great

resource for learning all about catching and eating fresh
United States Fish and Wildlife Service, part of the Dep
the Interior. The Fish and Wildlife Service has a website at *www*
*.fws.gov* that details all of this information. Each state will have different types of fish and a list of regulations for fishing for them.
Florida, for example, has a website full of information to help experienced and novice fishermen at *www.myfwc.com*.

## Houseboat Rentals

One of the biggest perks to renting a houseboat for your family
vacation is the opportunity to sleep on the water. The term "sleep
like a baby" applies to the experience, plus you'll be able to wake
up to unforgettable sunrises and doze off to breathtaking sunsets.

## ☂ Rainy Day Fun

The sound of the rain on the roof of a houseboat is so relaxing that
on a houseboat vacation, you might just pray for rain. The sound of
the rain combined with sleeping on the water creates a nap like none
other. Be sure to take full advantage.

Marina life is also part of the fun on houseboat vacations.
Wherever you rent your houseboat is likely to have a thriving
marina. Look there for fresh seafood restaurants and supply stores.
When you rent a houseboat, you'll need to decide whether to rent
a mobile houseboat or moored houseboat. The marina in the area
you'll be traveling to will be able to help you with this decision,
but for families looking for a true houseboat adventure, renting a
mobile or un-moored houseboat is the more attractive option. A
mobile houseboat is one that allows you to change locations on
the water, explore scenery, and try a variety of activities. Nonmotorized houseboats are moored to someone's permanent home
and don't allow for the freedom associated with houseboating.

If you're new to the idea of houseboating, you'll need to familiarize yourself with areas that provide houseboat rentals and see if any are within your travel comfort zone and budget. Some houseboats come with personal watercraft available for rent such as jet ski or dingy for getting to and from islands in shallow waters. Two great resources to get you started are *www.houseboating.org* and *www.all-about-houseboats.com.* Here you'll find multiple resources on houseboat rentals, areas, and options for every budget.

## Popular Houseboating Locations

There are several houseboating lakes in North America. Each is as unique as the houseboats available to rent. Details and boat rental information at each of the following lakes can be found on the Houseboating.org website.

Lake Powell is in the western United States in southern Utah. The lake water is flanked by red cliffs, impressive scenery, and almost 2,000 miles of coastline for exploration. There are three marinas at Lake Powell.

Trinity Lake on the west coast in northern California is great for fishing families who love trout and salmon. Trinity Lake is bordered by trees, sandy beaches, and private coves. There is one marina at Trinity Lake.

Oregon's Lake Billy Chinook sits between extraordinary canyon walls and is fed by three rivers. This lake is deep and filled with bull trout and kokanee salmon. There is one houseboat marina along a shoreline of more than seventy miles.

Lake Koocanusa in Montana and British Columbia is surrounded by the majesty of the mountains. Here families could virtually go for days without seeing another soul. This is natural solitude at its best and includes sandy beaches, forests, and alpine wildlife. There is one marina along Lake Koocanusa's 250 miles of shoreline.

Kentucky Lake in Kentucky is engulfed in woods and coves. Kentucky Lake provides a nearly endless array of adventures thanks to a whopping 2,400 miles of shoreline. Despite its size, Kentucky Lake has just one houseboat marina.

Bull Shoals Lake in the mighty Ozarks in Arkansas and Missouri is one of America's clearest lakes thanks to the mountain terrain that juts up around the entire lake. The scenery here is powerful thanks to the Ozark Mountains that loom over the lake from almost every viewpoint. There is one houseboat marina along the more than 1,000 miles of shoreline on Bull Shoals Lake.

## Learning to Sail

Another form of boating that families are going crazy over is sailing, and you don't even need your own boat to do it. Learn-to-sail adventures are on the rise thanks to programs that includes kids for free with two paying adults. Sailing often requires more than just one person, and that means it's an experience whereby family members must work together to learn the craft. Learning to sail is an incredible bonding experience that families will remember and learn from long after they leave the boat.

### ≡ Fast Fact

Learning to sail can include classroom and on-the-water experiences. Regardless of whether or not your family has ever sailed, each family member will have the opportunity to learn the basics they need to take the helm. Sailing is fun—and just learning how to sail is part of the fun.

Companies like Offshore Sailing (*www.offshoresailing.com*) offer "Learn to Sail" vacations that can include kids in the package for free with two paying adults. This is a great value, since learning to sail is the activity. Offshore Sailing offers "Learn to Sail" vacations leaving from the following ports:

- Captiva Island, Florida
- Ft. Myers Beach, Florida
- The Florida Keys
- St. Petersburg, Florida
- British Virgin Islands
- Chelsea Piers, New York City
- Jersey City, New Jersey
- St. Michaels, Maryland

## U.S. Space and Rocket Center

Outer space may be the final frontier, but at the U.S. Space and Rocket Center, families can get a glimpse of what it would be like to be in outer space if only for a moment. Home to Space Camp, Aviation Challenge, and X-Camp, U.S. Space and Rocket Center offers the Spacedome Theater, Rocket Park, and Education Training Center, which is home to the Educator Resource Center for NASA.

There is so much to experience at the U.S. Space and Rocket Center. The G-Force Accelerator gives guests an idea of what it would feel like to blast off into outer space. The Kids Cosmos Energy Depletion Zone allows kids (and perhaps future astronauts) to creep through the Space Station. The Apollo Cockpit Trainer is a Command Service Module Apollo mission simulator. And the Discovery Theater is fun for all ages. Discovery Theater shows include interactive demonstrations and live presentations. Kids won't want to miss Mars Climbing Wall at the Mars Mission attraction.

In the museum, families can explore original Mercury and Gemini capsule trainers, the Apollo 16 capsule, Casper, and a life-size replica of the Apollo 11 Saturn V. Kids five and under are admitted free of charge. One-day tours are available and each package includes entry into the Museum, Shuttle Park, Rocket Park, and public simulators. Space Camp simulators are in addition to package prices. Visit *www.spacecamp.com* for more information.

# Survival Schools

What if your family was suddenly stranded in the wild? Would you have what it takes to survive? You and your family can learn skills to make sure you could survive at one of many family-friendly survival schools. Survival school activities include learning about building a shelter, finding and purifying water to drink, making fire, and becoming adept at wilderness survival.

The Mountain Shepherd Wilderness Survival School in Catawba, Virginia, is a great place where parents can learn with their children what they need to know about surviving in the wilderness. At Mountain Shepherd Wilderness Survival School curriculum focuses on seven survival priorities:

- Having a positive attitude
- First aid in the wilderness
- Shelter
- Making fire
- Signaling
- Gathering food
- Finding and preparing water

## ≡ Fast Fact

Mountain Shepherd Wilderness Survival School offers a "Wild Comforts" course in which children ages ten to seventeen and a parent learn how to be safe in the woods, cope with wilderness emergencies, develop camping skills (including cooking in the wilderness), and have fun as a family in the outdoors.

Before families complete the Wilderness College, the parent and child students also learn about knots and lashings, how to read a map, and how to use a compass. The Mountain Shepherd Wilderness Survival School offers beginning courses that teach life-saving wilderness skills. But even more importantly, the courses inspire confidence and help students of all ages overcome fears and learn about nature. Go to *www.MountainShepherd .com* to learn more.

# CHAPTER 15

# All-Inclusive Resorts
# and Cruises

One of the best things about all-inclusive resorts is not having to dip into your wallet while you're there. And that's the whole point! How many times have you been at the beach and had to schlep your purse or wallet to pay for a snack or beverage? It's very freeing to go on vacation, lock your valuables and wallet in a safe, and be done with them until you're ready to return home. At many all-inclusive resorts, all you need is a bracelet and you're good to go for the duration of your stay. On cruises, accommodations vary, as does the dining. The ship itself is an attraction—a floating, fully autonomous amusement bastion.

## Planning Your All-Inclusive Resort Vacation

All-inclusive resort packages can vary but most include lodging, drinks, dining, entertainment (usually provided at night), facilities like swimming pools and playgrounds, and nonelectric or nonmotorized water sports.

Gratuities should also be included in your package—after all, isn't that the point of being able to leave your wallet in the room? Many all-inclusive resorts also offer packages that cover airfare and transfers to and from the property. Other packages can include off-site and on-site activities such as scuba diving or a tour of nearby ruins.

Dining at all-inclusive resorts can be an adventure of the best and worst kind. All-inclusive resorts will feed you 'til you want to burst. The dining at many resorts is excessive, but it ensures your family won't ever be hungry. The quality of the dining, however, can vary wildly. When you're researching an all-inclusive resort, review resort menus before you book. Also be sure to check dining times. Some resorts offer dining at all hours, while others have set meal times.

If you decide to venture off property during your vacation, to visit a local town, for example, be sure your resort knows where you are. Ask them to provide transportation to and from your off-property destination. Find out before you leave the resort how late resort transportation can pick you up.

## ■ Travel Tip

If your resort cannot provide transportation, ask them to call a reputable cab company for you and tell the driver where to take you. In countries such as Mexico, where English is not the first language, a language barrier can mean high fares or worse if you wind up in the wrong neighborhood.

When dining on resort property, you should be safe from parasites and other creepy crawlies that may be found in undercooked food and can make you and your family very sick. Guests who leave a resort to dine in a nearby town should make sure the food they consume is thoroughly cooked and served in a clean restaurant. A hole in the wall is fine—in fact, such places often have the best food. Just be sure the place looks clean and the food is thoroughly cooked.

Never ingest food cooked on household barbeques on the street. If you eat such foods, chances are you'll be fine, but why risk your health on vacation for a couple of ribs? Dining on vacation is part of the fun. Just be smart about what you put in your mouth, and bon appétit!

# Mexico, Costa Rica, and the Dominican Republic

Dreams Cancun Resort and Spa in Cancun is surrounded on all but one side by the Caribbean Sea. Like its resort cousins all over the Caribbean, Dreams is beautiful and relaxing. Dreams goes out of its way to welcome kids, though, and that means a lot when you're traveling with them. The Explorer's Club is for kids aged three to twelve and includes science and nature projects. The Club also includes a weekly beach camping adventure. Also a popular attraction at Dreams is the dolphinarium, a lagoon that's home to several dolphins. You can even book a "dolphin view" room. Guests can also register for the Dolphin Experience, which allows them to swim with the dolphins. (*www.dreams resorts.com*)

Paradisus Resorts is a luxury all-inclusive resort chain that has four properties: Costa Rica, Mexico, and two in the Dominican Republic. The all-inclusive price includes lodging, all food, and beverages—and that even includes room service! Many of the resort chains' premium activities like golf and scuba are also included. Paradisus Resorts also feature a Family Concierge—a trip planner with kids and families in mind. Here's a hint: turn-down service for this crowd includes milk and cookies. (*www.paradisus.com*)

Breezes Puerto Plata in the Dominican Republic offers kids-stay-free and single-parent promotions. These packages include lodging of course, meals, and SuperSnacks. In addition, families really can travel here stress free, since the resort offers packages that include cocktails, land and water sports activities with equipment and instruction, and daily scuba dives. Kid's Club activities and other recreational activities along with airport transfers are all included and no tipping is allowed. As if that wasn't enough to tempt you, the resort's Lighthouse Spa is the grandest in the Dominican Republic.

## St. Lucia, St. Kitts, and Antigua

Families can't wait to arrive in beautiful St. Lucia at the Coconut Bay Beach Resort & Spa. Parents know the resort was *Caribbean Travel & Life* magazine's 2007 Reader's Choice for Best Large Hotel. But kids could care less about the hotel. They know Coconut Bay Beach Resort has the island's largest water park and a paintball facility. "Splash" is the resort's own tropical playground, where kids have a whopping eighty-five acres to play around in. The resort also features the CocoLand Kidz Klub. Parents love the Harmony side of the resort where hammocks, spa, and adults-only pool whisks away their cares. Kids ages two to thirteen can stay free at Coconut Bay Beach Resort, and the resort also offers a single-parent promotion that waives single supplements. (*www .cbayresort.com*)

Kitts is for kids at the St. Kitts Marriott Resort & The Royal Beach Casino. The four-star resort features eight restaurants, casino, spa, and championship golf along with the requisite fitness center. The real family attraction here is the teen game room and Kid's Club. When the family goes sightseeing together, a rainforest tour or visiting the Monkey Sanctuary at the Lodge Great House is just the ticket. The Royal St. Kitts Golf Club offers a "Kids Golf-4-Free" program after 3 P.M. whereby children accompanied by a paying adult play free. (*www.marriott.com*)

Jolly Beach Resort in colorful, glorious Antigua has daily activities for families to enjoy. The Jolly Beach Resort goes above and beyond to keep kids busy, engaged, and having fun. Nightly entertainment keeps parents rocking until bedtime. The Jolly Kidz Club features a jam-packed listing of games and activities. The Jolly Teenz Club is for teens thirteen to sixteen, the Kidz Soirée teaches children about fine dining, and the Spa for Kidz and Teenz offers age-appropriate spa services. (*www .jollybeachresort.com*)

# Jamaica, Aruba, and the Turks and Caicos

FDR Holidays Pebbles resort in Jamaica (*www.fdrholidays.com/ Pebbles*) is like the vacation version of Santa Claus. This resort has the requisite white sand beaches, great food, and amazing views, and it promises to deliver a "worry-free, cashless vacation." But what Pebbles does that most other resorts do not is provide a vacation nanny for every arriving family. Talk about free time for parents! The nanny, who is on duty during the day, can also babysit in the evening at a rate of just $4 an hour. Plus, teens and preteens get to do their own things (supervised, of course) with field trips including activities like camping, fishing, sailing, windsurfing, hiking, and mountain biking. Pebbles also encourages multigenerational travel by offering packages that allow families to bring grandparents on vacation for free deals. There are even families-fly-free packages to choose from.

## ≡ Fast Fact

Pebbles is a thirty-minute ride east of Montego Bay at the heart of Jamaica's historic north coast in New Court, Trelawny. Nestled between the beautiful Caribbean and the picturesque green mountains, it offers plenty of opportunity for all sorts of family adventures.

Beaches Resorts has long been known to attract families for their multitude of family-friendly activities and programs dedicated just to families. Beaches has properties in Jamaica and the Turks and Caicos. They offer three family-oriented properties in Jamaica and another in the Turks and Caicos. What makes these resorts great for families, especially families with young children, is their exclusive deal with Sesame Street, which allows kids to eat and play with the their favorite *Sesame Street* characters. Children can participate in Crayola Art camps and play at the large water parks the resorts have built just for kids. There are kids-only pools and day camps that are managed by certified nannies. The resort also has family suites that can sleep as many as five people. The teen disco helps keep teens busy at night so parents can enjoy an evening on their own. (*www.beaches.com*)

## Cruises—The Basics

Depending on the package you choose, an all-inclusive cruise should include lodging, any meals or snacks, and mealtime beverages. The package should also include ship facilities, entertainment, and any activities you enjoy while on board, though spas are a typical exception to that rule and are usually extra. Transportation to and from the ship for all ports of call should be covered in your package. While you're off the ship you're likely to have to pay for any beverages, including alcoholic beverages, and food you consume. Your gratuities will also be at your expense as will other shore excursions. Airfare and transfers to and from the airport and ship can also be your responsibility unless otherwise specified on your package in advance.

Cruises are known for their food and beverage service. Passengers have lots of dining choices on cruises, including in-room dining, and even dining by assigned table. Head waiters handle seating. Dining "freestyle" requires reservations or often waiting in line. Most cruises offer a buffet at every meal and most dinners are casual dress.

Upgrades are rare these days. Repeat customers and customers who reserve earlier usually get priority when it comes to upgrades.

## Top Cruises for the Money

Carnival's Ecstasy Cruise goes from Los Angeles to Baja, Mexico, for four days. The food is great and the cabins on this cruise are actually roomy. The ship has the usual suspects of a gym and spa and entertainment promenade. Kids are not just welcome; the cruise provides many supervised activities for them to enjoy, including dinner parties by the pool. (*www.carnival.com*)

Celebrity's Horizon Cruises leave from Philadelphia or Norfolk, Virginia, and travel to Bermuda on a seven-night cruise. This line is known for service, and the cruise features gourmet cuisine, spa, and casino along with live entertainment. The Parents Night Out program is just what it implies, free time without the kids. Kids can enjoy pizza parties, Summer Stock Theater, and magic shows while parents kick up their heels. (*www.celebrity cruises.com*)

One of the best cruises a family can take together is a cruise around Alaska. The *Sikumi* is a wonderful cruise ship that only sleeps twelve people, but it is a family vacation that your family will remember forever. Families choose destinations, the cruise length, and the activities in which they engage. Because *Sikumi* is a small boat, passengers get access to many areas of the Alaskan shoreline and coves that the giant cruise ships can't reach. Passengers can enjoy fishing, kayaking, and hiking among other activities on these fun family cruises. (*www.sikumi.com*)

## ≡ Fast Fact

On Royal Caribbean cruises to Alaska, passengers can enjoy the sea cruise and spend some time on land touring waterfalls and rain forests. Passengers can even make arrangements to tour the Juneau Ice Field by helicopter or go dogsledding. The cruise lasts for nine to thirteen nights. (*www.royalcaribbean.com*) On Royal Caribbean's Destinations cruises, there are many activities to enjoy on land: climbing Jamaica's Dunn's River Falls, mountain biking in Costa Rican rain forests, or diving 800 feet below sea level in a research submarine. A tour of the Mayan pyramids is also on the list. (*www .royalcaribbean.com*)

# Cruises Kids Love

It's no surprise that Disney Magic and Disney Wonder cruises are popular with kids. Nearly a whole deck on these cruises is dedicated to kid-friendly activities. They are age specific with additional activities available for teens. In fact, teenagers get their own clubhouse at the top of the ship! From Goofy's Detective School to Mexican cooking lessons held on cruises to Mexico, only Disney could facilitate so much family fun for kids. Nightly entertainment is also family oriented and includes contests and other ways for families to participate. An on-site nursery is provided for babies aged three months and up.

## 💼 Travel Tip

Disney also offers seven-night land-and-sea packages that include accommodations before the cruise at one of the Walt Disney World resorts. These packages include unlimited admission to Disney theme parks, water parks, Downtown Disney, DisneyQuest Indoor Interactive Theme Park, and Disney's Wide World of Sports Complex.

As another great amenity, Disney offers a number of kids clubs. The Oceaneer Club is for kids aged three to seven and is designed to look like Captain Hook's ship. The Oceaneer Lab, for kids aged eight to twelve, focuses on the universe in a lab setting and an interactive play area. Add live shows and Disney characters who are liable to interact with kids at any given moment to the mix, and Disney Cruises and all inclusive resorts for traveling families just can't be beat. (*www.disney.com*)

It's the massive waterslides, outside movie nights, and video game arcades that make Carnival Liberty and Carnival Freedom cruises such a hit with kids. Activities are divided into five different age groups so no one gets bored, and a softer play area and wading pool are on deck for the tiny ones. (*www.carnival.com*)

Norwegian Pearl and Norwegian Gem cruises travel to Alaska, the Bahamas, Bermuda, Canada, Central America, and South America. These floating palaces even have bowling alleys. Youth activities on these cruises are led by youth counselors. The boats also have "teen clubs," each with its own juice bar. (*www.ncl.com*)

# CHAPTER 16

# Affordable Island Destinations

It's hard to justify vacationing in the islands when there's so much to do at home and so many places to go. And when you think of white sand beaches, water sports, and luxury lodging, it's hard to believe a trip to the islands is possible on a budget. Even the word "islands" is an all-encompassing term many travelers use to describe island destinations anywhere in the Caribbean, Mexico, South Pacific, Hawaii, and similar such glorious places. The islands have a heartbeat all their own, and many island vacations are affordable!

## Antigua

Ahhh, Antigua. Where the beaches are like heaven and the sea goes on forever. Among the greenest trees set against the ocean and white sand, it's practically impossible to have a care in the world when you're here. Antigua is a perfect place to have a family holiday. Family-friendly sites are many here, and the lodging and dining options are stellar. And in some places it seems you can walk the length of a football field before the Caribbean water is too deep to stand.

Antigua is the main island in the country of Antigua and Barbuda, located in the West Indies in the Caribbean. Touring ancient sugar mills is on the calendar one day, and swimming with sting rays is next on the list. Scuba diving is a favorite sport and sailing is a religion here.

History abounds at colorful places like Nelson's Dockyard. Nelson's Dockyard was built around 1725 and functioned as the maintenance home for Royal Naval warships. After restoration in 1951, the dockyard was renamed in honor of Admiral Horatio Nelson. This busy tourist attraction and yacht marina welcomes thousands of people in April for Antigua's sailing week. During sailing week, visitors can see some of the finest yacht racing in the islands and celebrate afterwards at Lord Nelson's Ball. (*www .antiguamuseums.org/nelsonsdockyard.htm*)

## Travel Tip

Another wonderful family attraction is sunset at Shirley Heights. Shirley Heights is not to be missed. The breathtaking view cascades over English Harbour. On Friday nights Shirley Heights is a fun party with barbecue and rum and is miles away from cubicles and yard work. (*www.shirleyheightslookout.com*)

Antigua is a very special place that has a rhythm all its own. Its beaches and lush mountain landscape make it one of most beautiful islands in the Caribbean.

### Where to Stay in Antigua

Rex Resorts at Halcyon Cove features a wonderful kids program called Rexplorers. It's available to kids ages four to twelve Monday through Friday except public holidays. When parents check in, they just alert the receptionist of their intention to register their child in the Rexplorers program. The property also has an outside play area where children can play supervised by mom and dad. The property arranges babysitting services with local sitters with twenty-four-hours notice. Visit *www.rexresorts.com* for more information.

The St. James Club is well known for an award winning Kidz Club. Kids ages four to eleven get to do creative activities that have a Caribbean touch, such as treasure hunts and crab races. Making masks and finger-painting are also part of the fun. The counselors are experienced and take children in the Kidz Club on nature walks, swimming, and even snorkeling. And of course just playing on the beach is always fun! The St. James Club Kidz Club facility has a large, fenced-in play yard. The Kidz Club doesn't close until 10 P.M. daily so moms and dads can stay out for a romantic dinner. The Kidz Club also shows a film with dinner. Parents can arrange for in-room babysitting as well for an additional fee. (*www.stjamesclubantigua.com*)

Jolly Beach Resort in colorful, glorious Antigua has daily activities for families to enjoy. Their Kidz Club features a jam-packed listing of games and activities to keep children busy by day, and nightly entertainment keeps parents rocking until bedtime. All-inclusive rates include accommodations, all meals, snacks and afternoon tea, house-brand beverages, land and water sports, Jolly Kidz and Teenz Clubs, evening entertainment, and all taxes and service charges.

## ≡ Fast Fact

Jolly Beach Resort has a special club just for teenagers. The Jolly Teenz Club is just for teens thirteen through sixteen years old. By day the Jolly Teenz Club includes games, flat-screen televisions, and Wii and Xbox video games. At night, the Club becomes a Dream Room with pizza, movies, and disco. The teens are also invited to participate in Bonfire Night, Antiguan Treasure Hunt, Moonlight Scavenger Hunt, and Mystery Night.

Of special note is the Jolly Beach Resort's Kidz Soirée. This off-the-beaten-path activity is for kids who like to eat and parents who like good manners. At the Kidz Soirée children have dinner at

Ristorante Bocciolo. While they're dining, restaurant management, servers, and the chef instruct the kids on proper dining etiquette. For the Kidz Soirée, children are asked to make their own reservation and dress well for dinner. P.S. . . . no parents are allowed at the Kidz Soirée! See *www.jollybeachresort.com*.

# Grand Cayman

A short plane ride south of Miami will land you in what many tourists have called the scuba diving capital of the world. It's no wonder, since Cayman's lack of rivers is responsible for the clarity of the clear blue waters. Located in the western Caribbean, Cayman is made up of three small islands. But big things come in small packages, and Grand Cayman is just that—grand!

Grand Cayman features world-renowned diving and snorkeling thanks to many reefs and walls, some of which people can access by swimming from the shoreline. In Grand Cayman if you don't go to "Hell" you'll miss all the fun. Cayman's "Hell" is a limestone formation that bears the moniker because, well, it looks like what one might imagine the real Hell would look like. It's fun to send a postcard to friends from "Hell" while you're visiting Grand Cayman.

Rated numerous times as the best shallow-dive site and the best snorkeling site in the world, Stingray City is just a short ride by boat from Grand Cayman. The shallow sand bars make for great lounging for stingrays. Here people can feed and even pet the gentle creatures who have long ago become used to the attention and happy to have a treat.

Families visiting Grand Cayman enjoy meandering along the Mastic Trail of the old-growth forests that used to cover the island. Keep your eyes open, though, for the beautiful blue iguanas and green parrots. After a nice walk, what could be better than a visit to the Butterfly Farm to see baby butterflies go through the chrysalis of the cocoon and take flight? Probably the most popular attraction on Grand Cayman is the Cayman Turtle Farm. Turtles, turtles, and more turtles live here along with blue iguanas and a caiman alligator. (*www.caymanislands.ky*)

### Where to Stay in Grand Cayman

Grand Cayman is so beautiful it's almost like a dream. Much of the lodging is the same—picturesque, charming, magnificent. New visitors to the island will almost certainly have a hard time making a choice in lodging, given so many special places to choose from. But repeat guests to the Turtle Nest Inn won't stay anywhere else, so if you decide on this enchanting place, you had better book in advance.

The polar opposite of big hotel chains, the Turtle Nest Inn (*www.turtlenestinn.com*) is an intimate inn on the beach and has amenities like a freshwater pool and fully furnished apartments. The apartments come with a complete kitchen so families can save big on meals. The price is right, too, as the Turtle Nest Inn costs less than a typical hotel room without a kitchen on Grand Cayman.

### ≡ Fast Fact

The Turtle Nest Inn has just eight apartments in its Spanish-style building. The beach in front of the Inn is largely uncrowded and since the Inn is in Bodden Town a few miles from George Town, guests get a loving dose of the local culture of the Cayman Islands.

Sunshine Suites is an all-suite hotel also with full kitchens, complimentary continental breakfast, and freshwater pool. The landscaped gardens are the star at this resort, which caters to divers with their convenient dive storage and rinse tanks. The Sunshine Suites also provides a weekly Caribbean barbecue sure to delight the taste buds. The Sunshine Grill is wildly popular for its tasty treats and the yellow and white architecture never fails to put a smile on your face. (*www.sunshinesuites.com*)

Just a hop, skip, and a jump from George Town, the Comfort Suites (*www.caymancomfort.com*) is a five-story all-suite resort about fifty yards from the beach. A big draw at this resort is the on-site diving it offers. The resort also has a complete kitchen and daily breakfast served compliments of the resort.

Cayman Beach Suites is truly a full-service all-suite resort. Everything you could possibly need to do, have, use or want you can get here. Best of all, the spectacular view is free!

On your way to the gargantuan beach steps away from your door, stop by the massive free-form swimming pools or take a dip in the hot tub. Kids will relish their time at the Lil Turtles Kids Camp. Parents will love the full kitchens and screened-in porches. (*www.grand-cayman-beach-suites.com*)

## Just for Parents

Mom will love Cayman Beach Suites European Style La Mer Spa just as much as dad will enjoy the Britannia Golf Course, a Jack Nicklaus design.

Location, location, location is what it's all about at Villas of the Galleon. These adorable alabaster condos are perfect for a traveling family. Situated between the Ritz Carlton and the Westin Casuarina on Seven Mile Beach, you just can't get a better location in Grand Cayman. The condos are affordable and are available with one, two, or three bedrooms. All have a full kitchen. (*www .villasofthegalleon.com*)

## The Bahamas

The Bahamas is the leading off-shore financial center worldwide. That means great lodging, great dining, and great medical care abound in this easy-to-get-to island paradise. It's been reported that every hotel has a doctor on call in case guests need assistance. Scuba divers and snorkelers come to the Bahamas from all over the world to witness the majesty of her coral reefs and water so clear it's like pool water. The sea life is renowned and easy to find in multiple diving sites. And best of all, the water is so warm and toasty most divers don't even need a wetsuit! Sailing is also a popular sport in the Bahamas because it can boast hundreds if not thousands of uninhabited coves accessible only by boat. Every island holds a boat regatta each year.

Nature lovers go gaga for the dozens of nature reserves like Great Inagua, where bird watchers wait with breathless anticipation for a glimpse of a flock of West Indian flamingos. Nearly every sort of water sport is yours for the asking in the Bahamas, including waterskiing, even on the ocean. Parasailing and windsurfing are also popular. In the Bahamas, kids stay for free at most major resorts.

## Where to Stay in the Bahamas

The tropical secret known as Chez Pierre Bahamas isn't so secret anymore now that so many guests want to return for repeat visits, especially the eco-friendly ones! Why? Because the resort is powered entirely by alternative energy, wind and sun. Room rates are inclusive of breakfast and dinner, but alcoholic beverages are extra. Guests can ride bikes, go kayaking, or take a cruise on a catamaran at no charge. But the coolest part of this unique resort is the lodging. Six private beach cottages are elevated on pillars to provide refreshing breezes and each one has a screened porch, not to mention panoramic views. (*www.chezpierrebahamas.com*)

Atlantis is a resort of incredible magnitude. Located on Paradise Island, it has the world's largest marine habitat and casino in the Caribbean. The complex includes the marina, lagoons, waterfalls, and underwater ruins of Atlantis. Three hotels provide elegant lodging for you to retreat to after you take the plunge on the Leap of Faith Water Slide—a sixty-foot, thirty-five-mile-an-hour vertical drop. Atlantis the hotel and casino is located adjacent to a recreated archeological dig site of the lost city of Atlantis. There are eleven swimming pools here and a seven-acre snorkeling lagoon.

But what makes Atlantis take the cake for an incredible kid-friendly Bahamas destination is the Atlantis Bahamas Children Activities program in partnership with The Discovery Channel. The two entities partnered to develop a program that allows children to truly appreciate the ocean and creatures of the sea. Kids aged four to twelve learn about shipwrecks, stingrays and jellyfish, ancient empires, and science with state-of-the-art technology. The camp allows kids to explore and learn about history, spend time in the technology lab and science outpost, and create nature crafts.

# Jamaica

There is so much to do in Jamaica it's hard to know where to start your journey. Just sit back, relax, and let this true island paradise take you in. It won't be long before you and your family figure out which activities are right for you. Jamaica is patient, and will happily accommodate.

Jamaica is home to horseback riding on sandy beaches. You can watch the sunset from Rick's cliff-side restaurant while divers cliff-dive right in front of you. It's about swimming with the dolphins in Dolphin Cove and all-terrain vehicle safaris.

Visitors to Jamaica love to fly through the air on the zip line Canopy Tour, thanks to decks and platforms installed at the tops of trees in Jamaica's lush forest.

Families especially should take a catamaran cruise while in Jamaica, and go early to snorkel or go late to witness a sunset that only Mother Nature could conjure. Kids will love Mobay Undersea Tours' trek aboard submarine *Coral See*. The tour of the underwater world cruises through the Montego Bay Marine Park. The Blue Mountain Bicycle Adventure takes riders through the Caribbean's highest mountain range.

The Rockhouse Hotel (*www.rockhousehotel.com*) is such a surprise. You don't know whether you'll be greeted with heavy metal music or a lot of rock formations (it's the latter). Situated across cliffs of Pristine Cove in Negril, thatched-roofed villas perch on the cliff's sixty-foot edge. Ladders and stairs are carved into the rock leading the way to swimming and snorkeling on the incredible reef. A new spa and daily yoga classes in the yoga room make the Rockhouse Hotel perfect for physically fit families. Best of all, Rockhouse is reasonably priced.

If there were an award for quaint, adorable Caribbean cottage village, Country Country would take top honors. All seventeen cottages are positively adorable and unique. The tropical gardens and brick-lined paths only serve to add to the already endearing property. Country Country is reasonably priced and located on Negril's Seven Mile Beach. Just when you thought you couldn't love this place more, you discover the open-air thatched-roof restaurant at the end of the beach. Visit *www.countryjamaica.com* for more information.

## A Quick Look at a Few More Amazing Island Destinations

There's no phone, television, or radio at Kona Village in Hawaii, but water sports, cultural and historic explorations, and the beach keep kids busy. The resort also has a children's program for kids aged five to twelve. (*www.konavillage.com*)

At the Renaissance Aruba Resort & Casino, buildings are separated into two areas, one for adults only and the other for families. The family area has a movie theater, kids' club, free-form pool, swim-up bar, artificial saltwater swimming lagoon, casual casino, forty shops, and fifteen restaurants. (*www .marriott.com*)

Grand Palladium Punta Cana Resort & Spa in the Dominican Republic is a favorite of moms who want to relax in the spa while dad and the kids play in the sand. Four outdoor pools offer plenty of room for kids to swim, and miniature golf, tennis, and other activities are supervised by staff. (*www.grandpalladiumpuntacanaresort.com*)

## Just for Parents

The spa at Grand Palladium Punta Cana Resort features sauna, spa tub and steam baths, and beauty and massage treatments.

The Moon Palace family resort in Cancun has two indoor pools and four swim-up bars! The two outdoor pools are flanked by six Jacuzzis and two pools just for kids. Aside from the ten restaurants, kids club, and mini-golf, the resort offers many choices of water sports. (*www.palaceresorts.com*)

The Wyndham Sugar Bay Resort & Spa in St. Thomas, U.S. Virgin Islands, has always been a great getaway for newlyweds, but families love this resort for all the same reasons. Voted Best Spa in the Virgin Islands for four years and Best Massage in 2007, it's easy to see why moms and brides would flock to the sugary sweet destination. What makes this place so special besides the incredible activities and accommodations is that the property sits on a thirty-one-acre tropical mountainside with a private beach. Never underestimate the view from an oceanside cliff looking out on Smith Bay's sapphire waters—you just might not be able to say goodbye when it's time to check out! (*www.wyndham.com*)

# CHAPTER 17

# Off the Beaten Path

Some of the best family vacations aren't listed in glossy travel magazines. Activities you and your family already enjoy make for grand getaways. Does your family have a soft spot for animals? Wildlife, nature, and eco-travel often allow tourists to get up close and personal with amazing animals. Love sports? Marketing companies have capitalized on America's obsession with sports and now offer team-oriented vacations that can include a pitching session with your favorite New York Yankee. Has your child shown an interest in history? Archaeological vacations provide opportunities to accompany field historians on actual digs. You might be surprised to discover how many great vacations are right in your backyard.

## BYOB—Bring Your Own Bike

Bicycling is fast catching up with camping as one of America's favorite vacation activities. It's easy once you learn how to do it, convenient, and inexpensive once you've purchased a bike. Plus, you can use your bike over and over again, and no two rides or trails are just alike. Plus, cycling is a sport most families can do together and many families already have bikes, which makes biking on vacation economical. Most national and local parks offer marked mountain biking trails appropriate for every skill level.

Mountain biking can be an aggressive sport, and not every trail listed on the Internet is clearly marked. When planning a cycling vacation it's best to stick with places that have mountain biking programs already in place.

## 🧳 Travel Tip

Trails.com is full of information on biking trails closest to your family's home. The site also includes reviews of trails from other bikers, so you can learn all about a trail, including any precautions you may need to take, before you even set foot on it. See *www.trails.com* to learn more.

Families don't have to trek across the country to enjoy the sport of mountain biking. But ski resorts that offer lift-operated mountain biking are usually located in areas best known for skiing. Unless you live near a well-known ski resort, don't expect to stay in your hometown. But if getting out of town is part of your plans, consider traveling to a winter ski resort area during the off-season. Ski resorts made famous for snowflakes are often synonymous with world-class mountain biking and other outdoor activities. During the summer months rates plummet and families of all ages and skill levels can bike together. Many resorts use the same chair lifts that haul skiers to transport bikers and their bikes to the top of the mountain. Descent is at the rider's own pace along dozens of trails. Scenery at ski resorts during the summer months is breathtaking. One of the perks of vacationing in a ski town in the off-season is the plethora of activities available for family members who don't bike.

### Colorado

Telluride, Colorado, regarded as a go-to ski destination for celebrities, transforms during the summer months. Here you get two towns in one trip with Telluride and Mountain Village, which are connected by a free gondola. The Victorian-era architecture of the National Historic Landmark District and hundreds of mountain biking activities and trails make the location perfect for families split by activity preferences. Families can plan a trip together using Telluride's itinerary builder at *www.telluride.com*.

A thriving mountain biking destination, the Aspen / Snowmass ski area in the off-season offers a mix of outdoor activities and culture for the whole family. It is home to the Aspen Institute, Aspen Music Festival and School, Theater Aspen, and other low-cost or free activities for the whole family.

## ⚐ Rainy Day Fun

The Aspen Recreation Center is an 82,000-square-foot facility with a climbing wall, pool, aquatic center, NHL-sized ice hockey arena, and batting cages. The Center is a perfect place to bring the kids when the weather doesn't cooperate in Aspen. (*www.aspenrecreation.com*)

The Aspen Center for Environmental Studies offers free guided nature walks atop Aspen Mountain. Othello's Sk8 Shop offers camps at the Rio Grande Skate Park. The Aspen Writers' Foundation sponsors the Scribes & Scribblers creative writing camp for kids between ages eight and fifteen. Fit-conscious family? Try a free yoga class on top of Aspen Mountain.

### Idaho

Idaho is home to downhill and single-track mountain biking trails throughout the entire state. Lift-assisted mountain biking is available at numerous ski resorts. Famous trails such as the Trail of the Coeur d'Alene and the Route of the Hiawatha attract thousands of cycling enthusiasts and novice bikers annually who come to Idaho just to ride. Vast Idaho still contains a lot of rough country. Though tourism is a big draw, its wilderness isn't littered with development—the perfect recipe for premium mountain biking. (*www.visitidaho.org*)

### New England

New England is a mountain biking mecca. The New England Mountain Bike Association (NEMBA) is a clearinghouse for the sport throughout New England. (*www.nemba.org*) NEMBA's Boston, Massachusetts, chapter supports Kid's Rides, the Massachusetts Dept. of Conservation and Recreation's "No Child Left Inside" cycling program with NEMBA Explorers. The program was designed to get children outside and engaged in a supervised physical activity.

Two of the most popular mountain biking destinations in the country are in Killington and Stowe, Vermont. Both destinations have many skiing-turned-mountain-biking resorts with family-friendly lodging and additional activities like scenic hiking tours and horseback riding.

### North Carolina

The Dupont State Forest in the Blue Ridge Mountains in North Carolina encompasses a 10,400-acre trail system of nearly 100 miles. Located in Brevard, North Carolina, experts have called it "ground zero for some of the best mountain biking in the eastern United States." Mountain biking in this forest rewards riders with unexpected delights along the way, including four outstanding waterfalls. The western North Carolina mountain biking website has a mass of information about seeing this legendary area of the country from atop a bike. (*www.mtbikewnc.com*)

## Educational Vacations

Edu-tainment is a term that was coined to describe the merging of education with entertainment. It caught on like wildfire in school programs in the late 1990s and has blossomed into a multibillion-dollar business. Edu-travel has closely followed. Many websites about educational travel provide information to teachers and students. Families who want to add an educational component to their vacations can benefit, too. Hey, you might even inquire with your child's teachers about extra credit!

Depending where your family wants to vacation, chances are an educational opportunity is available there. Be creative. Observe. Does your child struggle with foreign language? Vacation someplace where she can practice the language and understand the culture. Is math a source of stress in your house? The Western Colorado Math & Science Center is in Grand Junction (*www.visitgrandjunction.com*), an area also known as Colorado's wine country and a vacation destination in itself.

Even if your child is a straight-A student, educational family travel is a perfect catalyst for learning about his interests and what he might like to be when he grows up. There are quite literally thousands of educational travel destinations and portals, but the following may help you formulate your own ideas for your family's next edu-vacation.

## Learning about America's First Citizens

Touring Native American sites is an incredible way to teach children about the history of America and a truly great people who inhabited this land before them. Several Native American tour outfitters are available to help you plan your journey into America's past. Go Native America in Billings offers tours of the Great Plains of the Dakotas, Montana, Wyoming, and Nebraska (*www.nativeamericantours.net*).

Indigenous tour guides tell tales of the Little Bighorn Battle, Crazy Horse, Deer Medicine Rocks, and the Medicine Wheel among others. Equestrian families will enjoy the Ride the Rez tour of a reservation on horseback. The Dances with Wolves tour takes families to areas where the movie was filmed, like spectacular Spearfish Canyon, the site of the winter scenes. Tribal history in the heartland takes families back to a time when Indians ruled the plains.

## Archaeological Tours

As they question the past and wonder about their future, young people have a growing interest in archeology. It might surprise you to know there are hundreds of archaeological tours and vacations all over the world. Such tours have become so popular, the Archaeological Institute of America (AIA), *Archaeology* magazine, and the Adventure Travel Trade Association have come together to protect archaeological sites from damage by repeat tourists. Their guide to best practices includes tips for tourists as well. A good place to begin your search for a tour near you is *Archaeology* magazine, published by the AIA (*www.archaeology.org*). Through AIA Tours, participants can explore archaeological sites alongside archaeologists. The ultimate learning vacation, families can choose between land, small ships, and other tours depending on budget and areas of interest.

### ≡ Fast Fact

Tour companies like Far Horizons Archaeological and Cultural Trips organize tours to Mexico and Central America, South America, Polynesia, Turkey, the Middle East, Europe, India, China and Southeast Asia, and Africa (*www.farhorizons.com.*)

Some of the best digs can be found in the American Southwest. Colorado's Crow Canyon Archaeological Center has been teaching campers how to dig, sift, sort, and clean artifacts for twenty-five years. In Cortez, Colorado, participants helped experts excavate a Pueblo village dating back to A.D. 1000. Crow Canyon also conducts archaeological and cultural tours throughout the American Southwest.

## Family-Friendly Museums

The City Museum of St. Louis, Missouri, is located in a 600,000-square-foot building, formerly the International Shoe

Company. Here kids will struggle trying to figure out what do to first. Part playground, part architectural phenomenon, twenty artisans constructed the museum from objects within the municipal borders of the city. Salvaged bridges, chimneys, cranes, tile, and abandoned planes were used. City Museum's Enchanted Caves exhibit, in which children can crawl, climb, and walk, were built within the shoe factory's spiral conveyor tunnel system. The second floor houses City Museum's World Aquarium, home to 10,000 creatures including stingrays, seahorses, and sharks. Visit *www*
*.citymuseum.org* for more information.

## ≡ Fast Fact

In yet another area of City Museum, you'll find the MonstroCity. The exhibit was crafted from a fire engine, castle turret, aircraft fuselages, cupola, and gigantic wrought-iron slinkies to become monkey bars of colossal proportion. Also of special interest to families with toddlers is Toddler Town, built for City Museum's small visitors, with miniature tunnels, ball pit, slide, places to crawl, and stackables.

Denver is home to many museums, but the Denver Museum of Nature and Science is one of the largest natural history museums in the world. Here, exploring Colorado's mining heritage is on the menu. Guests can take a tour of the Coors Gem and Mineral Hall and Hall of Life health sciences exhibit, and get to know some Egyptian mummies in the process. One of the most interesting museums in the United States is Denver's Molly Brown Museum. Molly married J. J. Brown, a man who struck the largest vein of gold known during their time, but that's not why she became famous. Molly became known around the world as "The Unsinkable Molly Brown" after she survived the sinking of the *Titanic*. The play *The Unsinkable Molly Brown* was based on her tenacity and conduct during the sinking of the mighty ship. (*www.denver.org*)

The American Museum of Natural History is located in Manhattan's bustling Upper West Side and is home of the Hayden Planetarium. Visitors to New York City with children between the ages of eight and twelve can experience "A Night at the Museum," a nocturnal adventure in which kids can spend the night in the American Museum of Natural History. The blockbuster movie *Night at the Museum* was based on this program. The expedition includes watching Dinosaurs Alive! in the Museum's LeFrak IMAX Theater, exploring guided live-animal exhibitions and creepy Museum quests.

The American Museum of Natural History has multiple programs for families and kids that rotate throughout the year. Check the website *www.amnh.org* frequently to plan your visit.

## 👥 Just for Parents

The Upper West Side of Manhattan is home to some of the world's best dining. While the kids are enjoying a supervised romp and slumber in the museum halls, parents can relax and enjoy some time alone in a swanky Manhattan bistro.

Families could easily spend the better part of a vacation walking through Washington, D.C.'s many museums. The International Spy Museum is just plain fun. Museum "spies" learn just how realistic the spy industry really is and can participate in museum workshops, which are all about the kids. In one workshop children ages eight to twelve can "go undercover" on a secret mission right in the museum including creating a cover identity, documentation, and disguise. Professional makeup artists, spy experts, and hairstylists help the new recruits before they're off to obtain top-secret intelligence. The workshop includes souvenir photos of the participants. Additional workshops are offered throughout the year, but even if your family doesn't participate, the International Spy Museum is a family must-do if you're in Washington, D.C. Go to *www.spy museum.org* to learn more.

## ≡ Fast Fact

The Washington Convention and Visitors Bureau is your best bet to find resources to help you decide which museums you and your family would like to visit.

Visiting Chicago? The Chicago Children's Museum is full of activities for kids of all ages. At the Museum, kids age five and under can learn what it's like to camp, climb trees, and explore caves in an enchanted forest setting called Treehouse Trails. After cavorting in the make-believe river or mountain waterfall, a tree house awaits. A cushioned make-believe baby pond is the perfect place for the tiniest visitors to romp. With a dozen permanent exhibits just for kids at Chicago Children's Museum, there's much more to do, so check the website for featured programs at *www .chicagochildrensmuseum.org*.

### Digging for Dinosaurs

It's safe to say Colorado saw a lot of dinosaur action. There is even a town called Dinosaur. Diplodocus, stegosaurus, brontosaurus, and allosaurus were first discovered at Dinosaur Ridge (*www.dinoridge.org*). The exposed rock face at the Dinosaur National Monument features more than 15,000 fossilized dinosaur bones. In Fruita, kids can hang out with full-scale dinosaur models and visit the paleontology lab at Dinosaur Journey (*www.dinosaurjourney.org*). Fossilized dinosaur bones await hand-holding at the Dinosaur Depot in Cañon City (*www.dinosaur depot.com*). Suspect a budding paleontologist in your family? This is the place for Jurassic family educational fun.

### Culinary Schools (for Kids!)

The Umstead Hotel and Spa in Cary, North Carolina, isn't a place you'd expect to find a bunch of children making a mess in the restaurant's kitchen. The property is adjacent to Umstead State Park and is the first hotel in North Carolina to receive the AAA "Five Diamond Award." But behind the luxurious exterior, the Ulmstead staff provides lots of fun, interactive programs for kids. The Umstead hosts an annual pumpkin carving event every fall, Tea with Santa at Christmas time, and a series of naturalist programs including a nature scavenger hunt. Visit *www.theumstead.com* for more information.

The Culinary School of the Rockies welcomes children age eleven and over to attend cooking classes with their parents. Their Totally Tween Holiday Baking class is pretty popular with teens, especially during the holidays. The one-day class takes place after school just once a year during the Christmas season. (*www.culinary schoolrockies.com*)

## Animals and Nature

Nature is captivating, especially to young people. Watching some of the world's most spectacular animals in their natural habitat can imprint a love of nature on a child that lasts a lifetime. As the world watches natural habitats destroyed acre by acre from development and pollution associated with global warming, travelers are increasingly rushing to view animals in their native surroundings while they still can.

### Please Do Feed the Animals

The squeal of a child upon feeding her first llama is hard to beat. With hundreds of petting zoos, butterfly pavilions, and animal exhibits across America, it's easy to find one near you. There's even a website to help you find it: *www.pettingzoofarm.com.*

Kids love bugs. Denver's Butterfly Pavilion & Insect Center can boast more than 1,200 butterflies (*www.butterflies.org*). More than thirty endangered species live at the largest mountain zoo in the country, the Cheyenne Mountain Zoo. Here giraffes wait anxiously in the African Rift Valley exhibit for kids to feed them (*www .cmzoo.org*). The Lazy 5 Ranch in Mooresville, North Carolina, is a 3.5-mile drive-thru zoo. Beware of the zebras; your child will want to bring one home (*www.lazy5ranch.com*).

## The National Audubon Society Nature Camp

There's no better teacher than Mother Nature herself. And at nature camps, families can interact with nature on a daily basis, often in spectacular locales. The National Audubon Society Nature Camp in Rockland, Maine, is accessible only by boat. Campers travel to a 330-acre island where they spend time learning from respected naturalists and environmental educators. For seafood-loving moms and dads, a fresh lobster feast at the close of camp could the best part of the trip. (*www.acadianationalpark.com*)

## Natural Habitat Adventures

Natural Habitat Adventures (*www.NatHab.com*) is a nature travel company. They specialize in tours on which families can truly experience animals up close and personal. Seeing giant polar bears, gray whales, and mountain gorillas is yours for the asking. Naturalist guides accompany tours, and Natural Habitat Adventures Family Adventures employs professional youth coordinators and expedition leaders to ensure a safe and worriless adventure.

## Wild Mustangs of the Outer Banks, North Carolina

Early explorers left the Spanish mustangs behind nearly five centuries ago. Their home now is 16,000 acres of dunes flanked on all sides by beaches and island terrain. Wild Horse Safari offered by Back Country Outfitters & Guides on the Outer Banks is a half-day expedition to see the wild horses of these barrier islands. (*www.outerbankstours.com*)

## Raptor Centers

There are hundreds of raptor centers across the United States that rescue and rehabilitate raptors, also called birds of prey, and educate the public about these often protected creatures. These avian predators are at the top of the food chain. They're influenced by and influence nature on a grand scale. Raptors have proven that they can provide early warning signs for humans—thanks to their sensitivity to such environmental changes as those caused by chemical pollution. Because they make excellent study subjects for understanding the ecological process and the health of the environment, they are worth protecting. Birds of prey are magnificent to behold, with many displaying wing spans greater than the height of an adult man. In the past few years, centers for birds of prey have increasingly begun sprouting up all over the world.

## ≡ Fast Fact

The World Center for Birds of Prey located in Boise, Idaho, is a global leader on the cutting edge of preserving, protecting, and understanding these magnificent animals. (*www.peregrinefund.org*)

The Medina Raptor Center in Spencer, Ohio, treats hundreds of birds annually with the goal of returning the birds to the wild once rehabilitated. (*www.medinaraptorcenter.org*) But not every raptor will be able to return to the wild. Raptors are used to educate the public about these incredible avian predators at the Carolina Raptor Center. The Carolinas are home to two raptor centers, Charlotte's Carolina Raptor Center (*www.carolinaraptorcenter.org*) and the Center for Birds of Prey (*www.thecenterforbirdsofprey.org*) on the outskirts of Charleston, South Carolina. Both facilities provide special care to injured birds and in the direst of cases, a home for the animals.

# Sports Vacations

In nearly every corner of the country you'll find a sport that's become one of America's most passionate pursuits—NASCAR. But even if you dislike racing, everyone has fun at racing schools. With minimal instruction, attendees suit up in regulation racing suits and drive authentic Nextel Cup cars. The Mario Andretti and Jeff Gordon Racing Schools have multiple locations (*www .andrettiracing.com*).

If baseball is your family's favorite all-American pastime, Heroes in Pinstripes may be the vacation for you. Here campers can learn and play baseball with some of history's Yankee greats. Campers get their own pinstripe uniforms and are allowed to live like they're in the major leagues. They even get their own baseball card. Coaches vary annually but have included coaches who have earned forty-five World Championship rings, fifty-four All-Star games, four World Series MVPs, ten Gold Glove Awards, two Cy Young Awards, and two Rookie of the Year Awards, among others. See *www.heroesinpinstripes.com* to learn more.

Is there a soccer mom in your family? At Joe Machnik's No. 1 Soccer Camps, young players have realized their true potential for more than three decades. (*www.no1soccercamps.com*) If you're vacationing in Sonoma County, California, the University of Sports offers sports camps in all the major categories.

Even Lance Armstrong needed a push when he was preparing for the Tour de France. Where did he get it? From cycling coach Chris Carmichael. Carmichael, who is also a veteran of the Tour de France, is the founder of Carmichael Training Systems, cycling camps that take people who love to ride bikes to the next level. Approximately half of participants at the camp are recreational cyclists, so even if your family doesn't have the stamina of Lance Armstrong, you'll be just fine. (*www.trainright.com*)

# Dude Ranches

From cattle wrangling to spa treatments, today's dude ranches are not what they used to be. And that's a good thing, because now families can take part in the fun of the old west. Yesterday's cowboys often had to kill and cook their own dinner while out on the range. Multiple dude ranch associations exist in most western states to help you plan your visit to a working ranch.

- The Dude Ranchers' Association (*www.duderanch.org*)
- Montana Dude Ranch Association (*www.montanadra.com*)
- Colorado Dude and Guest Ranch Association (*www.coloradoranch.com*)
- Wyoming Dude Ranchers Association (*www.wyomingdra.com*)
- Arizona Dude Ranch Association (*www.azdra.com*)
- Idaho Dude and Guest Ranch Association (*www.idahodra.com*)

At many of today's dude ranches, you can still eat on the range, but chances are your meal will be cooked by a chef and served to you. Visiting a dude ranch can be a wonderful family adventure.

## Red Horse Mountain

Red Horse Mountain is located in Harrison, Idaho, near Coeur d'Alene. Families will enjoy the beautiful terrain and multiple activities such as horseback riding, biking, fishing, kayaking, hiking, and archery. Red Horse Mountain also offers sporting clays, challenge courses, swimming, rock climbing, and whitewater rafting. Before they arrive, families have the option to fill out "Family Planners" and are assigned two licensed adventure guides. Then guides, wranglers, and ranch hands fit guests with equipment for whichever adventure or activity they've chosen. Parents and kids can spend time together, or find their own adventures separately.

The full kids' program runs from May through November for children ages three to eleven. Red Horse Mountain's kids' program adventures help develop children's sharp senses, teach them respect for nature, and even contribute to team-building skills. (*www.redhorsemountain.com*)

## Hidden Meadow Ranch

Arizona's White Mountains are home to Hidden Meadow Ranch. This all-inclusive dude ranch has twelve private cabins that accommodate as many as five guests per cabin. Cabins are outfitted with fireplaces, board games, and XM radio. There are no televisions, and families enjoy three gourmet meals a day. Best of all, meals and activities such as the Kids Korral program are included in the all-inclusive price of the stay. Hidden Meadow Ranch has all the requisite ranch activities like horseback riding, fishing, canoeing, and archery, with a few extras including leather-making, arts and crafts, and woodworking. Wintertime means it's time for cross country skiing and sleigh rides. Kids so love Hidden Meadow they've made many of the ranch staffers and even ranch horses into pen pals. (*www.hiddenmeadow.com*)

## Bar W Guest Ranch

The Bar W Guest Ranch in Whitefish, Montana, is like something out of a western movie, with one exception. At most ranches, a dog is the ranch's four legged favorite. Instead of a family dog, the Bar W has Carlos the goat. Carlos is the welcome wagon at the Bar W, and just like a dog, he comes and goes as he pleases. Carlos loves treats, petting, and having his tummy scratched. After saying "hello" to Carlos, it's time to ride majestic mountain trails with incredible Montana scenery in the background. Bar W has more than just trail rides—it's a full-service guest ranch. Women come from all over the world for the Bar W "Cowgirl Up" event each summer. The Bar W serves world-class cuisine courtesy of chefs that have been in some of America's finest kitchens. Kids will love the accommodations and family-style activities, while parents can enjoy time in one of Montana's friendliest towns. (*www.thebarw.com*)

## 💼 Travel Tip

To visit a dude ranch, you will need a good pair of comfortable boots, a bandana, nonslip socks made from wicking material to prevent blisters, and sunscreen.

### Grand County

Grand County, Colorado, in the Colorado Rockies has earned the moniker of "Dude Ranch Capital of the USA." On their website (*www.dude-ranch.com*) families can examine maps and activities of six world-class dude ranches throughout Grand County located about an hour and half west of Denver. All of the ranches listed offer families traditional western experiences such as trail rides and square dancing as well as golf and gourmet cuisine. Affordable lodging at these ranches varies from rustic cabins to elegant lodges.

### Canadian Dude Ranches

Canada also has its share of dude ranches. Echo Valley Ranch and Spa in Jesmond, British Columbia, is one of the world's finest examples of an eco-friendly, soft-adventure ranch. (*www.evranch.com*) In northeastern British Columbia, Canada, Larry Warren and his wife Lori manage Tuchodi River Outfitters. Here, old-school horse-packing trips are all the rage. Larry runs approximately 150 horses that live in the mountains year-round. When Larry or Lori need a horse, they go out and catch one. (*www.tuchodiriveroutfitters.com*)

A dude ranch is a great place to have a family vacation. Talk with your family about what everyone expects from the trip. It can be as grueling as herding cattle, or as laid back as simply enjoying scenery. Many ranches now welcome tourists and can provide services that are either rustic or luxurious depending on what guests want. Select your dude ranch vacation from ranches that make a point of marketing to families with children and have a whole host of activities that appeal just to them.

# CHAPTER 18

# Attractions, Festivals, and Fairs

So many things to do, so many different places to do them. Trying to plan activities on a family vacation can be frustrating. Do you choose a destination because of the attractions it has to offer? Or do you choose the attractions because they happen to be located near your destination? Some attractions are so good, families plan entire vacations around them. Others are just plain fun, and happen to be near someplace you're already going. Regardless of how you plan your trip, be on the lookout for family-friendly festivals, attractions, and fairs. They can enhance your trip and fill your days with memories that will last a lifetime!

## Mother Nature's Coolest Attractions

Whether made by Mother Nature or man, America is full of amazing attractions. Families interested in the natural wonders of the world have hundreds of attractions to choose from. Families who like to stop at quaint roadside attractions off the beaten path will also find many choices.

### Old Faithful

Old Faithful is the world's most predictable geyser. Located in Yellowstone National Park, the geyser has drawn visitors for decades. Plus, Yellowstone National Park is reason enough to visit!

See if your family can stay at the rustic Old Faithful Inn, built in 1904. At the Old Faithful Inn you won't find TV or radio, air conditioning or the Internet. The main attraction is right outside your window and promises to blow on time.

### Niagara Falls

Niagara Falls isn't the tallest waterfall in the country. It isn't even close. But compared to all the others, Niagara Falls is a magnificent site to behold. The volume of these falls is a whopping 85,000 cubic feet of water per second with a maximum recorded volume of 292,000 cubic feet per second. That's a lot of water! Multiple family-friendly lodging options are available at Niagara Falls, along with affordable dining options for every member of the family. (*www.infoniagara.com*)

### Alaska

The northern lights, or the aurora borealis, are a sight to be seen—especially when they can be combined with a fun trip to Fairbanks, Alaska! Being able to see the lights is largely dependent on how dark the sky is, so careful planning is needed. That doesn't stop families from planning aurora borealis vacations throughout the viewing time, which is between August and April. Activities like snowshoeing, watching sled dog races and sleigh rides complement Alaska's incredible beauty. Kids will love visiting the Ice Park where they can crawl through ice mazes and slide down massive ice slides. Animal-loving families will also enjoy visiting sled dog kennels where you can pet the working canines.

### Chimney Rock

Chimney Rock in the North Carolina Mountains (*www .chimneyrockpark.com*) is home to the breathtaking Hickory Nut Falls. Chimney Rock is twenty-five miles from Asheville, North Carolina. Views from Chimney Rock are unforgettable, particularly during the fall when foliage explodes through the mountains. Geological formations formed three and half miles of trails, one of which was featured in the film *The Last of the Mohicans* starring Daniel Day-Lewis and Madeleine Stowe. Seventeen minutes of the film were shot along the Cliff Trail at the top of Hickory Nut Falls.

## Ruby Falls

Chattanooga, Tennessee, is home to Ruby Falls. They're the tallest, deepest underground waterfalls accessible to the public in the United States. It's part of Lookout Mountain, a family destination that offers many family-friendly activities and lodging options. See *www.lookoutmountain.com*.

One of the best times to visit Ruby Falls is around Halloween. The Ruby Falls Haunted Cavern Halloween event features a shrieking ride in the cavern's "hellevator" and numerous above- and below-ground tricks guaranteed to scare guests silly. The Haunted Cavern is open shortly before Halloween and closes shortly after. Discounts and additional information are available online at *www.hauntedcavern.com*.

## California Redwood Forest

The California Redwood Forest in Humboldt County is one of those places you hear about and wonder if it's worth the trip to see. Well, it is. If you're planning to visit Humboldt County, you might want to invest in a neck pillow for the ride home. Here you'll spend much time gazing upward at the incomprehensible heights of the California redwoods.

On your visit to the Redwood Forest, you'll travel along the Avenue of the Giants. This is a scenic drive you won't want to miss, but also be sure to get out and explore the Humboldt Redwoods State Park, home of the largest remaining location of virgin redwoods in the world. The Avenue of the Giants extends about thirty-one miles on Hwy. 101. The area is perfect for stopping to picnic, camp and hike, or just walk among trees that are hundreds of years old and hundreds of feet tall.

## Other Sites of Interest

Some other wonderful natural attractions:

- It's not hard to convince someone to visit Hawaii. It's a tropical, beautiful paradise. One of the most impressive things to do in Hawaii is to take a tour of a live volcano. Companies like Big Island Volcano Tours can take visitors close to craters to see firsthand some of the newest places on earth. Visit *www.bigislandvolcanotours.com* to learn more.
- The Rollins Planetarium at Young Harris College in Young Harris, Georgia, offers thirty free shows throughout the year on Friday nights. The show features the GOTO Chronos Space Simulator star projector, the first installation of this simulator in the world. If the skies are clear, the Observatory is also open. (*www.yhc.edu*)
- Cave of the Winds near Manitou Springs, Colorado, was discovered by two brothers accidentally in the late 1800s. If you go, be sure to take the lantern tour to see what it might have been like if your family were to happen upon such an amazing attraction. (*www.caveofthewinds.com*)

## Just-for-Fun Attractions

While you're in the neighborhood of the Northern California Redwood Forest, allow enough time to stop by Campbell Bros. Confusion Hill. Built in 1949, Confusion Hill is all about altering your normal perception. The starring act here is Gravity House, where visitors can solve the mystery of Confusion Hill for themselves. The other attraction is a thirty-minute Mountain Train Ride. The ride travels through second- and old-growth Redwoods. (*www.confusionhill.com*)

## ≡ Fast Fact

Some of the just-for-fun mysteries that you can experiment with at Confusion Hill include a trough in which water seems to be flowing uphill, rolling golf balls out a window and having them come back to you, standing on the walls, and trying to get out of the gravity chair. Also there are height variations in the Gravity House that make you seem to shrink at one end of a room and grow taller at the other end.

Headed to Florida? Check out the Miami SkyLift attraction in Miami's Bayfront Park. The 500-foot helium balloon ride suspends riders above Bayfront Park for fifteen minutes while a tour guide narrates a description of Miami.

### Colorado's Railroad Attractions

Kids love trains, and sightseeing by train is great family fun with a hint of education added to the mix. Colorado is a veritable train activity destination. The Durango and Silverton Narrow Gauge Railroad (*www.durangotrain.com*), a train tour of mining days, has been featured in over twelve films including *Butch Cassidy and the Sundance Kid*. Coal-fired steam locomotives take riders forty-five miles from Durango to Silverton, Colorado, on a 3,000-foot climb.

Katherine Lee Bates was inspired to write "America the Beautiful" thanks to the views she saw at the top of Pikes Peak, 14,110 feet high. Thankfully, the Pikes Peak Cog Railway (*www.cograilway.com*) has been taking visitors to the top of Pikes Peak to see those same views since 1891. And families with serious railroad buffs can stop by the Colorado Railroad Museum (*www.coloradorailroadmuseum.org*) in Golden, Colorado. It includes a replica of a depot, and more than 100 historic locomotives and cars on fifteen acres.

### America's Coolest Corn Mazes

Corn mazes are creepy, fabulous fun. The annual Corn Maze at The Old Frontier in Thomson-McDuffie County, Georgia, is laid out over a whopping five acres. The Old Frontier welcomes birthday parties and family reunions. (*www.exploremcduffiecounty.com*)

Richardson Farm in Spring Grove, Illinois, is a massive farm where visitors can climb a fifty-foot-tall tower to try and map in their minds how they'll find their way out of Richardson Farm's massive corn maze, the largest in America. Families can picnic on site, and don't forget the marshmallows. The farm provides free campfires. (*www.richardsonfarm.com*)

### The Biltmore Estate

You might question whether or not your children would enjoy visiting America's largest private residence, The Biltmore Estate in Asheville, North Carolina. It's just a house and grounds, right? Wrong! Biltmore is an adventure for the whole family, complete with a Land Rover Experience Driving School, mansion, restaurants, petting zoo, historic horse barn, and summer concert series.

### 👥 Just for Parents

At the Biltmore Winery parents can enjoy complimentary wine tastings and tours of the winery following a romantic dinner at the winery's Bistro. The Inn on Biltmore Estate is a four-star property perfect for reconnecting on vacation.

And families looking for a Christmas vacation should think of traveling to the Biltmore Estate. During the holidays, Biltmore displays 100 decorated trees, 1,000 wreaths and bows, nearly 2,000 poinsettias, miles of evergreen garland alongside thousands of ornaments and lights, and 35 Fraser fire Christmas trees in their 72-foot banquet hall. (*www.biltmore.com*)

# America's Zoos

America's zoos are some of the best in the world, and there are thousands to choose from. Most major cities have zoos, while some of the most interesting zoos are located off main routes in smaller towns and communities. It's easy to find a zoo near your home via the Internet Visiting a nearby zoo makes for a great last-minute or weekend getaway. And many zoos have unique qualities or programs that make them attractive to the vacationing family.

More than 4,000 animals call the Denver Zoo home (*www.denverzoo.org*) in Colorado. Here, the eight-acre Predator Ridge replicates part of Kenya's Sambura National Reserve down to the smallest detail.

The Pueblo Zoo in Pueblo, Colorado, includes among its 350 animals unique native sandstone buildings that have a prominent place on the National Register of Historic Places. (*www.pueblozoo.org*)

The Zoo Boise in Idaho wants to be sure you get enough to eat and have a great zoo experience. Their "Breakfast at Zoo Boise" program offers an inside glimpse of what happens at the zoo before the general public is allowed in. The behind-the-scenes tour includes a breakfast, and then participants learn about some of the animals, have an animal encounter, and witness an animal feeding or enrichment. Games and other activities follow the Beastly Breakfast, which includes a continental breakfast and souvenir to take home. (*www.zooboise.org*)

Against the backdrop of the world's most recognized city are polar bears, alligators, and all sorts of creatures normally found on other continents. Manhattan's Central Park Zoo is a family frenzy of activity and demonstrations with the animals. It's billed as the "wildest ticket in town," and in dashing New York City, that's saying a lot! (*www.centralparkzoo.com*)

The Mill Mountain Zoo in Roanoke, Virginia, is one of America's most charming zoos and is just off the picturesque Blue Ridge

Parkway. Kids love the Zoo Choo, a little train that winds and bends around the zoo for perfect viewing. (*www.mmzoo.org*)

South Carolina is for the birds and alligators. The Birdhouse at Riverbanks Zoo in Columbia, South Carolina, is one of a kind. But it's the Caribbean flamingos housed in front of the exhibit that steal the show every spring. Their "elaborate ritualized courtship displays" are spellbinding. These birds, like pink cotton candy bodies on sticks with long necks, endear families for hours on end. (*www.riverbanks.org*).

Myrtle Beach's Alligator Adventure has been one of the state's top attractions for decades. Mesmerizing live shows feature, you guessed it, alligators. When the gators are busy, out come the snakes for a hands-on lesson. Here guests can learn how to tell the difference between venomous and nonvenomous snakes. Galapagos tortoises (who love attention) also live at Alligator Adventure. Some weigh as much as 450 pounds and are forty years old.

The climate is what helps make Miami Metrozoo so successful, tolerable to a multitude of animals from Asia, Australia, and Africa. At the Miami Metrozoo exhibits have no cages. Based on geographic territory, animals at the Miami Metrozoo who are neighbors in the wild are roommates in the zoo's exhibits. The zoo features more than 1,000 animals and hundreds of species. A children's zoo, wildlife carousel, guided tram, and zookeeper lectures keep visitors busy between animal watching. (*www.miamimetrozoo.com*)

## Food Festivals

If your family likes to experience the culinary arts, virtually everything you need to know about food festivals—when, where, what and how—is available at FoodReference.com (*www.foodreference.com*). In fact, most festivals feature great regional food that can't be found anywhere else.

## Seafood Festivals

In the United States, Apalachicola hosts the Florida Seafood Festival. The festival includes an oyster-eating contest during which participants can consume as many as 300 oysters, and of course, an oyster-shucking contest. The Florida Seafood Festival features a parade, Blessing of the Fleet, and RedFish Run. (*www* *.floridaseafoodfestival.com*)

New York's Oyster Bay Rotary Club puts on one of the eastern seaboard's biggest seafood and waterfront festivals. This festival includes a massive food court of over thirty booths featuring everything from stews, fritters, pupusas, and gumbos along with the traditional oysters and other seafood. The Oyster Bay Festival's own buccaneers, called "Kings of the Coast," put on a pirate show in which kids can participate in treasure hunts and the performance, and later take a camel ride.

Every October, 45,000 people attend the North Carolina Oyster Festival. This festival also features live entertainment and arts and crafts along with incredible food, road race, shucking championships, and their oyster stew cook-off competition. (*www.brunswick* *countychamber.org/of-nc-oyster-festival.cfm*)

The king of all oyster festivals takes place in Ireland at the Galway Oyster Festival where participating countries worldwide compete in the world's largest oyster-opening contest. Home of the Guinness World Oyster Opening Championships, the festival is located in West Ireland. (*www.galwayoysterfest.com*)

The Maine Lobster Festival is all about, what else, Maine lobster! Overlooking the Penobscot Bay, Rockland is the scene where more than 20,000 pounds of lobster are prepared along with clams, shrimp, and mussels. The Maine Lobster Festival is a great place to bring the kids thanks to the festival's Children's Tent. The tent includes family-friendly activities like lobster eating, cod fish carrying, the diaper derby, and a costume parade. The festival also offers U.S. Navy ship tours, unlimited pancakes,

cooking contests, and provides a free shuttle service. (*www
.mainelobsterfestival.com*)

### Unique Food Festivals

The Napa Valley Mustard Festival takes place in the first quarter
of the year. That's when vineyards are sweatered in wild mustard—
think of it as a wine country mustard foliage tour! Napa Valley community participants feature the culture of the Napa Valley, which
includes striking introductions to the region's agriculture. National
sponsors and mustard companies round out the event that is sure
to tempt the taste buds of any mustard-loving family. (*www.mustard
festival.org*)

Texas shows off its Texas-sized culinary chops at the Houston
Rodeo Barbecue Festival. The Houston Rodeo is the world's larg-
est livestock show . . . no wonder they have so much barbecue!
Hundreds of barbecue chefs compete for three days in the World's
Championship Bar-B-Que Contest. (*www.hlsr.com*)

Charleston's Food and Wine Festival takes place in March and
welcomes chefs from all over the world. The festival includes two
"Grand Tasting Tents" with more than seventy culinary companies
offering food and wine tastings. (*www.charlestonfoodandwine.com*)

Super-healthy families will love Mendocino County, California,
in August. The Vibrant Living Expo in Ft. Bragg is a raw food festival whereby visitors can view demonstrations and hear presentations by noted raw food authors, medical and health professionals,
and culinary artisans. The raw food festival includes a small film
festival, raw pie contest, and "Rising Star Chef Showcase." (*www
.rawfoodchef.com*)

## Festivals and Fairs

If your family loves attending festivals and events like state fairs,
it's a good practice to use the Internet to find a state fair or festival nearest to your travel destination. Festivals and state fairs

make for easy weekend getaways. Festivals and fairs can be a great addition to any destination vacation. They can be educational and add a touch of culture to your family vacation. If you can time your vacation with a fun festival or fair your family will enjoy the trip all the more. Festivals and fairs have something for every member of the family, regardless of their ages. Families who love animals can find all sorts of petting zoos and pony rides at most state fairs.

Wyoming's Grand Targhee Music Festival and Virginia's Old Fiddlers Convention in Galax feature current artists and up-and-comers. Because of the locations of these festivals and the caliber of artists they attract, both are destination events, meaning families travel from all over just to attend. Both places have many activities the whole family can enjoy when the festivals are over. At the Grand Targhee Music Festival, the "Kidzone" features crafts and puppet shows, and children twelve and under are admitted free. (*www.grandtarghee.com*) And every performer at the Old Fiddlers Convention receives a free camp site, taking the cost of lodging out of the equation. (*www.oldfiddlersconvention.com*)

Charleston's Southeastern Wildlife Exposition and Harbor Festival attract tens of thousands of families annually. The Southeastern Wildlife Exposition (SEWE) takes place in February and is America's largest wildlife nature and art event. World-class original art is featured along with nature exhibits and educational presentations. (*www.sewe.com*) The Charleston Harbor Fest in June celebrates Charleston's maritime culture. For kids who love ships, the Charleston Harbor Fest is a sure winner. Tours of the tall ships, pirate camp, boat building, and sailing lessons, which are offered free of charge, make up the bulk of the activities along with extreme water sports demonstrations. (*www.charlestonharborfest.org*)

The Georgia Mountain Fair in July is one of America's most fun family fairs. Held at the Georgia Mountain Fairgrounds in Hiawassee, Georgia, about two hours from Atlanta, the eleven-day event is a carnival, and has an authentic Pioneer Village and musical performances. An agricultural element is included at the Georgia Mountain Fair along with pony rides, antique shows, and memorable foods like barbeque and smoked trout. (*www.georgia mountainfairgrounds.com*)

If you can't travel all the way to Key West, La Belle Amie Vineyard's Key West Music and Wine Fest in South Carolina is located on the outskirts of *über* family-friendly North Myrtle Beach. The festival, which takes place in May, includes a tour of the vineyard, tropical beverages, music, and barbecue. Best of all, kids under age eighteen are admitted free of charge (*www .labelleamie.com*).

## Theme Parks

Does your family love theme parks? Can you identify with Clark Griswold's obsession to visit Walley World in National Lampoon's *Vacation*? Do waterslides make your kids dizzy with excitement? Were you a zookeeper in a former life? If you answered "yes" to any of these questions, a theme park vacation might be just the ticket for your family. And thanks to a state directory of theme parks, amusement parks, water parks, and zoos, it's easy to plan theme park vacations. ThemeParkCity.com (*www.themeparkcity.com*) offers a state-by-state listing of parks and zoos. Locate your own state or a state where you'd like to travel, and you'll find links to several you can choose from. There are thousands of theme parks, amusement parks, and zoos to visit, but here are a few to consider if you're vacationing in these areas.

### 👪 Just for Parents

Adults love Sesame Place too! Nothing brings back the innocence of childhood like seeing Bert and Ernie or Oscar the Grouch, or hearing how your favorite character's skit was sponsored by the letter *H*.

Younger children will absolutely love Sesame Place. It's where kids can see that Sesame Street is real—complete with their favorite Sesame Street friends. Kids and parents can enjoy rides, shows, and water slides. Can't miss activities include Big Bird's Beach Party, Bert's Slip-n-Slide, Cookie Mountain, and the Teeny Tiny Tidal Wave. Sesame Place is north of Philadelphia and an hour and a half from New York City. (*www.sesameplace.com*)

The Northwest's largest theme park is Silverwood Theme Park in Northern Idaho. Silverwood has more than sixty-five attractions and rides, a water park, steam engine, and entertainment. (*www.silverwoodthemepark.com*)

## 💼 Travel Tip

Families who love history should make a stop at the Kit Carson County Carousel in Burlington, Colorado. The attraction is a National Historic Landmark from 1905 with forty-six hand-carved animals. (*www.kitcarsoncountycarousel.com*)

Wisconsin's Wisconsin Dells owns the registered trademark of the "The Waterpark Capital of the World." A year-round water park in Wisconsin might seem a little chilly, but Wisconsin Dells has indoor and outdoor water parks. Inside the thermostat stays set at 85° F. Resorts are attached to some of the parks so families really can make a whole vacation out of visiting the area, not just the park.

Ohio's Cedar Point in Sandusky is on the speed dial of roller coaster lovers. For eleven years it's won the Golden Ticket Award as "Best Amusement Park in the World" by *Amusement Today*. Hundreds of activities and rides including mind-numbing and easygoing roller coasters may be why you choose to come to Cedar Point. But the area is also a great destination for a full-on family vacation. Lake Erie's shores and islands are full of family activities. For destination information visitors can contact the Sandusky/Erie

County Visitors and Convention Bureau online. (*www.shoresand islands.com*)

# Aquariums

The ocean is a magical place. The creatures of the sea are hard to spot unless your family lives near the ocean. And even then, the elusive animals are usually too deep underwater for children to see and come to understand. It's a fact that children learn to respect and protect what they know. The survival of the oceans of the world is going to depend on coming generations. That's why it's so important that every child be able to see and understand the ocean's most precious commodity—its residents! Thankfully there are numerous aquariums and oceanic adventure parks throughout America for kids to be able to learn about and appreciate the oceans of the world.

The National Aquarium in Baltimore is one of the world's most visited aquariums. The aquarium has hundreds of exhibits and more than 16,500 animals. (*www.aqua.org*)

There are several Sea World locations where kids from all over the country can witness the majesty of the ocean's animals. Each park has different features, so check online before you go to be sure the park you're thinking of visiting is right for your family. Parks include Adventure Island in Tampa, Florida; Sea World in Orlando, Florida; San Antonio, Texas; and San Diego, California. Access all of the parks under an online umbrella at WorldsOfDiscovery.com. (*www.worldsofdiscovery.com*)

The Miami Seaquarium has an outdoor aquarium that features shows and exhibits. Kids who visit this park make friends with killer whale "Lolita," television star "Flipper," and a sea lion named "Salty." (*www.miamiseaquarium.com*)

Myrtle Beach's Grand Strand has been a family vacation destination for decades. Thanks to reasonable below-market lodging rates and a large percentage of activities just for children, tourism has continued to boom in this area. The addition of the Ripley's Aquarium has only served to increase it, with hundreds of neighboring town residents, schools, and church groups making day trips to interact with the marine animals that live there. One of this attraction's most unique highlights is the "Sleep with the Sharks" event. The sleepover adventure takes place in the aquarium's Dangerous Reef Tunnel and is geared for kids ages five and up. The event includes a scavenger hunt, crafts, educational presentation, aquarium tour, late-night snack, and continental breakfast. Each group of ten attendees must have a chaperone for the duration of the stay. (*www.ripleysaquarium.com*)

## 👥 Just for Parents

"Sleep with the Sharks" slumber party at Ripley's Aquarium provides the perfect opportunity to learn to "shag dance" at one of Myrtle Beach's popular beach music clubs. Child care is widely available throughout the Grand Strand. Better yet, for your trip to Myrtle Beach, bring a sitter.

The Georgia Aquarium in Atlanta features a week-long summer camp experience called Summer Camp H2O that allows kids to capture the behind-the-scenes story of the aquatic animals who live there. Camp H2O combines learning with animal encounters. Campers get to meet the Georgia Aquarium animal husbandry team. (*www.georgiaaquarium.org*)

# CHAPTER 19

# Unique Family-Fun Vacations

B udget family travel is about as broad a topic as you can get! And many families start the vacation planning process without knowing where to go—they just want to get away. When planning a vacation, starting from scratch can be challenging, but there are several places that strike it rich every time as great family vacation destinations. If your family is just itching to hit the road, but you're not sure where you want to land, check out these great vacation options. They may not fit in any specific category, but they are memorable destinations with something for every family to enjoy.

## Culinary Travel

The term "foodie" is a popular culture label used to describe someone who is a connoisseur of food and beverage. Nowadays there are foodie families too, with kids who love gourmet treats and drinks just like their parents do. Foodie parents are likely to have foodie children, and thankfully, travel providers are taking notice.

### Kid-Friendly Wine Country—Not Just for Parents Anymore!

Food and wine have always gone hand-in-hand. Among the more famous of wine regions, the Napa Valley is home to well over 300 wineries. Here, vineyard owners have realized that just because wine connoisseurs have children doesn't mean they have stopped enjoying their favorite Cabernet Sauvignon. In the past, typical vacations to wineries didn't include kids. But with expenses skyrocketing and disposable income dwindling, many families find it hard to justify vacationing twice—one vacation with the kids, and another vacation without. Now, many culinary and wine vacation packages also include activities for children.

Business-savvy vintners are stepping up to the plate and have begun to include programs that cater to the whole family. Since winemaking is in many instances a family business, at vineyards there are lots of fun things for all ages to enjoy. Some wineries have even gone so far as to offer child care while parents enjoy an afternoon or early evening tasting.

## Mendocino County, California

Mendocino is in wine country. If ever there were an award competition for family-friendly culinary travel, Mendocino would take top honors. On the cutting edge of culinary family travel, Mendocino is brimming with too many activities, festivals, and gourmet and roadside treats to name.

### ≡ Fast Fact

The first grapes in Mendocino were grown by failed gold prospectors in the 1850s. Today Mendocino is known for producing serious varietals like zinfandel and pinot noir, long-time favorites of wine drinkers everywhere.

Some visit Mendocino County just for the wine, but there are so many other activities that every family member can find a niche. Complete listings of events and festivals, wineries, lodging, and transportation in Mendocino County can be found online on *www.gomendo.com.*

Mendocino County, part of California's famous North Coast wine region, begins about ninety miles north of San Francisco and is located directly north of Sonoma County.

Aside from great wine and food, while you're in Mendocino don't miss world-famous Drive-Thru Tree, Confusion Hill, and the Skunk Train, an ancient steam locomotive that makes daily trips between Willits and Fort Bragg. Anderson Valley is all the rage with parents and kids thanks in part to the Philo Apple Farm. Families can sample dozens of varieties of apples and frolic through the farm chasing the farm animals, which include pigs and goats. Brutocao Cellars in Hopland offers bocce courts and a playground for kids.

For families who abstain completely, Navarro Vineyards, which is also located in Philo, serves a nonalcoholic Pinot Noir Gewürztraminer grape juice in their tasting area. Do your kids like animals? Milano Winery in Hopland has a petting zoo that includes tortoises, pygmy goats, and pot-bellied pigs. And at Handley Cellars, kids can stroll through the folk art garden and enjoy a natural soda.

### Wine and Dogs in Virginia

Families who love dogs love to visit Virginia's mountainous Chateau Morrisette winery, which is located in Floyd County between mileposts 171 and 172 on the magnificent Blue Ridge Parkway. The owners are big dogs lovers, and their favorite four-legged friends enjoy greeting wine lovers and their families. The winery also boasts a world-class restaurant and acres of natural beauty. (*www*
*.thedogs.com*)

### Iowa Wineries Welcome Families

Iowa isn't a name one might typically associate with a wine destination. But Iowa has such a large selection of wineries and wine growers the Iowa Wine Growers association is divided into three categories: eastern, central, and western Iowa wineries. The Iowa wineries website also features wine trails for parents who take the fruity beverage so seriously they enjoy traveling to experience various vintages. (*www.iowawinegrowers.org*)

The Heart of Iowa Wine Trail (*www.heartofiowawinetrail.com*) is extensive, but still only covers about a third of the state, from top to bottom. Iowa is a beautiful state with a multitude of activities for the whole family, making it a great wine and family destination in general. Numerous event schedules are listed on the Iowa wineries and Heart of Iowa Wine Trail and other wine trail websites, along with recommendations for memorable cuisine and shopping.

## Washington State's Olympic Peninsula

The Olympic Peninsula in Washington State is making a splash in American culinary travel. For families traveling to this area, or who are looking for an off-the-beaten-path culinary vacation, the Northwest has a plethora of culinary experiences that include: coastal seafood; local fruits, vegetables, and berries; culinary lavender and indigent mushroom farming; handmade cheeses; and local wines.

Farm tours, one-of-a-kind farmer's market events, and the harvest season offer focal points for tourists who love good food and beverages. And along with great culinary travel, around many culinary destinations incredible sight-seeing opportunities abound. Adjacent to Olympic Peninsula are old-growth forests and a breathtaking coastline with snowcapped mountains in the background. Historic national park lodges now cater to culinary traveling families.

For example, Lake Quinault Lodge offers culinary packages that serve up multicourse gastronomic dining experiences complete with regional wines and cooking demos (*www.visitlake quinault.com*). This area is sure to be a hit with teenagers; "Forks" is the home of the tween- and teen-sensation book *Twilight* by Stephanie Myer. Visitors can take the Twilight Tour before heading out for rafting on the Hoh River. Parents will love visiting five artisan wineries between Port Angeles and Sequim, Washington.

# Kennedy Space Center, Florida

The John F. Kennedy Space Center is where NASA launches their space vehicles. Located in Florida near Cape Canaveral, families can reach the space center easily via Miami or Jacksonville. Families interested in space exploration, astronauts, and science can build a wonderful vacation out of a trip to the Kennedy Space Center. There is so much for everyone to do and learn, and so many activities to ignite a spark of learning in the minds of the space center's young visitors.

## ≡ Fast Fact

The Florida Kennedy Space Center vacation website, *www.kennedy spacecenter.com*, has an abundance of information about planning a vacation centered around a visit to the Kennedy Space Center. The official government website for the Kennedy Space Center is *www .ksc.nasa.gov.*

### Family-Friendly Activities

The Kennedy Space Center Visitor Complex itself is a tourist destination. Tours leave from the visitor complex and can include touring NASA facilities. Tours include stops to see gargantuan launch pads, and the colossal Vehicle Assembly Building, which is so large that it's almost hard to believe it's real! Families won't want to miss seeing the Apollo/Saturn V Center.

## ⚊ Rainy Day Fun

Even when it's raining there's enough to do to keep everyone entertained at the Kennedy Space Center. The visitor complex offers live-action theater. Shows have included "Mad Mission to Mars," and "Astronaut Encounter" starring a NASA astronaut who has been in space.

On another stop on the tour of the space center, you'll see the rockets that tower several stories about ground. The rockets represent the different eras of space exploration in a place called the space center's Rocket Garden. Visitors can stroll through a full-size model of the Space Shuttle and view a real Gemini program capsule from the early days of space exploration.

The Kennedy Space Center Visitor Complex has an Astronaut Hall of Fame and bus tour. The bus tour lasts about two hours and departs frequently, but the last tour leaves in mid-afternoon. To be sure you don't miss the bus tour, arrive early to the space center. As you might expect, security is tight at the space center, and there are a lot of items on the prohibited items list. Obviously all firearms and ammunition are prohibited as are all weapons including mace, knives, and even pocket knives and nail clippers with knife blades. Alcohol is prohibited and there is no cooking or fire allowed on property. Pets, swimming, wading, and fishing are all also not allowed. If you go to the Kennedy Space Center, leave your bags and cooler at the hotel. Coolers, baggage, and large purses or backpacks aren't permitted past the front gate. And, everything else you bring in will be inspected. In addition, if your personal communication device such as cell phone or BlackBerry, or camera or video recorder cannot be powered on even because the battery is dead, it won't be permitted through the front gate. These rules are for the safety of the space center and everyone who passes through.

## ≡ Fast Fact

The Kennedy Space Center has two giant IMAX theaters that show thrilling space films. With a five-story screen, realistic 3D images, a wall of sound, and images shot during actual space missions, you'll feel like a real astronaut yourself.

Tickets to the Kennedy Space Center are good for admission for two days, so if you can't see everything in one day, don't worry! You can go back the next day at no extra charge. Tickets do expire after seven days. Admission is not valid for shuttle launch days or on Christmas Day when the center is closed. Admission only to the U.S. Astronaut Hall of Fame is less than admission to the complex, and tickets to the U.S. Astronaut Hall of Fame are good for just one day.

Tours of the space center are also not included in the general admission price, but are well worth the extra cost, so be sure to save enough vacation dollars to take one of the incredible tours at the Kennedy Space Center. Tours have to be purchased with admission tickets.

## Tours

Discover KSC: Today & Tomorrow (*www.kennedyspacecenter .com/discover-nasa.aspx*) includes a visit to NASA headquarters, with the closest possible view of the shuttle launch pads. Tour guides answer questions about how the shuttles were made and launched and how astronaut crews are trained.

Cape Canaveral: Then and Now (*www.kennedyspacecenter .com/visitKSC/NASAtours/thenNow.asp*) is a look at the history of Cape Canaveral up until today. This tour covers the launch of the first American way back in the sixties and includes a visit to the Air Force Space and Missile Museum, as well as witnessing today's unmanned rocket program.

## ■ Travel Tip

Perhaps the most fun for families at the Kennedy Space Center is having lunch with an actual astronaut in the Lunch with an Astronaut tour. Lunch is included and consists of a space briefing with a NASA astronaut. Tour participants also leave with an autographed souvenir.

One of the top attractions at the Kennedy Space Center is the Shuttle Launch Experience. In the Shuttle Launch Experience visitors go into the six-story Shuttle Launch Simulation Facility as veteran shuttle astronauts give their testimony about what it was like to blast off into space. Visitors get a play-by-play experience of the shuttle launch sequence they'll never forget.

## Youth Education Programs

Youth and education programs are available at the Kennedy Space Center. In these programs young people get to tour NASA areas, meet astronauts, and watch IMAX films among other activities.

The Visitor Complex provides youth education programs that include:

- Camp Kennedy Space Center
- Overnight Adventures
- Field Trips
- Girl Scout and Boy Scout Days
- Homeschool Days

During Overnight Adventures, young people camp out at the Kennedy Space Center Visitor Complex. Activities include meeting a NASA astronaut, seeing the "Magnificent Desolation" IMAX film and taking part in fun projects like the "Great Rocket Scavenger Hunt." Activities are led and supervised by an Overnight Adventure instructor team. Program includes dinner and a midnight snack and breakfast. The Kennedy Space Center welcomes youth, scout troops, and school groups but groups must have a minimum of ten kids to have a group and all kids must be between ages eight and fourteen.

The Salute to Scouts program honors the fact that more than half of astronauts were active boy scouts or girl scouts. Kennedy Space Center Visitor Complex salutes scouts with special events each year. This program is specifically for troops who get a full day of Kennedy Space Center shows and exhibits and get to learn about the latest accomplishments at NASA. Scouts get to take bus tours of launch areas, meet an astronaut, and take the Shuttle Launch Experience. The Salute to Scouts program also encompasses visiting the U.S. Astronaut Hall of Fame where scouts try their skills in the motion-based space simulators. They also get to experience special hands-on activities that are arranged to support the requirements scouts need to acquire Space Exploration and Aerospace Merit badges.

## ≡ Fast Fact

Homeschool Days is provided at the Kennedy Space Center for homeschool students and their families and teachers. Homeschool participants get to do many of the same activities as the scout troops in the Salute to Scouts program, and packets of NASA education materials are available to homeschool teachers.

## Rocking Horse Family Fun Ranch, New York

The Rocking Horse Ranch (*www.rhranch.com*) is one of less than a hundred all-inclusive resorts in the United States. Located about an hour and a half from New York City, the Rocking Horse Ranch sits on 500 acres and the activities here are practically endless. The year-round activity schedule is so intensive, even the most challenging kids will fall into their beds at night exhausted from a day of fun.

Originally created in 1958 by Toolie and Gloria Turk, the Rocking Horse Ranch has stayed in the Turk family. Over the past fifty years they have welcomed guests in droves from all over the country—including children and grandchildren of the first guests who stayed at Rocking Horse Ranch.

Winter time activities include snow tubing and skiing, ice skating, and sleigh rides. The Rocking Horse Ranch also has an indoor pool with fountains and a geyser. Horseback riding, water skiing, fishing, archery, and paddle boats are just a few things kids can get into during the warmer months.

At the Rocking Horse Ranch, meals are included, as well as parties (of the ice cream and cocktail variety) and the ranch makes coffee, hot cocoa, and snacks available twenty-four hours a day. Entertainment includes Wild West acts, magic, the circus, and other shows. Performances that get families involved and musical revues are also part of the fun. A disc jockey provides music for dancing, and bonfire sing-a-longs get everyone involved. And what family ranch vacation would be complete without marshmallow roasts and hot chocolate? The Rocking Horse Ranch also puts on a fireworks show three times per year.

For the equestrian-loving family, there are horses galore at Rocking Horse Ranch. From basic horseback riding to pony rides for young kids, families can also receive riding instruction. And of course hay rides drawn by horses and tractors are all part of the fun.

The giant water slide is always a hit with the kids, along with children's heated pool and spray fountain. The jumbo slide for young ones allows family members of all ages to join in the fun. The Rocking Horse Ranch has its own private lake that features water skiing, banana boats, kayaking, paddle boating, and fishing.

## ☂ Rainy Day Fun

If the weather outside is frightful while you're visiting the Rocking Horse Ranch, kids can make a beeline for the video arcade and Wii room.

During the winter months, Rocking Horse Ranch opens up its Winter Fun Park, which includes a ski area with two ski lifts and a massive snow tube run. Instruction is optional, and thanks to snowmaking there's never a worry about enough snow for winter activities. Ice skating and horse-drawn sleigh rides followed by s'mores around a bonfire complete the cold-weather festivities.

Aside from seasonal activities, the Rocking Horse Ranch offers a variety of activities and sports for every member of the family. Lighted tennis courts, beach volleyball, basketball, shuffleboard, and softball are complemented by a climbing wall with four stations so the lines are kept to a minimum.

The Rocking Horse Ranch even has its own western "mining town" where kids can mine for "gems and minerals." Bocci, mini golf, a BB gun shooting gallery, and an archery range bring out the competitors in the family.

The Fun Barn at the Rocking Horse Ranch is a gigantic indoor facility that includes a "foam factory" for interactive soft play. Ten air-powered cannons make for hours of busy time for kids, along with the climbing wall and bounce assembly. There is a fitness center for mom and dad and saunas.

The Rocking Horse Ranch provides age-appropriate activity directors for children of all ages, teens, and adults so families can interact together and go off on their own. Parents can choose from several children's programs like day camps that include supervised programs such as sports, hiking, playing games, swimming, and arts and crafts. There is a kids nursery for tiny tots, and babysitting can be arranged. The "Fort Tiny Playground" for the littlest guests and the massage and facial center for parents form a perfect combination of activities!

## Alaskan Adventure

Alaska is one of Mother Nature's greatest gifts to the world. A vacation to Alaska isn't just a weekend jaunt; it's 500 miles from the closest state, Washington. A visit to Alaska requires extensive planning in order to take advantage of all this incredible place has to offer. However long it takes to save or plan for the trip, visiting Alaska is a family adventure you'll remember for a lifetime!

Alaska is full of undisturbed habitats for a multitude of animals. For families who like to combine vacation with education, or for families who enjoy animals, there's no better destination than Alaska. The wildlife viewing in Alaska is like nothing else on the planet—polar bears, birds of prey, both blue and humpbacked whales, wolves, bears, and moose are just a few whose fierce beauty will take your breath away.

Fishing is a great family activity in Alaska, and one that has a variety of choices. Families visiting in Alaska can learn to fly-fish, go freshwater fishing, or even go ice fishing. Alaska has more than a million lakes along with thousands of rivers and innumerable fish-filled streams.

One way to see Alaska is by taking a day cruise in places like Glacier Bay, through the Kenai Fjords, or the Prince William Sound. The coast of Alaska includes mountain landscape, glaciers, and many kinds of wildlife. These are just a few of the animals your family might see on a day cruise in Alaska:

- Whales
- Seals
- Sea lions
- Orcas
- Sea otters
- Mountain goats
- Bears
- Puffins

Boating sports such as kayaking and rafting are popular activities in Alaska. Touring Alaska on foot is also popular along with wildlife viewing. However, no family wants to get caught in the wilderness of a place like Alaska without a guide! That's why it's always best to use an experienced outfitter who can safely accompany you and your family on the many activities Alaska has to offer. Alaska is the wilderness—and while visiting can be a once-in-a-lifetime opportunity, the last thing you want to do is to wander off on your own.

Alaska Outdoors offers a classic family tour that's perfect for families with kids who are age eight and older. Tour options can vary, but an example of a Travel Alaska Outdoors tour is the Classic Alaska Family Tour. This tour starts with two nights in the Kenai National Wildlife Refuge. Here families can get up close and personal with lakes, glaciers, and wildlife—on foot and in a canoe. The tour continues through the Kenai Fjords National Park and Denali National Park. Best of all, the tour includes an expert guide who stays with you throughout your tour.

Hotel accommodations are provided along with state-of-the-art camping equipment, and all meals are included with the exception of meals purchased in restaurants. Tour activities include canoeing, wildlife viewing via bus tours within Denali National Park and at Mt. McKinley, and hiking. More adventurous families can attempt river rafting, mountain biking, glacier cruises, dog sledding, "flight seeing" from an aircraft, and sea kayaking. (*www.travelalaskaoutdoors.com*)

# Top Ten Scenic Drives

Scenic splendor, animals on parade in their natural habitats, and virtually every kind of outdoor recreation imaginable are yours when you go on a Top Ten Scenic Drives of the Northern Rockies vacation (*www.dDrivethetop10.com*). This is a trip that fosters connection—with nature, history, and even culture and volunteerism for those families who so choose. The Top Ten Scenic Drives in the Northern Rockies extend over five states including Idaho, Montana, Wyoming, Washington, and Oregon as well as two Canadian provinces, British Columbia and Alberta.

### Getting to Your Destination

Since a Top Ten Scenic Drives vacation covers so much distance, it's a good idea to decide where you'll begin your journey and research areas to stop, stay, and dine before leaving home. This will determine your lodging and dining options. The Top Ten Scenic Drives in the Northern Rockies is made up of four all-American roads, ten national parks and recreation areas, and four connecting national historic trails including:

1. Hot Springs Circle Tour (British Columbia)
2. International Selkirk Loop All-American Road (Washington, Idaho, and British Columbia)
3. Waterton-Glacier International Peace Park Loop (Montana, Alberta, and British Columbia)
4. Montana Scenic Loop (Montana)
5. Northwest Passage All-American Road (Idaho)
6. Hells Canyon All-American Road and National Recreation Area (Oregon and Idaho)
7. Salmon-Sawtooth Scenic Byways (Idaho)
8. Yellowstone-Grand Teton National Parks Grand Loop (Wyoming, Montana, and Idaho)
9. Beartooth Highway All-American Road (Montana and Wyoming)
10. Circle the Continental Divide Driving Tour (Wyoming)

The Top Ten Scenic Drives National Historic Trails include the David Thompson Historic Route, which winds through British Columbia, Montana, Idaho, and Washington. The Lewis & Clark National Historic Trail is located in Washington, Idaho, and Montana. The Nez Perce National Historic Trail can be found in Oregon, Idaho, Montana, and Wyoming. And the Oregon Trail is in Oregon, Idaho, and Wyoming.

Families can fly to a multitude of airports and rent vehicles or if they're near any one of the access points, they can drive their own vehicles. Thanks to the stunning scenery and wildlife viewing, RV and motorcycle enthusiasts love Top Ten Scenic Drives vacations. Taking a Top Ten Drives vacation presents a kind of nostalgia for many visitors—like traveling through a North America that existed before discount stores and fast food restaurants dotted landscapes. These drives showcase North America in its purest state, and for many visitors, strikes a chord that is life changing.

Along the way on a Top Ten Drives vacation, families can enjoy and choose from nearly every outdoor activity a traveler could image. Just a few include:

- Hiking
- Mountain biking
- Kayaking
- Fishing
- Hunting
- Skiing
- Snowmobiling
- Snowboarding
- Horseback riding
- Golfing
- Birdwatching
- Dining
- Arts and crafts
- Wineries
- Regional cultures
- Historical experiences

An added bonus to a Top Ten Scenic Drive vacation is its status as a green tourism vacation. Such a trip promotes green travel in that these authentic destinations showcase the beauty of the local environment and are proof that conservation is worth every effort.

On a Top Ten Scenic Drive vacation, families will find opportunities to volunteer in communities along the way, giving each family member a chance to leave each place they visit on the Top Ten Scenic Drives better than they originally found it.

# Small Town Charm

In fairy tales kids can still leave home at daybreak and not be home until dusk without their parents worrying about where they are. Families can freely walk to and from their hotel to quaint shops and restaurants all within five minutes of each other. Horse drawn carriages are still a viable mode of transportation. Kids can ride bikes along the streets and throughout greenways that connect the township. In some of America's quaintest small towns, fairy tales are true!

In the tiny town of Pinehurst, North Carolina, about an hour south of Raleigh, it's as if time stopped somewhere in the mid-twentieth century. The safety kids go without in metropolitan areas is ever-present in this miniature town. Pinehurst and its surrounding towns may be small, but affordable family activities are as substantial as are their many charms.

### Family-Friendly Activities

Pinehurst has long been called the golf capital of the world. And though golf is one of its most valuable commodities, tennis, horseback riding, water sports, resort activities, world-class dining, spas, nature, and festivals offer something for every family member to enjoy.

## Travel Tip

If you're traveling by car, bring a blanket and cooler so you can spend an afternoon lounging in Pinehurst's Village Arboretum after strolling around the Village of Pinehurst. Visiting families can grab an order to go from many different restaurants and have a picnic on the Arboretum meadow.

The Village Arboretum is a greenway project and public park with a magnolia garden, meadow for picnicking, and paths. The

Arboretum pays homage to the style of Frederick Law Olmsted, who designed the original Village of Pinehurst way back in 1895. Visitors to Pinehurst, especially those staying at the Carolina Hotel, Pine Crest Inn, Holly Inn, or other nearby lodging in the Village of Pinehurst are encouraged to use the park for outdoor recreation like walking, jogging, or biking on the many trails that meander through the Arboretum. (*www.VillageOfPinehurst.org*)

Another great thing for families to do in Pinehurst is to attend the Pinehurst Labor Day Food and Wine Festival. The celebration includes guest chefs and wineries and a stay at the Manor Inn in the heart of Pinehurst. The wine festival offers social, golf, and accompanying spa packages. Families traveling together should ask about Pinehurst's KidsClub rates which are available throughout the festival.

The Spa at Pinehurst is also welcoming to kids. In addition to the regular service most adults expect to find at a world-class spa, the Teen Spa Lounge is for kids aged twelve to seventeen with corresponding services. The Spa at Pinehurst Kid Spa requires the presence of a parent or guardian and kids must be at least age six to participate. (*www.pinehurst.com*)

## ☂ Rainy Day Fun

Seeing a film or play might be in order on your visit to Moore County. If so, be sure to check out what's playing at the historic Sunrise Theater in Southern Pines. (*www.sunrisetheater.com*)

Next to seeing a show or film at the Sunrise Theater, Southern Pines is known for its colorful shopping and one-of-a-kind boutiques that yield treasures you'll keep for a long, long time. Strolling down the sidewalks of cheery Southern Pines is all about stopping into several of the many shops like A Wild Hare (*A Wild Hare 910-692-7096*). A Wild Hare is for people who love bunnies, but this is no pet store. Rabbits come in all shapes and sizes here, from lamps to holiday ornaments and everything in between. Need a bunny-shaped serving tray? How about a rabbit teapot or maybe a bunny dairy dispenser? If you've ever read Beatrix Potter's Peter Rabbit tales to the kids, put A Wild Hare on your list of shops where you must stop. Along the way, a paint-your-own-pottery shop, a wine store, unique clothing boutiques, and equestrian hobby shops among numerous others offer exceptional gifts that will solidify memories without breaking the bank.

No visit to Pinehurst would be complete without a horse-drawn carriage ride. On this ride, which only lasts about a half an hour, visitors can learn a century of history about Pinehurst. The carriage picks riders up at the Carolina Hotel or the nearby and equally charming Magnolia Inn. A carriage tour from Carriage Tours of Pinehurst Village is by far the best way to see the Village of Pinehurst and hear about all of its secrets, transporting visitors back in time to the turn of the century in another one of Pinehurst's heydays. (Carriage Tours of Pinehurst Village 910-235-8456)

## Lodging

Pinehurst has many places to stay. The Carolina Hotel and the Holly Inn were built in 1895 and restored to their original grandeur several years ago. Both properties are on the luxury side, but special deals are available at various times of the year. Pinehurst is a golf mecca, so prices are typically higher during golfing season. (*www.Pinehurst.com*)

The Pine Crest Inn is also located in the Village of Pinehurst. This village property has a long history too. Built in 1913, the Pine Crest Inn's previous owner was legendary golf course architect, Donald Ross, who died in 1948. Today it's still privately owned. (*www.pinecrestinnpinehurst.com*)

Staying in Pinehurst is part of the historic fun, but if your family is on an absolute budget, just on the outskirts of Pinehurst is a little town called Southern Pines where you'll find budget-friendly hotel chains that are more reasonably priced. These hotels lack the charm and character that is so much a part of the Village of Pinehurst lodging. (*www.moorecountychamber.com*)

### Family-Friendly Dining

Moore County might be located in a remote area for world-class dining, but that's just what this little corner of the earth offers. From an ice cream parlor that serves the world's best crinkle-cut French fries to pubs to fine dining, the towns of Pinehurst and Southern Pines make the culinary cut.

On Broad Street, The Ice Cream Parlor is a kid- and family-friendly eatery that's almost always packed with kids and families! At 176 Northwest Broad Street, home of the all-the-way hot dog, The Ice Cream Parlor is also mobbed for its delicious ice cream and black-and-white malted milkshakes. (Southern Pines Ice Cream Parlor 910-692-7273).

On West Pennsylvania Avenue just around the corner from Broad Street in Southern Pines, Italian fare packs Coach Light Trattoria every night. The Coach Light Trattoria is not just family-friendly, surprisingly it's also wallet-friendly.

## Just for Parents

Coach Light Trattoria entrees are part of a three-course meal that includes soup, salad, and an enormous entrée.

The Coach Light Trattoria offers a great menu for kids, but where's the fun in eating chicken tenders when authentic Italian dishes are so large, three kids can easily split one? Parents will love the amount of food they get for the price, and the wine list is extensive. (*www.coachlighttrattoria.com*)

Elliott's on Linden, located on Linden Road on the outskirts of Pinehurst, is a restaurant and culinary destination that includes a cooking school. Chef/owner Mark Elliott is known for colorful cooking. His dishes have been sampled repeatedly by the rich and famous from all over the world who come to Pinehurst to play in golf tournaments or who have mega-vacation houses in the area. For families who enjoy cooking together, Elliott's offers cooking classes for all ages. (*www.elliottsonlinden.com*)

There's just something about coffee in Moore County, with more quaint coffee shops scattered across the county than you can shake a stirrer at. Two notable coffee shops are Poppy's and the Java Bean Plantation and Roasting Company.

No visit to Pinehurst would be complete without a stop at Poppy's for a coffee and homemade ice cream. Poppy's is located in the middle of all the action in sleepy Pinehurst at 601 Cherokee Road (910-235-0383). In Southern Pines, visitors can enjoy a cup (or five or six) of coffee made from homemade roasted coffee at the Java Bean Plantation and Roasting Company, located at 410 Southwest Broad Street (910-685-2326).

## Christmas in Mendocino County, California

When you think of Christmas, the thought of holiday travel is almost too scary to contemplate. If you're looking for snow there are lots of obvious places to go. But if you're planning a trip around the holiday season that doesn't include skiing or other such winter sports, Mendocino County, California is serving up a capital Christmas.

Fort Bragg is home to events like the Holiday Lights Parade in early December (*www.FortBragg.com*) closely followed by the Mendocino Coast Candlelight Inn Tour of Mendocino County ocean-side towns (*www.mcn.org*). Ukiah, California hosts Small Town Christmas (*www.cityofukiah.com*).

## Don't Miss This

The Skunk Train Christmas Train in Willits, California (*www .skunktrain.com*), is an enchanting hour and a half ride with Santa and the elves, but the terrain is no North Pole. This ride takes lucky guests through a tour of the impressive redwood forest where trees have been strung with lights. Mouths will be agape at the glory of the ancient redwoods. This fun ride even welcomes people in pajamas! Hot chocolate and cookies, strolling musicians and storytellers are part of the fun. The train leaves Willits Station twice daily.

Families traveling on or throughout the Christmas holidays can enjoy time at Gualala, California's "Festival of Nine Lessons and Carols" on Christmas Eve. The tradition dates back to performances given at King's College Chapel in Cambridge, England since 1919. (*www.gualalaarts.org*)

The Christmas Day Open House at the Ford House Museum in Mendocino Village, California, is home to some of the world's best homemade cinnamon buns and spiced cider. (*www.mendoparks .org*) Going on a Christmas Day Whale Watch at the Point Cabrillo Lighthouse Museum in Mendocino Village is another amazing thing to do if your family is spending Christmas together in Mendocino County. (*www.pointcabrillo.org*)

# Key West

Key West is an island at the southern tip of Florida. Part of the Florida Keys, it's been the location for many bestselling books and movies. Thanks to its unique personality, Key West has a heartbeat and atmosphere all its own. One of the most popular activities in Key West is exploring the amazing architecture of old Key West. Many visitors prefer to see the city via a bicycle or walking tour. Popular tour stops include Key West Cemetery, Mallory Square's Sunset Celebration, and the Duval Street dining and nightlife district.

## Family-Friendly Activities in Key West

There is much to do in Key West, which is why so many families make it a dedicated destination. Just a few attractions include:

- Key West Butterfly and Nature Conservatory featuring a 5,000-square-foot glass-domed tropical butterfly habitat (*www.keywestbutterfly.com*)
- Mel Fisher Maritime Museum displays spoils and treasure from international shipwrecks (*www.melfisher.org*)
- Key West Historic Seaport (*www.fla-keys.com*)
- Key West Aquarium (*www. keywestaquarium.com*)
- Key West Shipwreck Museum (*www.shipwreckhistoreum .com*)
- Sunset Culinaire Gourmet Sunset Cruise, kids under age two are free (*www.sunsetculinaire.com*)
- Snorkeling or kayaking through the Key West National Wildlife Refuge to see animals like turtles, starfish, stingrays, and fish (*www.fws.gov*)
- Key West Ghost Tour, a guided tour by lantern light (*www .hauntedtours.com*)
- Dolphin shipwreck and snorkel tours (*www.dolphinecho .com, www.bestonkeywest.com*)
- Conch Tour Train (*www.conchtourtrain.com*)
- Ripley's Believe It or Not! Key West (*www.ripleyskeywest .com*)
- Key West Pirate Soul Museum, showcasing pirate artifacts including plunder, weapons, and confessions (*www.pirate soul.com*)

Tours of Key West are especially popular, thanks to the island's rich history. Local transportation includes the Old Town Trolley. The tour is narrated by Key West experts and covers a multitude of sites. Plus, there are nearly ten stops on the tour for easy hop-on, hop-off shopping and dining fun. The Ghosts and Legends of Key

West Tour is a narrated, guided tour of Key West, also known as "Bone Island." (*www.historictours.com/KeyWest*)

Another cool attraction in Key West is the Light House and Keeper's Quarters Museum. The lighthouse was constructed in 1847 to help ships navigate the deadly reefs of the lower Keys. It was powered by fifteen oil lamps with reflectors each more than a foot wide. Visitors can trek the eighty-eight steps to an observation deck to see the spectacular view. The lighthouse and Keeper's Quarters have been restored and maintained to showcase historic rudiments in period style. Historic furnishings and photography provide a peak into life in Key West during that time. (*www.kwahs.com/Lighthouse.htm*)

### Family-Friendly Lodging

Parrot Key Resort Waterfront Hotel is one of the newest properties in Key West. Near the historic district, the resort is on the Florida Bay. Several things about this resort beckon families: its connection with Turtle Island Watersports, and the children's adventure program keep kids busy and happy on vacation. Parrot Key also has four swimming pools. It's a relaxing atmosphere that includes sunbathing terraces surrounded by lush landscaping. The Parrot Key Resort offers one-, two-, and three-bedroom houses and vacation rentals large enough for families and families traveling together to spread out. All of Parrot Key Resort's vacation cottages have a view of the pool or sunsets, and each has private porches, full kitchens with flatware, appliances, serving ware, and cookware, so families on a budget can shop nearby for groceries and save a bundle on food costs. Parrot Key Resort also has an Adventure Concierge who can help families book local activities and attractions on the resort, in town, and in surrounding areas.

### Family-Friendly Dining

Hogfish Grill on Stock Island serves up one of Florida's favorite seafoods, hogfish! Caught by spearfishing rather than pole fishing, this delicacy is not to be missed on a trip to Key West. (*www.hogfishbar.com*) Conch Republic Seafood Co. is a great stop for conch fritters. (*www.conchrepublicseafood.com*) And what visit to Key West would be complete without key lime pie? Kermit's Key West Key Lime Shoppe serves all sorts of Key lime treats including chocolate-covered key lime pie on a stick. (*www.keylime shop.com*)

# CHAPTER 20

# Savor the Moments, Remember the Journey

As the years go by, chances are you've saved family photos that captured important events such as a birth, graduations, or other such milestones. Every vacation your family takes is an important event. And preserving those memories is a fun way for you to spend quality time together. As time marches on you'll be able to look through a treasure trove of memories your family created when traveling together. Plus, keeping good records of your family vacations can save valuable dollars. Every time you plan a trip, your family can take a few moments to look back at previous journeys and decide which activities to repeat, and which ones weren't so great after all.

## Chronicling Your Travels

Chronicling your past vacations is helpful for planning new ones. A chronicle, or report about your vacation, captures important information, facts and experiences your family might accidentally overlook in planning the next trip.

The most important thing a traveling family can bring on a vacation is a travel folder. Your family travel folder should contain all of the documents you need to travel. In this day and age where so much documentation is online, it's even more important to print online receipts and carry them with you on your trip.

What's more, if logistical issues arise with your airline, car rental, or other vendor that could require a refund or credit, your vacation papers are like precious gems. Most often, good documentation is the only way travelers can prove they are entitled to receive a refund from a vendor.

Travel document folders are great for carrying those important documents needed to get from point A to point B, and everywhere in between. Travel document folders hold and protect important documents for easy access when you're traveling. Plus, they make for quick work when you have to constantly retrieve and store things such as your and your family members' identification cards or passports.

## 🧳 Travel Tip

You can customize your family's travel document folder with your name and select a theme for your folder through a company called Company Folders. You can even select your travel document folder design online (*www.companyfolders.com*).

Throughout your trip, collect mementos like ticket stubs, brochures, small souvenirs, menus, and receipts. These not only document your journey, but also make creative, memorable additions to travel keepsakes like scrapbooks. You can even scan them to add a creative slant to electronic albums for interactive photo-sharing programs.

## Preserving Your Vacation Memories

All of these mementos are like gold and silver when it comes to remembering your family vacation. By the time your family returns from vacation, you could have a suitcase full of mementos that your family will treasure for a lifetime.

Collect things you come across on vacation. You can use them in scrapbooking, scan them to use on a family vacation calendar, or just put them in the sleeves of a photo album and refer back to them when you want to remember the fun times your family had together on vacation. Some of the things you might want to collect include photography, writings, clips from local newspapers and magazines, restaurant menus, fortune cookie messages, airline tickets, passport documents, and brochures from fun attractions you visited.

Getting your mementos home in one piece can be challenging, no matter where you go on vacation. When it comes to bringing anything home from vacation, shipping might be your best option. When airlines are charging a small fortune to check extra baggage, shipping can be more economical than checking an additional bag at the airport.

## ≡ Fast Fact

Ask your child's teacher if anything they do on vacation could possible earn them extra credit. In some cases, kids can even use their writings in classroom projects like geography reports for example, for extra credit.

Journaling is a great way for the kids in the family to embrace the journey and glean an understanding of the places you visit on your vacation. Consider purchasing an inexpensive journal for every member of the family. Or, you can purchase a diary in which everyone can contribute their thoughts while on vacation. Consider inserting tabs for each family member. Encourage everyone to write about interesting foods they tasted, or funny people they meet. Maybe your family made lifelong friends while on vacation. Make notes about them, and put addresses and e-mails next to their names so everyone can keep in touch.

Your images can be easily converted into a wonderful coffee table book that anyone who comes to your home can enjoy. And with today's digital technology, there's no glue, cutting, or pasting necessary.

A family vacation calendar on your refrigerator is a constant reminder of your vacation fun, and it's relatively easy to create. There's another great thing about custom family calendars:

They make wonderful personalized gifts for grandparents, friends, and teachers.

Crayola's souvenir suitcase is a fun project for kids of all ages. The following instructions and all sorts of other Crayola projects can be found on the company's website at Crayola.com (*www.crayola.com*).

1. Let your child choose a sneaker box for your suitcase with the lid attached.
2. Cut construction or white paper into rectangles with Crayola Scissors.
3. Draw pictures of places you have visited or hope to visit on your travel stickers.
4. Use Crayola Crayons and Crayola Washable Markers to create scenes of parks, picnics, famous places, cities, beaches, or mountains. You could also include vehicles such as cars or planes.
5. Write travel words or destinations on more rectangles. Have fun! Visit the Big Apple! Customs! are some examples. Make up more words of your own.
6. Attach stickers to your Souvenir Suitcase with Crayola Glue Sticks. Point them in different directions to cover your suitcase.
7. To make a suitcase handle, ask an adult to poke two holes through one end of the box. Thread ribbon through the holes, and knot the ends inside the box.

Children can glue mementoes and dictate stories for mom or dad to write in their vacation memory book. Older kids may draw or write about their experiences on the trip and embellish their journal with postcards and photographs.

Look for opportunities on your trip to have some quiet time for your child to draw, write, and glue in his vacation memory book. If she has a hard time getting started, a few prompts will help her think of ideas for her book. Start by asking about her favorite or most memorable thing on that day. Let her draw and color a picture about it. Take plenty of photos. You can even print some favorites at kiosks during your trip.

Digital video is a great way to preserve travel memories. Nowadays many digital cameras also have features that allow you to capture video and download it to your personal computer, or upload it to a video- or photo-sharing website. Families can even edit vacation videos into short films. Microsoft's Digital Image Suite PLUS or Apple's iMovie is a starting point for beginners new to video editing. With these programs, you can also match clips with tracks of music.

## Vacation Photography

One of the most important things to remember when you're packing for vacation is to remember to bring your camera! Photos are key to chronicling your vacation so you and your family can reflect back on your journey through the years that follow. Having a good camera is a great start. There are several options that take great pictures and are also very affordable.

If you've been capturing your family's memories on a disposable camera, you already know it can be inconvenient to have your photos developed. With the cost of developing your film and making copies, it won't be long before you've spent enough money to purchase a digital camera. Plus, using a digital camera will dramatically increase the chances you'll return home with quality photos. They're easily transferred from your camera to a home computer, and easily shared via the Internet.

When choosing a camera, image quality and additional bells and whistles determine the price point. Knowing the language will help you when you shop. A pixel is one single point in any given image. One million pixels equal a megapixel. Less expensive cameras are five megapixels or less. The more pixels your camera has to offer, the better an image will appear when it's enlarged. If you are going to limit your photography to taking a few photos for a family album, a smaller megapixel point-and-shoot camera should meet all of your needs and budget, and allow you to take great pictures. A digital camera that has five megapixels will provide enough resolution so prints won't be grainy when enlarged to eight by ten inches for example.

The next level for point-and-shoot compact cameras are seven, then nine megapixels. Companies like Nikon and Canon offer a wide selection of point-and-shoot cameras that are so small they can fit into pockets and pocketbooks. Many of these cameras provide features similar to more bulky models.

## 💼 Travel Tip

Everyone hopes their photos develop beautifully. But in the event yours don't measure up to album standards, most visitors' bureaus of the country or state your family visited will have images they can share. If your family's photos don't come out, at least you'll have some of the area you visited for your collection.

Taking great pictures may seem difficult, but on the Internet you'll find incredible free tips for taking better photos. You'd be surprised to find that if you can point and click, you can probably take great photos of your family vacation.

## Scrapbooking Fun for the Whole Family

A travel-themed scrapbook is a great way to preserve your family's travel memories. They showcase your journey in a fun way, and best of all, making your own travel-themed scrapbook is a project the family can do together. Travel scrapbooks come in a variety of sizes along with entire scrapbook kits that make it easy for anyone to do. Even smaller travelers can pitch in.

Another fun thing about creating a travel scrapbook with your family is the wide assortment of cool additives you can get to make your scrapbook really special. All kinds of plane-, train-, and automobile-themed embellishments, along with maps and luggage stickers, make for great additions to your family travel scrapbook. There are practically as many kinds of travel scrapbooks and scrapbooking kits as there are places to go. Many of them are available online at reasonable prices.

- *www.hellotraveler.com*
- *www.scrapbook.com*
- *www.scrapyourtrip.com*
- *www.bee-utifulscrapbooking.com*
- *www.fabulousscrapbook.com*
- *www.scrapbooking-warehouse.com*

There are many ways to create a scrapbook that the whole family can enjoy. Perhaps each family member can build his own page with favorite mementos from your family vacation. Or, perhaps each family member can contribute something to each page.

Before you begin making your scrapbook, gather all of your vacation photos. Find a large space on which you can spread them out for everyone to see. The kitchen table and even the living room floor are both great places to get a bird's-eye view of your photo collection. Each family member can select her favorites. Be picky, because too many photos will clutter the pages and make it hard to handle. Document each photo with a little note on the back or a Post-it. Label them with names and dates, places and anything special that made you take the picture in the first place. You'll need this later when you actually start assembling your scrapbook. Once everyone has selected and labeled her favorites, you're ready to start building your scrapbook!

The next step is to decide what size your scrapbook will be. After selecting your photos, lay them out on a table separated as if you were laying them on the page of a photo album. Leave room for fun mementos. For example, put all of one family member's photos together. More than one page may be required to accommodate all of them. Count the number of photos you have, and using a tape measure, see how many inches you'll need to include all of the photos and whatever creative additions you want to use. Write down all of the specifics in a notebook.

Choosing your travel scrapbook is part of the fun. Measuring your photos will help you decide how large your scrapbook needs to be to accommodate your memories. A two-week trip will require a much larger scrapbook than a weekend getaway.

## ≡ Fast Fact

Websites like Smilebox (*www.smilebox.com*) offer free downloadable scrapbooking layouts for families who already have a theme in mind.

Your new scrapbook is a blank canvas, and your family members are the artists. There are a few basic tools you'll need that can be purchased at a discount store, and many might already be in your kitchen drawer. They include two-sided adhesive tape, card stock paper, small and large scissors, pens, and magic markers.

If you need guidance on how to build a scrapbook, sites like Scrapbook.com (*www.scrapbook.com*) contain helpful tips on how to create scrapbooks and albums. The website's message boards allow scrapbookers to communicate with each other and share resources. Things like an up-to-date listing on discount scrapbooking stores, tips on how to start or finish a scrapbook, and where to find coupons for discounted scrapbooking supplies can be found on the message boards. Scrapbookers leave messages with clever ideas for scrapbooking as well, like one that suggested using pretty leftover wallpaper border to trim a scrapbook for a girl's bedroom. For your travel scrapbook, you might consider using an old map you no longer need, or even menus from favorite restaurants your family visited on vacation.

## Interactive Sharing and e-Photo Albums

Interactive photo sharing websites allow for moving photos from a digital camera or camera phone to create a digital photo album you can share online with anyone you choose. Best of all, most of them are free.

Shutterfly is a photo storage and picture sharing website (*www.shutterfly.com*). Like other photo sharing websites, account holders get unlimited picture storage and it's free. Images at Shutterfly are stored at full resolution so the photo quality remains intact, and they carry a customer satisfaction guarantee. Shutterfly also offers promotional rewards like free prints. Shutterfly offers cards to celebrate birthdays, birth announcements, and other kinds of greeting cards and invitations, all using your original photos. And families can create their own photo sharing website on which they can share photos from their travels. For the family who really wants a showpiece of their journey, Shutterfly also offers professionally bound hard and soft cover photo books.

At Snapfish, another photo sharing website, account holders can upload photos through their Snapfish account with a one-click system. Photos can also be e-mailed to Snapfish and they'll upload your photos for you. For families who plan to create multiple digital albums, Snapfish provides free software, called PictureMover, that you can download. The software allows you to upload photos directly from a camera or USB drive. First-time users of a Snapfish account get twenty prints free of charge as an incentive to use the service. (*www.snapfish.com*)

Yahoo's Flickr.com is a popular photo sharing website and storage option (*www.flickr.com*) that links with Yahoo's "Trip Planner." Trip Planner is a separate website that allows users to build travel itineraries including lodging, dining, things to do, maps, and directions. Trip Planner allows you to create a photo album when your family returns from your vacation and share it on Flickr with friends and other family members.

## ≡ Fast Fact

New to online photo sharing? You and your family can download instruction manuals for most photo sharing applications online in the help or customer service sections of each site.

Teenagers are flocking to PhotoBucket.com (*www.photo bucket.com*) to upload all photos and videos. This site makes it easy to create slide shows and share videos. One reason it's so popular with teens is the sharing of MySpace icons for the purposes of profile layouts.

Some of the options on the photo album website BlueMelon .com include the freedom to choose between three separate uploaders to retain stored photos online in their original size. Photo albums can be titled and organized into dedicated categories and customized for visitors to view with narratives and keywords, so visitors to your album can easily download it with minimal clicks. (*www.bluemelon.com*)

## Recap and Reminisce

Once you've returned from your vacation, you'd be surprised at how quickly you and your family will forget details. Something your waiter said that made everyone laugh. The sandcastle your son or daughter built, and accidentally wiped out when they tripped over the sand bucket. There are many ways for everyone to reminisce—from looking at family photo albums together to playing games and watching a slide show of your vacation on your DVD player.

One way to recreate the fun you and your family had on vacation is to do "Dinner and a Movie" relating to the trip. It's a fun way to enjoy your vacation photographs and pay homage to wherever you and your family traveled, especially if the destination is known for a special cuisine.

Did your family visit Kansas City, Missouri, or Memphis, Tennessee? If so, chances are you tried the barbecue both cities are known for. Wherever your family vacationed, you can find easy recipes online to recreate your favorite dishes at home. Before dinner, using an application like PowerPoint, make a family photo slide show of your vacation and burn it to a DVD. Many DVD players can play slide shows of your photos for you to watch while enjoying the cuisine your family loved on vacation.

Decorate for the holidays with things you found on vacation. Seashells are especially good for this project, and make wonderful Christmas tree ornaments! A family beach vacation should yield enough shells to cover your beach-themed holiday tree. Candy wreaths made from candy purchased on a family vacation make great gifts.

Whether you and your family go on a weekend getaway or an extended vacation, remember to chronicle your travels, preserve your memories on film and take time when you get home as a family to reflect on your journey. Family time is special, especially, when you're traveling together.

# Attractions and Sites by Region

## Northeast

### Mountains of Fun

**POCONO MOUNTAINS**
Poconos Tourism Clearing House
*www.800poconos.com*

Split Rock Resort
*www.splitrockresort.com*

Woodloch Resort
*www.woodloch.com*

Great Wolf Lodge
*www.greatwolf.com/Locations/Poconos*

**VERMONT MOUNTAINS**
Vermont Vacations
*www.vermontvacation.com*

Stowe Mountain Lodge
*www.stowemountainlodge.com*

Stoweflake Resort and Spa
*www.stoweflake.com*

Smugglers' Notch Resort
*www.smuggs.com*

Greenview Cottages
*www.smuggsvacationhomes.com*

Nye's Green Valley Farm
*www.nyesgreenvalleyfarm*

Sterling Ridge Log Cabin Resort
*www.sterlingridgeresort.com*

Summit Lodge & Resort
*www.summitlodgevermont.com*

Mountain Meadows Lodge
*www.mountainmeadowslodge.com*


**WHITE MOUNTAINS OF NEW HAMPSHIRE**
New Hampshire Mountain Hiking
*www.nhmountainhiking.com*

Visit White Mountains
*www.visitwhitemountains.com*

Ski NH
*www.skinh.com*

Mount Washington Observatory
*www.mountwashington.org*

New Hampshire Travel & Tourism Guide
*www.mountaintravelguide.com*

New Hampshire Mountain Peaks & Summits
*www.mountainzone.com/mountains/state.asp?s=NH*

**MAINE MOUNTAINS**
Maine Office of Tourism
*www.visitmaine.com/region/lakes*

## Water, Water Everywhere

**NEW ENGLAND**
Massachusetts Beaches
*www.masstraveljournal.com/beaches*

Raft Maine
*www.raftmaine.com*

Inn by the River
*www.innbytheriver.com*

Maine Beaches
*www.visitmaine.net/beaches.htm*

Maine Lakes
*www.visitmaine.com/region/lakes*

New Hampshire Beaches
*www.eastern-beaches.com/new-hampshire-beaches*

New Hampshire Lakes Region
*www.lakesregion.org*

Rhode Island Beaches
*www.visitrhodeisland.com/what-to-do/beaches*

Connecticut Beaches
*www.eastern-beaches.com/connecticut-beaches*

**MID-ATLANTIC BEACHES**
Ocean Place
*www.oceanplace.com*

New Jersey Shore
*www.newjerseyshore.com*

Virtual New Jersey Shore
*www.virtualnjshore.com*

Wildwoods at the Jersey Shore
*www.wildwoodsnj.com*

Maryland Beaches
*www.eastern-beaches.com/maryland-beaches*

Ocean City, Maryland
*www.ococean.com*

Delaware Beaches
*www.eastern-beaches.com/delaware-beaches*

## America's Coolest Family-Friendly Cities

**NEW YORK CITY**
Chelsea Piers
*www.chelseapiers.com*

Broadway Theater
*www.broadway.com*

Statue of Liberty and Ellis Island
*www.nps.gov*

Central Park
*www.centralparknyc.org*

Gem Hotels
*www.thegemhotel.com*

Grand Hyatt Hotel Midtown Manhattan
*www.grandnewyork.hyatt.com*

Explore Chinatown
*www.explorechinatown.com*

Little Italy
*www.littleitalynyc.com*

**BOSTON**
Boston Convention and Visitors Bureau
*www.bostonusa.com*

Boston Duck Tours
*www.bostonducktours.com*

Freedom Trail
*www.nps.gov*

Colonnade Hotel
*www.colonnadehotel.com*

Seaport Hotel and World Trade Center
*www.seaportboston.com*

Legal Seafood
*www.legalseafoods.com*

Vinny T's Restaurant
*www.vinnytsofboston.com*

**PHILADELPHIA**
Philadelphia Visitors Bureau
*www.gophila.com*

Comfort Inn Penns Landing
*www.comfortinn.com*

Best Western Independence Park Hotel
*www.independenceparkhotel.com*

Dalessandro's
*www.dalessandros.com*

Ralph's Italian
*www.ralphsrestaurant.com*

**WASHINGTON, D.C.**
Washington D.C. Walking Tours
*www.washingtonwalks.com*

DC by Foot
*www.dcbyfoot.com*

*Washington.org*
*www.washington.org*

Library of Congress
*www.loc.gov*

Madame Tussauds Wax Museum
*www.madametussaudsdc.com*

National Air & Space Museum
*www.nasm.si.edu*

National Museum of Natural History
*www.mnh.si.edu*

National Cherry Blossom Festival
*www.nationalcherryblossomfestival.org*

International Spy Museum
*www.spymuseum.org*

Washington Convention and Visitors Bureau
*www.washington.org*

L'Enfant Plaza Hotel
*www.lenfantplazahotel.com*

Old Glory Barbeque
*www.oldglorybbq.com*

ICI Urban Bistro
*www.iciurbanbistro.com*

## A Taste of the Past—Historic Destinations

### HISTORIC DESTINATIONS NORTHEAST

Salem Witch Museum, Massachusetts
*www.salemwitchmuseum.com*

Plimoth Plantation, Massachusetts
*www.plimoth.org*

Old York, Maine
*www.oldyork.org*

New England Visitors Bureau
*www.visitnewengland.com*

York Microtel, Maine
*www.yorkmicrotel.com*

Bunker Hill Bed and Breakfast, Massachusetts
*www.bunkerhillbedandbreakfast.com*

Salem Waterfront Hotel, Massachusetts
*www.salemwaterfronthotel.com*

Walking Tours of Historic Philadelphia
*www.theconstitutional.com*

Gettysburg National Park, Pennsylvania
*www.nps.gov/gett/index.htm*

Historic Delaware: The First State
*www.visitdelaware.com/history.htm*

## Winter Wonderlands

### STOWE, VERMONT
Stowe Commodores Inn
*www.commodoresinn.com*

Trapp Family Lodge
*www.trappfamilylodge.com*

GoStowe.com
*www.gostowe.com/KidsZone*

Stowe
*www.stowe.com*

### VERMONT
Ski Vermont
*www.skivermont.com*

Winter Tourism in Vermont
*www.travel-vermont.com/seasons/winter.asp*

### MAINE
Ski Maine Association
*www.skimaine.com*

Winter Tourism in Maine
*www.visitmaine.com/seasons/winter/*

### NEW HAMPSHIRE
Ski New Hampshire
*www.skinh.com*

Winter Tourism in New Hampshire
*www.visitnh.gov/best-time-to-visit/winter-activities*

**NEW YORK**
Winter Tourism in New York
*www.iloveny.com/Outdoors/WinterActivities.aspx*

**PENNSYLVANIA**
Pennsylvania Ski Areas Association
*www.skipa.com*

## Camping: America's #1 Vacation

Boston Harbor Islands
*www.bostonharborislands.com*

Maine's Sebago Lake Family Campground
*www.sebagolakecamping.com*

Northwaters Wilderness Program
*www.northwaters.com*

Maine Camping Guide
*www.campmaine.com*

New Hampshire Campground Owners Association
*www.ucampnh.com*

New York State Campgrounds
*www.visitnewyorkstate.net/campgrounds*

Pennsylvania Campground Owners Association
*www.pacamping.com*

Vermont Campground Association
*www.campvermont.com*

Delaware Outdoor Recreation
*www.visitdelaware.com/outdoor.htm*

Maryland Family-Friendly Trails
*www.visitmaryland.org/Pages/FamilyFriendlyTrails.aspx*

## Attractions, Festivals, and Fairs

Top 10 Scenic Drives
*www.drivethetop10.com*

Niagara Falls
*www.infoniagara.com*

Manhattan's Central Park Zoo
*www.centralparkzoo.com*

New York's Oyster Bay Seafood and Waterfront Festival
*www.theoysterfestival.org*

Maine Lobster Festival
*www.mainelobsterfestival.com*

Six Flags New England
*www.sixflags.com/newEngland*

ThemeParkCity.com
*www.themeparkcity.com*

Sesame Place
*www.sesameplace.com*

National Aquarium Baltimore
*www.aqua.org*

Polar Caves Park, Plymouth, New Hampshire
*www.polarcaves.com*

Trusted Tours
*www.trustedtours.com*

Story Land, Glen, New Hampshire
*www.storylandnh.com*

# Southeast

## Mountains of Fun

### NORTH GEORGIA MOUNTAINS
Majestic Mountain Getaways
*www.majesticmountaingetaways.com*

Brasstown Valley Resort and Spa
*www.brasstownvalley.com*

Glen-Ella Springs Inn & Meeting Place
*www.glenella.com*

Georgia State Parks
*www.georgiastateparks.org*

### BLUE RIDGE MOUNTAINS
Earthshine Mountain Lodge
*www.earthshinemtnlodge.com*

Best Western Asheville
*www.bestwestern.com*

### GREAT SMOKY MOUNTAINS
Gatlinburg's Fort Fun Family Center
*www.smokymountainfun.com*

Lookout Mountain
*www.lookoutmountain.com*

Nantahala Outdoor Center (NOC)
*www.noc.com*

Gatlinburg Vacations
*www.gatlinburg.com*

Great Smokies Vacation Rentals
*www.greatsmokies.com*

Carolina Mountain Vacations
*www.carolinamountainvacations.com*

## Water, Water Everywhere

**FLORIDA**
Florida Beaches
*www.visitflorida.com/beaches*

Paradise Coast
*www.paradisecoast.com*

Naples Beach Hotel & Golf Club
*www.naplesbeachhotel.com*

Naples Grande Beach Resort
*www.naplesgranderesort.com*

The Lemon Tree Inn
*www.lemontreeinn.com*

Marco Island Marriott Beach Resort Golf Club & Spa
*www.marriott.com*

Marco Beach Ocean Resort
*www.marcoresort.com*

Watercolor Inn and Resort
*www.watercolorresort.com*

The Everglades
*www.florida-everglades.com*

## SOUTH CAROLINA
South Carolina Beaches
*http://beaches.discoversouthcarolina.com*

Wildwater, Ltd.
*www.wildwaterrafting.com*

Nantahala Family Outdoor Center (NOC)
*www.noc.com*

Caribbean Resort and Villas
*www.caribbeanresort.com*

## NORTH CAROLINA
North Carolina Beaches
*www.ncbeaches.com*

Nantahala Family Outdoor Center (NOC)
*www.noc.com*

Oceanana Family Resort
*www.oceanana-resort.com*

The Outer Banks
*www.visitob.com*

## TENNESSEE
Nantahala Family Outdoor Center (NOC)
*www.noc.com*

Tennessee Lakes
*www.tennesseelakeinfo.com*

**GEORGIA**
Explore Georgia
*www.exploregeorgia.org/At-The-Beach*

Mountain Aire Cottages and Motel
*www.mountainairecottages.com*

Jekyll Island: Georgia's Jewel
*www.jekyllisland.com*

Tybee Island: Savannah's Beach
*www.tybeevisit.com*

**LOUISIANA**
Alligator Bayou Adventure Tours
*www.alligatorbayou.com*

Louisiana Tour Company—Swamp and Airboat Tours
*www.louisianaswamp.com*

Mississippi Riverboat Tours
*www.neworleansonline.com/neworleans/tours/riverboattours.html*

**VIRGINIA AND WEST VIRGINIA**
Virginia Beaches
*www.virginia.org/site/features.asp?featureID=114*

All Day River Adventure Cruises
*www.misshamptoncruises.com*

Alliance Tall Ship Day Sails
*www.schooneralliance.com*

Virginia Wildlife Refuges
*www.fws.gov/northeast/easternshore*

Virginia Beach
*www.vabeach.com*

West Virginia White Water Rafting
*www.wvwhitewater.com*

West Virginia Lakes Region
*www.westvirginia.com/lakes*

Resort at Glade Springs, West Virginia
*www.gladesprings.com*

**MISSISSIPPI**
Canoeing and Kayaking
*www.visitmississippi.org/outdoor_rec/outdoor_kayaking.asp*

Fishing
*www.visitmississippi.org/outdoor_rec/outdoor_fishing.asp*

**ALABAMA**
Alabama Beaches
*www.alabama.travel/activities/alabama-beaches*

Alabama Water Sports
*www.alabama.travel/activities/outdoor-activities/water-sports*

**ARKANSAS**
Canoeing, Rafting, and Kayaking
*www.arkansas.com/outdoors/canoeing-rafting-kayaking*

Fishing
*www.fishing-arkansas.com*

## America's Coolest Family-Friendly Cities

**NASHVILLE**
Grand Ole Opry
*www.opry.com*

Bluebird Café
*www.bluebirdcafe.com*

Country Music Hall of Fame and Museum
*www.countrymusichalloffame.com*

Ryman Auditorium
*www.ryman.com*

Visit Music City
*www.visitmusiccity.com*

Gaylord Opryland Resort
*www.gaylordhotels.com*

Wildhorse Saloon
*www.wildhorsesaloon.com*

Loveless Café
*www.lovelesscafe.com*

**ORLANDO**
Orlando Tourism
*www.orlandoinfo.com*

Universal Studios, Orlando
*www.universalorlando.com*

Walt Disney World
*www..disney.go.com*

Sea World Orlando
*www.seaworld.com/orlando/default.aspx*

**ATLANTA**
Atlanta Travel Guide
*www.atlanta.net*

Georgia Aquarium: The World's Largest Aquarium
*www.georgiaaquarium.org*

**ST. AUGUSTINE**
St. Augustine Tourism
*www.oldcity.com*

Ghost Tours
*www.ghosttoursofstaugustine.com*

St. Augustine Alligator Farm
*www.alligatorfarm.us*

St. Augustine for Kids
*www.staugustine4kids.com*

## A Taste of the Past—Historic Destinations

Colonial Williamsburg, Virginia
*www.colonialwilliamsburg.com*

Civil War Discovery Trail
*www.civilwardiscoverytrail.org*

James Madison's Montpelier, Virginia
*www.montpelier.org*

Bentonville Battlefield State Historic Site, North Carolina
*www.nchistoricsites.org/Bentonvi*

Chickamauga Battlefield, Georgia
*www.nps.gov/CHCH*

Historic Savannah, Georgia
*www.visit-historic-savannah.com*

America's Best Value Inn Savannah, Georgia
*www.americasbestvalueinn.com*

Crowne Plaza Williamsburg Hotel, Virginia
*www.cpwilliamsburghotel.com*

Inn on Poplar Hill Virginia near Montpelier
*www.innonpoplarhill.com*

Arkansas Fort Smith National Historic Site
*www.fortsmith.org*

River Cove Cabins North Carolina
*www.rivercovecabin.com*

Historic Tours of Key West
*www.historictours.com/KeyWest*

Key West Historic Seaport
*www.fla-keys.com*

## Winter Wonderlands

Snowshoe Mountain Ski Resort, West Virginia
*www.snowshoemtn.com/index.htm*

Wintergreen Resort, Virginia
*www.wintergreenresort.com*

Sky Chalet Mountain Lodge, Virginia
*www.skychalet.com*

Ober Gatlinburg, Tennessee
*www.obergatlinburg.com/ski.htm*

## Camping: America's #1 Vacation

Ozarks State Park Campground, Arkansas
*www.ozarkmountainregion.com*

Miami Everglades Campground
*www.miamicamp.com*

Falling Waters Resort
*www.fallingwatersresort.com*

Nantahala Outdoor Center
*www.noc.com*

Blue Ridge Parkway
*www.blueridgeparkway.org*

## Attractions, Festivals, and Fairs

Rollins Planetarium at Young Harris College in Georgia
*www.yhc.edu*

Chimney Rock in the North Carolina Mountains
*www.chimneyrockpark.com*

Miami SkyLift
*www.miamiskylift.com*

Corn Maze at The Old Frontier in Thomson-McDuffie County, Georgia
*www.exploremcduffiecounty.com*

Richardson Farm in Spring Grove, Illinois
*www.richardsonfarm.com*

Biltmore Estate, North Carolina
*www.biltmore.com*

Charleston's Southeastern Wildlife Exposition and Harbor Festival (SEWE)
*www.sewe.com*

Charleston Harbor Fest
*www.charlestonharborfest.org*

Georgia Mountain Fair
*www.georgiamountainfairgrounds.com*

La Belle Amie Vineyard's Key West Music and Wine Fest in South Carolina
*www.labelleamie.com*

Sea World Orlando
*www.seaworld.com/orlando/default.aspx*

Miami Seaquarium
*www.miamiseaquarium.com*

Myrtle Beach's Grand Strand Ripley's Aquarium
*www.ripleysaquarium.com*

Georgia Aquarium
*www.georgiaaquarium.org*

South Carolina Riverbanks Zoo
*www.riverbanks.org*

Myrtle Beach's Alligator Adventure
*www.alligatoradventure.com*

Miami Metrozoo
*www.miamimetrozoo.com*

Florida Seafood Festival
*www.floridaseafoodfestival.com*

North Carolina Oyster Festival
*www.brunswickcountychamber.org/OF-NC-Oyster-Festival.cfm*

Charleston's Food and Wine Festival
*www.charlestonfoodandwine.com*

Trusted Tours
*www.trustedtours.com*

Four Seasons Family Fun at Bryce Resort, Virginia
*www.bryceresort.com*

# Central United States

## Mountains of Fun

The Aspen Chamber
*www.aspenchamber.org*

Idaho's Payette River Mountains
*www.payetterivermountains.com*

Boise, Idaho
*www.boise.org*

Swan Mountains Fly Fishing
*www.bigskyfishing.com*

Limelight Lodge, Aspen, Colorado
*www.limelightlodge.com*

Aloft Hotels
*www.starwoodhotels.com/AloftHotels*

Gateway Canyons
*www.gatewaycanyons.com*

Steamboat Resorts, Colorado
*www.steamboatresorts.com*

Redfish Lake Lodge, Idaho
*www.redfishlake.com*

The Duck Inn, Montana
*www.duckinn.com*

Grand Targhee Resort, Wyoming
*www.grandtarghee.com*

## Water, Water Everywhere

ROW Adventures, Idaho
*www.rowadventures.com*

River Expeditions
*www.RaftingInfo.com*

Lodge at Whitefish Lake, Montana
*www.lodgeatwhitefishlake.com*

Bear Lake, Utah and Idaho
*www.bearlake.org*

Great Lakes Region Geocaching
*www.nmg-geocaching.org*

Alpena
*www.alpenacvb.com*

Lake Erie
*www.thelakeerieguide.com*

Shilo Inn
*www.shiloinns.com*

South Beach Resort Hotel and Marina, Ohio
*www.sbresort.com*

Thunder Bay Resort, Michigan
*www.thunderbayresort.com*

## America's Coolest Family-Friendly Cities

### CHICAGO
Chicago Tours
*www.chicagotours.us*

Chicago LEGOLAND Discovery Centre
*www.legolanddiscoverycenter.com*

Kohl Children's Museum
*www.kohlchildrensmuseum.org*

Chicago Brookfield Zoo
*www.brookfieldzoo.org*

Lincoln Park Zoo
*www.lpzoo.org*

Chicago Navy Pier
*www.navypier.com*

Holiday Inn Hotel and Suites Downtown Chicago
*www.ichotelsgroup.com*

Best Western Grant Park Hotel
*www.bwgrantparkhotel.com*

Giordanos Pizza
*www.giordanos.com*

Chicago Pizza and Oven Grinder Company
*www.chicagopizzaandovengrinder.com*

**ST. LOUIS**

St. Louis Tourism
*www.explorestlouis.com*

St. Louis for Kids
*www.explorestlouis.com/kids/index.asp*

St. Louis Hotels Guide
*www.hotels-stl.com*

The Gateway Arch
*www.gatewayarch.com/Arch/index.aspx*

St. Louis Zoo
*www.stlzoo.org*

St. Louis Forest Park
*www.slfp.com/ForestPark.html*

St. Louis Fine Restaurant Guide
*www.diningstl.com*

## A Taste of the Past—Historic Destinations

Holiday Inn Express, Rapid City, South Dakota
*www.holidayinnexpress.com*

Spirit of the Old West
*www.thespiritoftheoldwest.com*

Native American Historic Destinations
*www.nanations.com*

Go Native America
*www.gonativeamerica.com*

Boothill Inn and Suites of Billings, Montana
*www.boothillinn.com*

Legends of America
*www.legendsofamerica.com*

## Winter Wonderlands

Aspen/Snowmass, Colorado
*www.aspensnowmass.com*

Silvertree Hotel at Snowmass Village, Colorado
*www.silvertreehotel.com*

Limelight Lodge, Aspen, Colorado
*www.limelightlodge.com*

Alta/Snowbird, Utah
*www.altalodge.com*

Beaver Creek, Colorado
*www.beavercreek.Snow.com*

Northstar at Lake Tahoe, Nevada
*www.northstarattahoe.com*

Kids Mountains of Discovery at Breckenridge Resort, Colorado
*www.breckenridge.Snow.com*

Idaho Winter
*www.visitidaho.org/winter*

Jackson Hole Ski Resort, Wyoming
*www.jacksonhole.com*

Ski Montana
*http://skimt.com*

## Camping: America's #1 Vacation

Colorado River & Trail Expeditions
*www.crateinc.com*

Southwest Colorado's Mesa Verde National Park
*www.nps.gov/MEVE*

Cortez, Colorado
*www.cortezchamber.com*

Jellystone Park Camp and Resort
*www.nashvillejellystone.com*

Glacier National Park, Montana
*www.nps.gov/glac/index.htm*

Yellowstone National Park
*www.nps.gov/yell/planyourvisit/camping-in-yellowstone.htm*

## Attractions, Festivals, and Fairs

Wyoming's Grand Targhee Music Festival
*www.grandtarghee.com*

Wisconsin's Wisconsin Dells
*www.wisconsindells.com*

Ohio's Cedar Point/Sandusky/Erie County Visitors and Convention Bureau
*www.shoresandislands.com*

Trusted Tours
*www.trustedtours.com*

The Mall of America, Minnesota
*www.mallofamerica.com*

The Rock and Roll Hall of Fame, Cleveland, Ohio
*www.rockhall.com*

Midwest Horse Fair
*http://midwesthorsefair.com*

Durango and Silverton Narrow Gauge Railroad
*www.durangotrain.com*

Pikes Peak Cog Railway
*www.cograilway.com*

Colorado Railroad Museum
*www.crrm.org*

Denver Zoo
*www.denverzoo.org*

Pueblo Zoo, Colorado
*www.pueblozoo.org.*

Kit Carson County Carousel, Colorado
*www.kitcarsoncountycarousel.com*

# Northwest

### Mountains of Fun
LaConner Channel Lodge and LaConner Country Inn,
Washington
*www.laconnerlodging.com*

Skamania Lodge, Stevenson, Washington
*www.skamania.com*

Suncadia, Cle Elum, Washington
*www.suncadia.com*

Resort at the Mountain, Mt. Hood, Oregon
*www.theresort.com*

## Water, Water Everywhere

Alaska Cruises
*www.alaskacruises.com*

Nenana Raft Adventures, Denali National Park, Alaska
*www.alaskaraft.com*

Pacific Coast Beaches
*www.pacific101.com/beaches.htm*

California Beaches
*www.beachcalifornia.com*

Half Moon Bay, California
*www.visithalfmoonbay.org*

Monterey Bay Aquarium, California
*www.montereybayaquarium.org*

Oregon Coast Visitors Association
*http://visittheoregoncoast.com*

Cannon Beach, Oregon
*www.cannon-beach.net*

San Juan Islands, Washington
*www.visitsanjuans.com*

Bird Rock Hotel, San Juan Island, Washington
*www.birdrockhotel.com*

Inn at Ship Bay, Orcas Island, Washington
*www.innatshipbay.com*

Susie's Mopeds, Friday Harbor, Washington
*www.susiesmopeds.com*

## America's Coolest Family-Friendly Cities

### SAN FRANCISCO
San Francisco Cable Car
*www.sfcablecar.com*

Best Western Tuscan Inn at Fisherman's Wharf
*www.tuscaninn.com*

Argonaut Hotel
*www.argonauthotel.com*

Palace Hotel
*www.sfpalace.com*

Scharffen Berger Chocolate Maker
*www.scharffenberger.com*

Charles Chocolates Factory Store & Chocolate Bar
*www.charleschocolates.com*

San Francisco Zoo
*www.sfzoo.org*

Rooftop at Yerba Buena Gardens
*www.yerbabuenagardens.com*

Alcatraz Island
*www.nps.gov/Alcatraz*

Golden Gate Park
*www.sfgate.com*

**SEATTLE**

Visit Seattle
*www.visitseattle.org/visitors/*

Go Northwest Travel Guide
*www.gonorthwest.com*

Seattle's Space Needle and Pacific Science Center
*www.pacsci.org*

Inn at the Market
*www.innatthemarket.com*

Seattle Watertown Hotel
*www.watertownseattle.com*

## A Taste of the Past—Historic Destinations

Jacksonville, Oregon
*www.jacksonvilleoregon.org*

Tillicum Village, Washington
*www.tillicumvillage.com*

Klondike Gold Rush National Historic Park
*www.nps.gov/klse/index.htm*

Pan for Gold in Columbia, California
*www.columbiacalifornia.com*

Old Town, San Diego, California
*www.oldtownsandiego.org*

Winchester Mystery House, San Jose, California
*www.winchestermysteryhouse.com*

## Winter Wonderlands

Alyeska Ski Resort, Alaska
*www.alyeskaresort.com*

World Ice Art Championships and Kid's Park, Alaska
*www.icealaska.com*

Ski Washington
*www.skiwashington.com*

Ski Oregon
*www.traveloregon.com/Ski-Oregon.aspx*

Oregon Ski Resorts
*www.skicentral.com/oregon.html*

California Snow
*www.californiasnow.com*

## Camping: America's #1 Vacation

Alaska Camping and RV Touring
*www.alaska.com/activities/camping/*

Washington State Parks
*www.parks.wa.gov*

Quarts Mountain Lookout at Mount Spokane State Park
*www.parks.wa.gov/yurtsandcabins/quartzmountain*

Oregon State Parks and Recreation
*www.oregon.gov/OPRD/PARKS/index.shtml*

Lake Owyhee, Oregon
*www.oregon.gov/OPRD/PARKS/tepees_wagons.shtml*

Umpqua Lighthouse State Park, Oregon
*www.oregonstateparks.org/park_121.php*

Joshua Tree National Park, California
*www.joshua.tree.national-park.com/camping.htm*

California State Parks
*www.parks.ca.gov*

## Attractions, Festivals, and Fairs

Anchorage Museum, Alaska
*www.anchoragemuseum.org*

Anchorage Folk Festival, Alaska
*www.anchoragefolkfestival.org*

Juneau Jazz and Classics, Alaska
*www.jazzandclassics.org*

California Fairs and Festivals
*http://californiafairsandfestivals.com*

Napa Valley Mustard Festival, California
*www.mustardfestival.org*

Vibrant Living Expo Raw Food Festival, Mendocino County, California
*www.rawfoodchef.com*

Silverwood Theme Park in Northern Idaho
*www.silverwoodthemepark.com*

Zoo Boise in Idaho
*www.zooboise.org*

Seattle International Film Festival
*www.siff.net*

Washington Festivals and Events
*www.wfea.org*

Washington State Autumn Leaf Festival
*www.autumnleaffestival.com*

Trusted Tours
*www.trustedtours.com*

# Southwest

## Mountains of Fun

Beaver Dam Mountain Wilderness, Arizona
*www.americansouthwest.net/arizona*

Grand Canyon National Park Hiking Guide
*www.grand.canyon.national-park.com/hike.htm*

New Mexico Hiking
*www.explorenm.com/hikes/*

## Water, Water Everywhere

White Water Rafting on the Rio Grande
*www.kokopelliraft.com*

Bill Dvorak's Kayak and Rafting Expeditions
*www.dvorakexpeditions.com/southwest_rivers.htm*

Southwest Paddler
*http://southwestpaddler.com*

## America's Coolest Family-Friendly Cities

**LAS VEGAS**
Visit Las Vegas
*www.visitlasvegas.com*

LasVegas.com
*www.lasvegas.com*

Las Vegas Kids
*http://lasvegaskids.net*

Adventuredome Theme Park
*www.adventuredome.com*

Circus Circus
*www.circuscircus.com*

Excalibur Hotel and Casino
*www.excaliburcasino.com*

Ballys Las Vegas
*www.ballyslasvegas.com*

**AUSTIN, TEXAS**
Austin Convention and Visitor's Bureau
*www.austintexas.org*

Austin Children's Museum
*www.austinkids.org*

City Guide
*www.austin360.com*

Iron Works BBQ
*www.ironworksbbq.com*

Austin Zoo and Animal Sanctuary
*www.austinzoo.org*

Texas State Capitol
*www.tspb.state.tx.us/spb/capitol/texcap.htm*

Lyndon B. Johnson Library and Museum
*www.lbjlib.utexas.edu*

Zilker Park
*www.ci.austin.tx.us/zilker*

## A Taste of the Past—Historic Destinations

Grand Canyon National Park
*www.nps.gov/grca/index.htm*

GhostTowns.com
*www.ghosttowns.com*

Montezuma Castle National Monument, Arizona
*www.nps.gov/moca/index.htm*

Sunset Crater National Monument, Arizona
*www.nps.gov/sucr/index.htm*

Tombstone, Arizona
*www.cityoftombstone.com*

Fort Union National Monument, Waltrous, New Mexico
*www.newmexico.org/explore/monuments/fort_union.php*

Aztec Ruins National Monument, Aztec, New Mexico
*www.newmexico.org/explore/monuments/aztec.php*

The Solano Starlight Ballroom, Solano, New Mexico
*www.newmexico.org/western/enjoy/starlight_ballroom.php*

The Alamo
*www.thealamo.org*

The Moody Mansion, Galveston, Texas
*www.moodymansion.org*

Fort Worth Western Heritage
*www.fortworth.com/visitors/western-heritage*

## Camping: America's #1 Vacation

Guide to Texas Outside
*www.texasoutside.com/campMain.html*

Wild Texas Camping, Parks, and Lakes
*www.wildtexas.com/parks*

New Mexico Camping
*www.explorenm.com/camping*

Camp Arizona
*www.camparizona.com*

## Attractions, Festivals, and Fairs

Albuquerque International Balloon Fiesta, New Mexico
*www.balloonfiesta.com*

Santa Fe Indian Market, New Mexico
*http://swaia.org*

Arizona Events—Office of Tourism
*www.arizonaguide.com/events-calendar*

Arizona Aloha Festival
*www.azalohafest.org*

Festivals of Texas Online
*www.festivalsoftexas.com*

Houston Rodeo Barbeque Festival
*www.hlsr.com*

Poteet Strawberry Festival, Texas
*www.strawberryfestival.com*

Trusted Tours
*www.trustedtours.com*

# Adventure Travel

New Hampshire's Sky Rider Treetop Canopy Tour
*www.visit-newhampshire.com*

Manhattan Sky Helicopter Tour
*www.allnewyorktours.com*

Niagara Falls Helicopter Tour
*www.niagara-helicopters.com*

Learn to Sail: New York, New Jersey, and Maryland
*www.offshoresailing.com*

Original Canopy Tour, Costa Rica
*www.canopytour.com*

Colorado Captain Zip Line Adventure Tours
*www.captainzipline.com*

Grand Canyon Helicopter Tours
*www.grandcanyon.com/GrandCanyonHelicopterTours.html*

Grand Canyon Tours
*www.grandcanyontourcompany.com*

Grand Canyon Helicopter & Sunset Ranch Adventure
*www.heliusa.com*

Helicopter Tours of Hawaii
*www.paradisecopters.com*

Houseboating
*www.houseboating.org*

All-About-Houseboats.com
*www.all-about-houseboats.com*

United States Space and Rocket Center
*www.spacecamp.com*

Mountain Shepherd Wilderness Survival School, Virginia
*www.mountainshepherd.com*

Salmon River Rafting, Idaho
*www.salmonriverexperience.com*

Paradise Ballooning over the Rio Grande
*www.taosballooning.com*

# Eco-Travel

Earthwatch Institute
*www.earthwatch.org*

Ocean Conservancy
*www.oceanconservancy.org*

International Ecotourism Society
*www.ecotourism.org*

EarthEcho
*www.earthecho.org*

SEE Turtles Baja Ocean Adventure
*www.seeturtles.org*

Crown of the Continent
*www.crownofthecontinent.net*

Mendocino County, California
*www.gomendo.com*

Alderwood Manor
*www.alderwood.org*

Stanwood/Camano Island
*www.sahs-fncc.org*

Western Heritage Center
*www.westernheritagecenter.org*

Flying Heritage Collection
*www.flyingheritage.com*

Snohomish County Arts
*www.artscouncilofsnoco.org, www.snohomish.org*

Forks, Washington
*www.forkswa.com/HomeofTwilighttheBook.html*

Quinault Valley
*www.rainforestgetaways.com*

Magical Misty Tour
*www.olympicpeninsulawaterfalltrail.com*

Lavender Growers of Sequim, Washington
*www.lavendergrowers.org*

Olympic Peninsula
*www.visitolympicpeninsula.org, www.olympicpeninsula.org*

Kalaloch Lodge of Forks, Washington
*www.visitkalaloch.com*

Tulalip Resort Casino and T-Spa
*www.tulalipresort.com*

Ariau Amazon Towers
*www.ariautowers.com*

Zegrahm and Eco Expeditions
*www.zeco.com*

## Off the Beaten Path Vacations

### Biking

Trails.com
*www.trails.com*

Telluride, Colorado
*www.telluride.com.*

Aspen Recreation Center
*www.aspenrecreation.com*

Coeur d'Alene and Route of the Hiawatha, Idaho
*www.visitidaho.org*

New England Mountain Biking Association NEMBA
*www.nemba.org*

Mountain Bike Western North Carolina
*www.mtbikewnc.com*

## Educational

Western Colorado Math & Science Center
*www.visitgrandjunctionGo Native America*

Archaeological Tours
*www.archaeology.org*

Far Horizons Archaeological and Cultural Trips
*www.farhorizons.com*

City Museum of St. Louis, Missouri
*www.citymuseum.org*

Denver Museum of Nature and Science and The Molly Brown Museum
*www.denver.org*

American Museum of Natural History
*www.amnh.org*

International Spy Museum
*www.spymuseum.org*

Chicago Children's Museum
*www.chicagochildrensmuseum.org.*

Dinosaur Ridge
*www.dinoridge.org*

Dinosaur Journey
*www.dinosaurjourney.org*

Dinosaur Depot in Cañon City
*www.dinosaurdepot.com*

## Culinary Schools for the Whole Family

Umstead Hotel and Spa of Cary, North Carolina
*www.theumstead.com*

Culinary School of the Rockies
*www.culinaryschoolrockies.com*

## Nature and Animals

Petting Zoo Farm reference
*www.pettingzoofarm.com*

Denver's Butterfly Pavilion & Insect Center
*www.butterflies.org*

Cheyenne Mountain Zoo
*www.cmzoo.org*

Lazy Five Ranch in Mooresville, North Carolina
*www.lazy5ranch.com*

National Audubon Society Nature Camp
*www.acadianationalpark.com*

Natural Habitat Adventures
*www.nathab.com*

Wild Mustangs of the Outer Banks
*www.outerbankstours.com*

World Center for Birds of Prey of Boise, Idaho
*www.peregrinefund.org*

Medina Raptor Center of Spencer, Ohio
*www.medinaraptorcenter.org*

Charlotte's Carolina Raptor Center
*www.carolinaraptorcenter.org*

Center for Birds of Prey of Charleston, South Carolina
*www.thecenterforbirdsofprey.org*

## Sporting Vacations

Mario Andretti and Jeff Gordon Racing Schools
*www.andrettiracing.com*

Heroes in Pinstripes
*www.heroesinpinstripes.com*

Joe Machnik's No. 1 Soccer Camps
*www.no1soccercamps.com*

Carmichael Training Systems and Cycling Camp
*www.trainright.com*

Fly Fishing in Santa Fe
*www.highdesertangler.com*

## Dude Ranches

Dude Ranchers' Association
*www.duderanch.org*

Montana Dude Ranch Association
*www.montanadra.com*

Colorado Dude Ranch Association
*www.coloradoranch.com*

Wyoming Dude Ranch Association
*www.wyomingdra.com*

Arizona Dude Ranch Association
*www.azdra.com*

Idaho Dude Ranch Association
*www.idahodra.com*

Red Horse Mountain Ranch in Harrison, Idaho
*www.redhorsemountain.com*

Hidden Meadow Ranch in Arizona's White Mountains
*www.hiddenmeadow.com*

Bar W Ranch of Whitefish, Montana
*www.thebarw.com*

Grand County in the Colorado Rockies
*www.dude-ranch.com*

Echo Valley Ranch and Spa, British Columbia
*www.evranch.com*

Tuchodi River Outfitters, British Columbia
*www.tuchodiriveroutfitters.com*

## Unique Family-Fun Vacations

**NORTHEAST**
Rocking Horse Family Fun Ranch, New York
*www.rhranch.com*

Mount Washington Cog Railway, New Hampshire
*www.thecog.com*

New England Fall Foliage Tours
*www.escortedfallfoliagetours.com*

The Berkshires, Massachusetts
*www.berkshires.org*

Haunted Boston Ghost Tours
*www.hauntedboston.com*

Canobie Lake Park, Salem, New Hampshire
*www.canobie.com*

Hershey Park, Hershey, Pennsylvania
*www.hersheypark.com*

**SOUTHEAST**
Key West Butterfly and Nature Conservatory
*www.keywestbutterfly.com*

Mel Fisher Maritime Museum
*www.melfisher.org*

Key West Aquarium
*www.keywestaquarium.com*

Key West Shipwreck Museum
*www.shipwreckhistoreum.com*

Sunset Culinaire Gourmet Sunset Cruise
*www.sunsetculinaire.com*

Key West National Wildlife Refuge
*www.fws.gov*

Key West Ghost Tour
*www.hauntedtours.com*

Dolphin Shipwreck and Snorkel Tours
*www.dolphinecho.com, www.bestonkeywest.com*

Conch Tour Train
*www.conchtourtrain.com*

Ripley's Believe It or Not! Key West
*www.ripleyskeywest.com*

Key West Pirate Soul Museum
*www.piratesoul.com*

Key West Light House and Keeper's Quarters Museum
*www.kwahs.com/Lighthouse.htm*

Parrot Key Resort Waterfront Hotel
*www.parrotkeyresort.com*

John F. Kennedy Space Center
*www.kennedyspacecenter.com, www.KSC.NASA.gov*

Village of Pinehurst, North Carolina
*www.villageofpinehurst.org*

Spa at Pinehurst, North Carolina
*www.pinehurst.com*

Historic Sunrise Theater, Southern Pines, North Carolina
*www.sunrisetheater.com*

Cabbage Patch Kids Babyland Tour
*www.cabbagepatchkids.com/index.html*

## CENTRAL UNITED STATES

The Wisconsin Dells
*http://wisdells.com*

Amana Colonies, Iowa
*www.amanacolonies.com*

Conner Prairie, Indiana
*www.connerprairie.org*

The Oz Museum, Wamego, Kansas
*www.ozmuseum.com*

Frankenmuth, Michigan's Little Bavaria
*www.frankenmuth.org*

Mammoth Site, Hot Springs, South Dakota
*www.mammothsite.com*

Mount Rushmore, South Dakota
*www.nps.gov/moru/index.htm*

## NORTHWEST

Christmas in Fort Bragg, Mendocino County, California
*www.fortbragg.com*

Ukiah, California, Small Town Christmas
*www.cityofukiah.com.*

Skunk Train Christmas Train in Willits, California
*www.skunktrain.com*

Craters of the Moon National Monument and Preserve, Idaho
*www.nps.gov/crmo/index.htm*

Alaska's Kenai Fjords National Park and Denali National Park
*www.travelalaskaoutdoors.com*

Gualala, California's "Festival of Nine Lessons"
*www.gualalaarts.org*

Mendocino Headlands State Park, California
*www.mendoparks.org*

Point Cabrillo, Mendocino Village, California
*www.pointcabrillo.org*

## SOUTHWEST

Native American Ruins in Sedona, Arizona
*www.visitsedona.com*

UFO Sightings: Roswell, New Mexico
*www.roswellnm.org*

The Taos Pueblo, New Mexico
*www.taospueblo.com*

Space Center, Houston
*www.spacecenter.org*

Houston Livestock Show and Rodeo
*www.hlsr.com*

Ripley's Believe It or Not! San Antonio, Texas
*http://sanantonio.ripleys.com*

Natural Bridge Caverns, Texas
*www.naturalbridgecaverns.com*

# Resorts, Cruises, and Island Vacations

## All-Inclusive Resorts and Cruises

Paradisus Resorts
*www.paradisus.com*

St. Lucia Coconut Bay Beach Resort & Spa
*www.cbayresort.com*

St. Kitts Marriott Resort & The Royal Beach Casino
*www.marriott.com*

Antigua's Jolly Beach Resort
*www.jollybeachresort.com*

Jamaica Holidays Pebbles
*www.fdrholidays.com/Pebbles*

Beaches Resorts
*www.beaches.com*

Royal Caribbean
*www.royalcaribbean.com*

Disney Cruises
*www.disney.com*

Carnival Liberty and Carnival Freedom Cruises
*www.carnival.com*

Norwegian Pearl and Norwegian Gem Cruises
*www.ncl.com*

# Affordable Island Destinations

Antigua's Nelson's Dockyard
*www.antiguamuseums.org/nelsonsdockyard.htm*

Antigua's Shirley Heights
*www.shirleyheightslookout.com*

Rex Resorts at Halcyon Cove
*www.rexresorts.com*

St. James' Club
*www.stjamesclubantigua.com*

Grand Cayman
*www.caymanislands.ky*

Turtle Nest Inn
*www.turtlenestinn.com*

Sunshine Suites
*www.sunshinesuites.com*

Comfort Suites
*www.caymancomfort.com*

Cayman Beach Suites
*www.grand-cayman-beach-suites.com*

Villas of the Galleon
*www.villasofthegalleon.com*

Chez Pierre, Bahamas
*www.chezpierrebahamas.com*

Atlantis
*www.atlantis.com*

Rockhouse Hotel, Negril
*www.rockhousehotel.com*

Country Country, Jamaica
*www.countryjamaica.com*

Kona Village, Hawaii
*www.konavillage.com*

Renaissance Aruba Resort & Casino
*www.marriott.com*

Grand Palladium Punta Cana Resort & Spa, Dominican Republic
*www.grandpalladiumpuntacanaresort.com*

Moon Palace Family Resort, Cancun
*www.palaceresorts.com*

Wyndham Sugar Bay Resort & Spa, St. Thomas, U.S. Virgin Islands
*www.wyndham.com*

# Helpful Travel Websites

**A BRIGGS PASSPORT SERVICES**
*www.abriggs.com*

Passport expeditors

**ADVENTURES IN TRAVEL EXPO**
*www.adventureexpo.com*

Travel trade show

**ALL-INCLUSIVE**
*www.all-inclusive.com*

Discount all-inclusive vacations

**AMAZON.COM**
*www.amazon.com*

Shopping website

**AMERICAN SOCIETY OF TRAVEL AGENTS (ASTA)**
*www.asta.org*

Industry association

**CRUISE DEALS**
*www.cruisedeals.com*

Reduced prices for cruise vacations

**ECO TRAVEL IDEAS/TRAVEL CHANNEL**
*www.travelchannel.com/Travel_Ideas/ Outdoors_and_Eco-Friendly*

Ecotourism and eco-friendly outdoor travel

**FESTIVALS**
*www.festivals.com*

Local event and world festival calendar of events

**THE FOOD ALLERGY & ANAPHYLAXIS NETWORK**
*www.foodallergy.org*

Information on food allergies

**GAP ADVENTURES**
*www.gapadventures.com*

Adventure tour company

**GO CITY KIDS**
*www.gocitykids.com*

Urban family adventure tips

**GORDON'S GUIDE**
*www.gordonsguide.com*

Travel publication

**HELLOTRAVELER.COM**

*www.hellotraveler.com*

Travel journals, photo albums, and scrapbooks

**HISTORICAL VACATIONS/TRAVEL MUSE**

*www.travelmuse.com/themes/historical-vacations*

Ideas for combining vacations with education

**HOME EXCHANGE**

*www.homeexchange.com*

Worldwide listings of home swap possibilities

**HOUSEBOATING**

*www.houseboating.org*

Houseboat rentals and vacations across the United States

**JOHNNYJET.COM**

*www.johnnyjet.com*

Travel portal and current travel destination website

**KAYAK.COM**

*www.kayak.com*

Travel booking website

**LAST-MINUTE TRAVEL**

*www.lastminutetravel.com*

Deals for flexible travelers

**NATIONAL PARK SERVICE: FIND A PARK**
*www.nps.gov/findapark*

Listing of all U.S. national parks by state

**NATURAL HABITAT ADVENTURES**
*www.nathab.com*

Nature tour company

**ORBITZ.COM**
*www.orbitz.com*

Travel booking website

**PASSPORTS, U.S. DEPARTMENT OF STATE**
*www.travel.state.gov/passport*

**PETTRAVEL.COM**
*www.pettravel.com*

Website about traveling with your pet

**PRICELINE.COM**
*www.priceline.com*

Travel booking website

**RESERVE AMERICA**
*www.reserveamerica.com*

Campgrounds and camping reservations

**ROADFOOD.COM**
*www.roadfood.com*

Suggested places to stop for food on the road

## SIDESTEP.COM
*www.sidestep.com*

Travel booking website

## SMARTERTRAVEL.COM
*www.smartertravel.com*

Travel booking website

## STATE FAIR DIRECTORY
*www.ncstatefair.com*

Links to official sites of U.S. state fairs

## THEMEPARKCITY.COM
*www.themeparkcity.com*

Theme park reference website

## THRILL PLANET
*www.thrillplanet.com*

Adventure travel website

## TOP 10 SCENIC DRIVES
*www.drivethetop10.com*

Information on traveling the top-ten scenic drives in the United States

## TRAVEL DOCUMENT FOLDERS
*www.traveldocumentfolders.com*

Folders specially made for holding travel documents like passports, itineraries, and the like

**TRAVEL.ORG**
*www.travel.org*

Travel website

**TRAVELING WITH KIDS**
*www.travelingwithkids.com*

Tips and information on traveling with kids

**TRAVELOCITY.COM**
*www.travelocity.com*

Travel website

**TRAVELZOO.COM**
*www.travelzoo.com*

Travel website

**TRUSTED TOURS**
*www.trustedtours.com*

National tour operator with tours in multiple cities

**USA ZOOS**
*www.officialusa.com/stateguides/zoos*

List of zoos, aquariums, safaris, wildlife sanctuaries, and preserves in the United States

# Travel Glossary

### All-inclusive vacation or cruise
A resort or cruise vacation that usually includes all of the costs of the trip in one overall price

### Booking buddy
A feature on travel websites that provides a web portal to help users search for fares and other travel destination information

### Currency calculator
Real-time online calculator that calculates the differences in destination currencies

### Cardholder travel rewards
Rewards, usually in the form of points or frequent-flier miles that cardholders can use in exchange for travel

### Credit card authorization
A "hold" credit card holders place on available credit, usually upon reserving and check-in at hotels, renting vehicles, and occasionally for restaurant reservations

### Day trip
Travel that begins and concludes in one day or less

### Eco-travel
Ecologically focused (Earth-friendly) travel also known as green travel, sustainable tourism, and ecotourism

### Educational travel
Vacations that are designed to encourage learning or destinations that specialize in teaching visitors a specific skill or topic

### Edu-tainment
Entertainment that is also educational, such as visiting a history museum that uses child-friendly tools to teach kids about history

### Emergency funds
Money, credit, or other sources of funding that are set aside before a trip for emergencies only

### e-Savers
US Airways weekly discount fares

### Flip chart
Large sheets of paper bound in a chart and usually placed on an easel that allows users to write in large letters for a group to read during a presentation

### Foliage
The period of time in autumn when leaves change color

**Food allergy**
A condition in which a person is allergic, sometimes fatally, to a certain type of food or liquid, such as peanuts

**Footwash**
Found at many public attractions and beaches, a small container usually equipped with a faucet located near a restroom where people can wash their feet

**Heli-tour**
Helicopter tour

**House sitter**
An individual or company hired to take care of or watch a home while a family or individual is out of town

**Imbibe**
To partake in drinking alcoholic beverages

**In-season**
The busiest time of year for a destination, hotelier, or merchant

**Long-term travel**
Travel plans that extend longer than a typical one-week vacation

**Meal planning**
The act of planning meals for an entire vacation in order to accurately estimate the cost of meals for the duration of the trip

### Multi-family travel
A trip where more than one family travels together to the same destination, usually to save money on hotel and transportation costs

### NetSAAvers
American Airlines regular discount fares

### Oceanfront
Lodging that is situated directly on the waterfront

### Oceanview
Lodging that provides a view of the ocean, but may not necessarily be directly on the beach

### Off-season
The time of year when a resort or destination is least busy

### Passport expeditor
A consultant who expedites travel visas and passports for travelers

### Pay-at-the-pump credit card authorization
A hold placed on a credit card by the credit card bank or company when purchasing gasoline at the pump with the respective credit card

### Redeye
Flights that typically leave the West coast around midnight and arrive at destinations the following morning

### Road food
Impromptu meals typically consisting of comfort food found at local diners and restaurants during road trips

### SingleParentTravel.com
a travel website devoted to single parents

### Snowbirds
Northern residents who travel south for cold-weather months

### Stay-cations
Vacations that are enjoyed close to your residence

### Tour operator
An individual or corporation who operates tours

### Transportation Security Administration (TSA)
The federal administration responsible for transportation safety

### Travel insurance
Temporary insurance travelers can obtain that covers travel expenses in the event of cancellation, illness, or loss of possessions and valuables

### Travel scammers
Individuals or companies who specialize in "scamming" or robbing travelers out of trips, expenses, or other goods and services

### Travel trade show
A trade show that features travel professionals and destinations like AdventureExpo.com where travelers can obtain valuable information

### Tweens
Children about to enter their teenage years

### Wilderness camping

Camping in a wilderness location without assistance from a guide or camping tour operator

### Ziplining

An activity in which people are hooked into a harness suspended by a pulley and ride a cable line from one end to the other on an incline

# Index

# A

# D

# E

# F

# G

# We Have
# EVERYTHING®
## on Anything!

**With more than 19 million** copies sold, the Everything® series has become one of America's favorite resources for solving problems, learning new skills, and organizing lives. Our brand is not only recognizable—it's also welcomed.

The series is a hand-in-hand partner for people who are ready to tackle new subjects—like you!

For more information on the Everything® series, please visit *www.adamsmedia.com*

The Everything® list spans a wide range of subjects, with more than 500 titles covering 25 different categories:

| | | |
|---|---|---|
| Business | History | Reference |
| Careers | Home Improvement | Religion |
| Children's Storybooks | Everything Kids | Self-Help |
| Computers | Languages | Sports & Fitness |
| Cooking | Music | Travel |
| Crafts and Hobbies | New Age | Wedding |
| Education/Schools | Parenting | Writing |
| Games and Puzzles | Personal Finance | |
| Health | Pets | |